GUIDES TO THE REFORMED TRADITION
Worship

GUIDES TO THE
REFORMED
TRADITION

John H. Leith

John W. Kuykendall

Series Editors

WORSHIP
Hughes Oliphant Old

THE CHURCH
Wallace M. Alston, Jr.

GUIDES TO THE REFORMED TRADITION

Worship

That Is Reformed According to Scripture

Hughes Oliphant Old

John Knox Press
ATLANTA

Library of Congress Cataloging in Publication Data

Old, Hughes Oliphant.
    Worship that is Reformed according to Scripture.

    (Guides to Reformed tradition)
    Bibliography: p.
    Includes index.
    1. Reformed Church—Liturgy. 2. Reformed Church—
Doctrines. 3. Public worship. I. Title. II. Title:
Worship. III. Series.
BX9427.0425 1984   264'.057   83-19616
ISBN 0-8042-3252-0

© copyright John Knox Press 1984
10 9 8 7 6 5 4 3 2 1
Printed in the United States of America
John Knox Press
Atlanta, Georgia 30365

To the memory of my uncle

Mr. A. C. Oliphant

and in honor of my aunt

Mrs. A. C. Oliphant

Series Preface

GUIDES TO THE REFORMED TRADITION have as their purpose the interpretation and explication of the Reformed tradition in a way that illuminates human experience in the last quarter of the twentieth century, in particular the experience of life and the world in the Christian community.

In the intention of the editors the exposition of the faith is to be (1) positive, critical but appreciative, (2) based upon the primary texts of the tradition, (3) related to the best work in allied fields such as the natural sciences, social sciences, aesthetics, and literature, and (4) written with scholarly competence but with a clarity that is intelligible to the generally educated reader. The purpose of the Guides is the building up of the worshiping, believing, obeying community which seeks to be Christian in the Reformed way.

Within the guidelines stated above the individual writers have been given the maximum freedom to express their convictions and conclusions in their own way. The writers have been chosen to include pastors of local congregations as well as seminary and university scholars. The books in the series will be united by a common perspective but not by common conclusions or styles. It is hoped that this variety will contribute to debate within the community.

Hughes Oliphant Old is uniquely qualified to write the volume on worship. In addition to his education at Centre College and Princeton Theological Seminary, Dr. Old spent seven years in Europe reading the sources of Reformed liturgy for his doctorate at Neuchatel under the direction of Jean-Jacques von Allmen. His dissertation was published as *The Patristic Roots of Reformed Worship*. Dr. Old has at his command facts that are not easily available from any other source. He has recovered forgotten sources of the Reformed tradition of worship. In addition he is a person of passion and conviction who practices the Reformed faith as pastor of Faith Presbyterian Church, West Lafayette, Indiana.

John H. Leith, Editor
Pemberton Professor of Theology
Union Theological Seminary in Virginia

John W. Kuykendall, Editor
Associate Professor and Head of the Department of Religion
Auburn University

Author's Preface and Acknowledgments

The book before us has, to be sure, a history. In the summer of 1979 Professor Donald Wardlaw asked me to do a series of lectures on worship for the pastors' institute at McCormick Theological Seminary in Chicago. After some discussion we chose as the subject, *The Biblical Roots of Reformed Worship*. At the end of the course Wardlaw asked if he might have the manuscript typed up and mimeographed for use in his introductory course on worship the following semester. The manuscript needed considerable work before it could be used for this purpose and with the editorial assistance and great patience of Mrs. Sue Armendariz, a manuscript was produced for Wardlaw's class in the spring of 1980. To this was given the title *Introduction to Reformed Worship*.

In the spring of 1981 I received an invitation to give a paper at the meeting of the International Colloquium of Calvin Studies held at Calvin College in Grand Rapids. It was at the suggestion of the late Ford Lewis Battles that I was asked to write something on Calvin's Theology of Worship. The first chapter of this book represents to a large extent a reshaping of that lecture. Professor Edward Dowey of Princeton Theological Seminary offered a number of comments and criticisms from which I have greatly profited.

The chapter on the Reformed discipline of daily morning and evening prayer is a very brief reworking of a considerable amount of research which I have done as a member of the North American Academy of Liturgics committee on the daily office. To Professor William Storey of the University of Notre Dame I owe considerable appreciation for encouraging me to dig deeply into the Reformed approach to the service of daily prayer. Much of the work on prayer I did in connection with my being on General Assembly's task force on prayer. Here I am particularly indebted to the sympathetic support of Dr. James Kirk, Director of the Advisory Council of Discipleship and Worship of the United Presbyterian Church.

Behind all of my work is the encouragement of my doctor Father at the University of Neuchatel in Switzerland, Professor Jean-Jacques von Allmen. In the five years I spent under his guidance I got to know a great amount about the Continental Reformed liturgical heritage. To him I am most grateful.

Two things I have been obliged to leave out of this study. I should have very much liked to have treated at length the liturgical contributions of the Middle Ages, both in the Eastern and Western churches. I think there would be genuine worth in a Reformed liturgical scholar treating this period sympathetically. Much happened in this period which is of great value. For example, I would like to have written at greater length about the monastic daily office and the eucharistic theology of the High Scholastic theologians. When one sees the variety of thought and practice during the Middle Ages the work of the Reformers is put in much clearer perspective. I should also have liked to have written about the developments in Reformed worship in more recent centuries. Charles W. Baird I have always regarded as a personal hero. Henry van Dyke was a much beloved cousin in my mother's family. The figure of Alexander Campbell has interested me for years. Here again many positive things happened. This book was supposed to be brief, and if something of substance was to be said, it seemed necessary to focus on those periods of our liturgical history which were crucial. The editor and I decided to leave these subjects aside for the present.

As it now stands the purpose of the book is to explicate the classical Reformed tradition in regard to worship. The heart of this tradition is the witness of the Reformers to the teaching of Scripture. It is therefore that Professor Leith and I were both in agreement that it was appropriate to spend a large part of each chapter presenting the relevant biblical passages. Particular attention has been given to the collegial nature of the Reformed tradition. The Reformed liturgical heritage has been shaped by many hands. It seemed important therefore to treat a variety of Reformers. Much attention has been given to the less well known Reformers of the first generation such as Oecolampadius, Capito, and Bucer as well as to the English Puritans of later generations. Apart from taking this wide angle lens it is really very hard to get the whole picture in focus. More and more I am fascinated by Peter Martyr Vermigli, William Perkins, and Thomas Manton. I did not realize we had such treasures in our attic! Our tradition is not very well known and what is known is badly misunderstood. My highest hope for the pages which lie ahead is not that they will constitute a "definitive work" but rather that they will inspire a more careful look at the subject treated. What I have written is only a report on what I have discovered up to this point. This is a fascinating field, and there is much yet to be brought to light.

Appreciation should be expressed to Christopher Borgert, a member of my congregation, who has now for the last two years acted as my research assistant. He chases down books for me in the library and performs innumerable other services. To him goes the credit for putting together the bibliography and the index. Even more important, he keeps a sharp eye on my spelling and syntax, and lets me know whether I have said what I really intended to say.

To my congregation go very special thanks for their being patient with my putting so much time into my research and writing. There is not much in this book which they have not heard in sermon form. Mrs. Grieke Toebes very kindly read through the manuscript before I sent it to the publisher to see whether it was readable. Our church secretary, Mrs. Peggy Downey, has usually typed up the first draft of whatever I have written. She keeps me up to date on my correspondence and generally keeps me in order. Without such practical saints there would be no doctors of theology.

Contents

I
Some Basic Principles

We worship God because God created us to worship him. Worship is at the center of our existence; at the heart of our reason for being. God created us to be his image—an image that would reflect his glory. In fact the whole creation was brought into existence to reflect the divine glory. The psalmist tells us that "the heavens are telling the glory of God; and the firmament proclaims his handiwork" (Ps. 19:1). The Apostle Paul in the prayer with which he begins the epistle to the Ephesians makes it clear that God created us to praise him.

> Blessed be the God and Father of our Lord Jesus Christ,
> Who has blessed us in Christ with every spiritual blessing in the
>   heavenly places,
> Even as he chose us in him before the foundation of the world,
> That we should be holy and blameless before him.
> He destined us in love to be his sons through Jesus Christ,
> According to the purpose of his will, to the praise of his glorious
>   grace . . .
>
> (Ephesians 1:3–6)

This prayer says much about the worship of the earliest Christians. It shows the consciousness that the first Christians had of the ultimate significance of their worship. They understood themselves to have been destined and appointed to live to the praise of God's glory (Eph. 1:12). When the *Westminster Catechism* teaches us, "Man's chief end is to glorify God and to enjoy him forever," it gives witness to this same basic principle; God created us to worship him. Surely it is here that we must begin when as Reformed theologians we ask what worship is. Worship must above all serve the glory of God.

Now there are those today who would justify worship for any number of other reasons. We are told that we should worship because it brings us happiness. Sometimes worship does make us happy, but not always. We are told that we should worship because it will give us a sense of self-fulfillment. Surely worship does fulfill the purpose of our existence but we do not worship *because* it brings us self-fulfillment. We are often told that we should worship in order to build family solidarity: "the family that prays together stays together." The high priests of the Canaanite fertility religions said much the same thing. All kinds of politicians have insisted on participation in various religious rites in order to develop national unity or ethnic identity. Queen Elizabeth I was not the first or the last who tried to consolidate her realm by insisting that the worship be in some way English. One can always find medicine men and gurus who advocate religious rites for the sake of good health, financial success, or peace of mind. True worship, however, is distinguished from all of these in that it serves above all else the praise of God's glory.

Not only did God create us to worship him, but he also commanded us to worship him. The first four of the Ten Commandments concern worship. The first commandment tells us, "Thou shalt have no other gods before me." Jesus tells us that the first and greatest commandment is that we are to love God with all our hearts, all our minds, and all our souls. The point is that our worship, our deepest devotion, our most ardent love is to be directed to God rather than to ourselves. Even before loving ourselves or our neighbor or any other worthy human cause we are to devote ourselves to God. John Calvin (1509–1564), one of the leaders of the Protestant Reformation, in his commentary on the Ten Commandments says that the first commandment means that we are "with true and zealous godliness . . . to contemplate, fear, and worship, his majesty; to participate in his blessings; to seek his help at all times; to recognize, and by praises to celebrate, the greatness of his works—as the only goal of all the activities of this life" (Calvin, *Institutes* II: viii, 16). The second commandment tells us that we are not to use images or idols in our worship, for as the Apostle Paul tells us, God is not represented by the art and imagination of men; God created *us* to be the reflection of his image (Acts 17:22–31). Taking this command-ment seriously has been fundamental to the Reformed understanding of worship. If today American Protestant worship services have confused worship with art, or even worse, if we have confused it with entertain-ment, it is because we have failed to fathom the meaning of the second commandment. The third commandment tells us that we are not to use the Lord's name in vain. Vain means empty. The commandment teaches us to worship God honestly and sincerely, to worship God "in spirit and in truth," to use the words of Jesus. The fourth command-ment tells us to remember, or observe, the worship of the Sabbath Day. This commandment makes the preceding three commandments very concrete. Without this commandment it might seem that the law had had something much more subjective in mind than actual services of worship. As we shall see in another chapter, Jesus too interpreted this commandment in a very concrete way when he told the disciples to celebrate the Lord's Supper in *remembrance* of him. All the way through Scripture we find commandments to worship God and com-mandments regarding worship. All these are in fact an unfolding and an interpretation of these basic four commandments. True worship is an act of obedience to the law of God. Reformed theology with its Augustinian sense for the continuity between the Old and New Testaments has taken very seriously what the first tablet of the law has to say about worship.

This then is the first characteristic of Reformed worship: it is wor-ship which is "according to Scripture." The Reformers did not mean by this a sort of Bible-pounding literalism although they have often been accused of this. Much more they had in mind that Christian worship should be in obedience to God's Word as it is revealed in Holy Scrip-ture. At the very beginning of the Reformation we find this principle put forth by Martin Bucer (1491–1551), the leading Reformer of the city of Strasbourg, one of the first cities of that day actually to attempt liturgi-cal reform. As Bucer put it, it is only the worship which God asks of us which really serves him. Bucer obviously did not understand worship as though it were some sort of creative art, as though the object of worship were to entertain God with elaborate liturgical pageants and dramas. As Bucer and his colleagues understood it, God directs us above all to worship him by the proclamation of his Word, the giving of alms, the celebration of communion, and the ministry of prayer. This Bucer gathered from the text of Acts 2:42 which tells of the worship of the primitive church, "And they devoted themselves to the apostles' teaching and fellowship, to the breaking of bread and the prayers."

John Oecolampadius (1482–1531), the Reformer of Basel, and one of the most highly respected scholars of his age, developed at considerable length what the early Reformed theologians meant by worship that was according to Scripture. As Oecolampadius well understood, the Bible does not provide us with any ready made liturgies or services of worship. Nevertheless the church should develop services of worship in accordance with whatever specific directions and examples are to be found in Scripture. When Scripture does not give specific directions, then in such matters we should be guided by scriptural principles. For instance, Oecolampadius taught that Christian worship should be simple and without pompous ritual and sumptuous ceremony because the manner of life which Jesus taught was simple and without pretense. As Oecolampadius understood it, the worship of the church should be consistent with such essential principles as justification by faith, prevenient grace, and above all Christian love.

This principle, that the worship of the church should be according to Scripture, has suggested to a large extent the arrangement of this book. One cannot readily appreciate what the Reformers had to say about worship unless one sees how they brought it out of the Scriptures. One has to understand their teaching as an interpretation of the Scriptures. We will therefore devote a great amount of attention to what the Scriptures have to say about various aspects of worship and then we will turn to the subject of how the Reformers understood the Scriptures. In order to understand what Reformed is, we must understand what Reformed according to God's Word is.

There is more. While the Reformers understood the Scriptures to be their sole authority they were very interested in how generations of Christians down through history had understood the Scriptures. Studying the history of Christian worship they found many good examples of how the church had truly understood Scripture. Often the Fathers of the ancient church had been most faithful witnesses to the authority of Scripture. The Reformers learned from Athanasius about Christian psalmody, from Ambrose about catechetical instruction, from John Chrysostom about preaching and from Augustine about the sacraments. In these pages we will need to say something both about the way the church through many centuries maintained a faithful witness, and also the way the church confused that witness. Otherwise it would be difficult to understand what the reform was all about and why it was necessary.

One often asks why today we should study the Reformers. We study the Reformers for the same reason the Reformers studied the Church Fathers. They are witnesses to the authority of Scripture. The Reformers studied the patristic commentaries on Scripture because it enriched their own understanding of Scripture. Today we study the Reformers because they throw so much light on the pages of the Bible. They were passionately concerned to worship God truly and they searched the Scriptures to learn how. We study the Reformers because their understanding of Scripture is so profound.

The second fundamental of Christian worship is that it should be in the name of Christ (Col. 3:17). We begin our worship as Christians by being baptized in his name (Acts 2:38). It is in his name that the Christian congregation is assembled, remembering the promise that when two or three are gathered together in his name he is present with us (Matt. 18:20). Jesus frequently taught his disciples to pray in his name (John 14:14; 15:16; 16:23). That we are to pray in the name of Jesus is a very important principle of Christian prayer. To do something in someone's name is to do it as the agent of someone else. It is to do something in the service of someone else. When we pray in the name of Christ we are praying in his service; we are continuing the ministry of intercession which Jesus himself began on the cross. The preaching and teaching of the Apostles was likewise in the name of Jesus (Acts 5:41). It was in the name of Jesus because he commissioned the church to continue that ministry of preaching and teaching which he began. The church is, as Jesus himself put it, "to teach all things whatsoever I have commanded you." In the same way our giving of alms and our good works are to be in the name of Christ (Matt. 18:5; Mark 9:38–41; Acts 3:6). In the Upper Room at the Last Supper Jesus commissioned the twelve to act as his agents, "Do this in remembrance of me." How often Jesus had broken bread with them and how often Jesus had fed the multitude! Now the Apostles were to go out and hold the memorial which he had appointed in his name.

Christian worship is in the name of Christ because worship is a function of the body of Christ and as Christians we are all one body. All of our worship must be in him! What an important New Testament concept this is that the church is the body of Christ, and how vividly the first Christians understood that they were all together one body, the body of Christ. They understood their worship to be part of the worship which the ascended Christ performed in the heavenly sanctuary to the glory of the Father (Heb. 7:23–25; 9:25; 10:19–22; 13:15).

If Reformed theology is concerned that worship be according to God's Word and in obedience to God's Word and if Reformed theology has made a point of worship being in the name of Christ and in the body of Christ, it is most surely because it has realized the importance of worship being far more than merely a human work. Worship is the work of the Holy Spirit. Here is the third principle we would like to advance. The Scriptures are particularly clear about prayer being the work of the Holy Spirit. As the Apostle Paul tells us it is the Holy Spirit who cries out within us when we pray (Rom. 8:15–27). The Apostle tells us that when we pray, "Our Father," it is the Holy Spirit praying within our hearts (Rom. 8:15). The hymns and psalms that are sung in worship are spiritual songs, that is, they are the songs of the Holy Spirit (Acts 4:25; Eph. 5:19). Even the preaching of the church is to be in the Spirit (1 Cor. 12:8). Jesus promised to us that when we present our testimony before the world it is not we who speak but the Holy Spirit who gives us utterance (Mark 13:11). Christian worship is inspired by the Spirit, empowered by the Spirit, directed by the Spirit, purified by the Spirit, and bears the fruit of the Spirit. Christian worship is Spirit-filled.

As far back as the eighth century before Christ the prophet Amos had insisted that true worship must be holy. It must come from a people whose lives are consecrated to God. God has no interest in the sacrifices of a wicked people or the praises of those who ignored the ethical demands of the law.

> I hate, I despise your feasts,
>   and I take no delight in your solemn assemblies.
> Even though you offer me your burnt offerings and cereal offerings,
>   I will not accept them,
> and the peace offerings of your fatted beasts
>   I will not look upon.

Take away from me the noise of your songs;
   to the melody of your harps I will not listen.
But let justice roll down like waters,
   and righteousness like an everflowing stream.

(Amos 5:21–24)

With these words, Amos announced God's displeasure with the worship of Samaria. Mistreatment of the poor, militarism, the luxury of the rich, bribery in the courts, sexual promiscuity, high interest rates, and oppressive taxes revealed the religious hypocrisy of the kingdom of Israel. Jesus must have had this prophecy in mind when he made very clear to a woman of Samaria that the day had finally come when the true worshiper would worship God in spirit and truth (John 4:1–26). For the Christian, holiness of life and sincerity of worship must go together; they must be of one piece.

For the Reformed theologian the integrity of the service of God and the service of the neighbor is essential. Dr. Thomas Manton (1620–1677), whom we might well reckon with the most brilliant of the Westminster Divines, tells us that when those who worship God live immoral lives the glory of God is obscured. On the other hand when Christians reflect the holiness of God and are in fact the image of God then God is glorified. When those who worship the holy God become through that worship holy themselves, they show forth the praises of him who has called us out of the darkness into his marvelous light (1 Peter 2:9). This does not mean that holiness is a prerequisite to worship. If it were, none of us could worship. Holiness is rather the fruit of worship. Dr. Manton tells us that God is sanctified by his people when they discover him to be holy, the source of all holiness, and when God sanctifies us by working grace and holiness in us, then we declare him to be a holy God (Thomas Manton, *Manton's Works* I, 84). It is the Holy Spirit who purifies our worship by his continual work of sanctification. By purifying the worshipers the worship is made pure. When we worship, having our minds enlightened by the Spirit, our lives cleansed by the Spirit, our wills moved by the Spirit, and our hearts warmed by the Spirit, then our worship is transformed from being a mere human work into being a divine work.

But if worship is a divine work, it is God's saving work among us. It is God's work of building up the church. It is this point which is made when the *Westminster Shorter Catechism* tells us that word, prayer, and sacraments are means of grace. "The outward and ordinary means whereby Christ communicateth to us the benefits of redemption . . . " (*Westminster Shorter Catechism*, Q. 88). From the very beginning Reformed theologians have been fond of speaking of worship as being edifying. Martin Bucer in particular liked to use this word to describe Christian worship. He had in mind that passage where the Apostle Paul tells us that everything in the service of worship should edify the church (1 Cor. 14:1–6), that is, it should teach or build up the church. Worship which puts first the praise of God's glory, worship which is according to God's Word, worship which serves God and God alone does in fact edify the church. It edifies the church because it is the work of the Holy Spirit in the body of Christ. When in the worship of the church the word is truly preached and the sacraments rightly administered, then God calls, teaches, and leads his people into a new way of life. It is in coming together for worship that we become the church (1 Cor. 10:16–17; 11:17–22). It is here that we are united together into one body by God's Spirit, that we are made participants in the coming kingdom. It is in worship that we hear the good news of our salvation, that we are saved from our sins and transformed into the image of Christ. If God has commanded us not to worship him by creating images of our own art and imagination it is because he wants us to be his image. Worship is the workshop where we are transformed into his image. When we are thus transformed into his image, we then reflect his glory. It is then through the ministry of praise and prayer, the ministry of word and sacrament that we are transformed to offer that spiritual worship which the Apostle Paul tells us is acceptable to God (Rom. 12:1–2). It is this which is meant when it is said that worship is the work of the Holy Spirit in the body of Christ to the glory of the Father.

II

Baptism

The Gospels tell us that God sent John the Baptist to prepare the way of the Lord. John prepared the way for the coming of Christ by calling the people of Israel to repentance and baptizing them in the Jordan River. It was significant that John carried out his ministry in the wilderness and that he baptized in the Jordan. The wilderness had always been a place of repentance, a place of preparation, a place of beginning anew. It was in the wilderness that God had for forty years prepared the children of Israel to enter the promised land. When the people had been prepared by learning the discipline of the law and by all the trials, wanderings, and testings that we read about in the story of the Exodus, then they were led by Joshua across the Jordan River into the promised land. That John exercised his ministry in the wilderness and baptized in the Jordan implies a new entry into the promised land. It implied the reconstituting of Israel and the establishment of the long-promised kingdom of God.

Jesus, as many Jews of his day, went out into the wilderness to hear John and accepted baptism at his hand. In doing this Jesus became the new Joshua, leading the new Israel into the new kingdom of God. It was by God's specific direction that Jesus had been given the same name as Joshua. The name Jesus, as is well known, is but the Greek form of the name Joshua. Jesus was baptized not because he needed to have his sins washed away but because it was part of his ministry to lead the new Israel into the new kingdom of God. It was through baptism that Jesus entered into the kingdom of God and it was through baptism that the disciples followed Jesus into the kingdom. Even today it is in baptism that we too enter into the kingdom of God. Baptism is a prophetic sign at the beginning of our Christian life that we belong to the people of God. It is our entrance into the church.

Entering the kingdom of God was an act of repentance and John made this clear in his preaching. When the Jews who went out to hear John were baptized, they were baptized "confessing their sins" (Matt. 3:6). John called on them to bear fruit that befit repentance, to share their goods with one another, and to carry out their business and professions with honesty and fairness (Luke 3:14–17). Baptism is a call to make the crooked straight but it is also a witness to Christ, the Lamb of God who takes away the sin of the world. It is not that the washing of water bears away the sin of the world but rather that it is a witness that in Christ there is the cleansing of sin. John the Baptist was very clear about how our sins are taken away. He told those whom he baptized, behold the Lamb of God who takes away the sin of the world. Christ is the Lamb of God. It is he by his sacrifice who cleanses us from sin. The baptism which the disciples received from John pointed them to Christ. When we are baptized the same thing happens to us. Our baptism points us to Christ.

When Jesus was baptized the Holy Spirit descended upon him and the voice of the Father from heaven identified Jesus, "This is my beloved Son." So our baptism is a sign to us that we, too, are sons and daughters of our heavenly Father. We become sons and daughters of our heavenly Father by receiving his Spirit. We know that we are his children because his Spirit dwells within us. In baptism the promise of the prophets is fulfilled, "I will sprinkle clean water upon you, and you shall be clean. . . . A new heart I will give you, and a new spirit I will put within you . . . and you shall be my people, and I will be your God" (Ezek. 36:25–28). With this, the New Covenant, which Jeremiah too had promised, had come into being (Jer. 31:31–34). As Joel had promised, God had indeed poured out his Spirit upon all flesh (Joel 2:28–32; Acts 2:17–21). In the baptism of Jesus the pouring out of God's Spirit became clearly visible but in our baptisms the same thing happens. The giving of the Spirit is the invisible spiritual reality to which the sprinkling, pouring out, or washing of water gives witness. Baptism with water is the sign and promise of the giving of the Holy Spirit.

At the end of his ministry, our Lord sent out the Apostles to make disciples of all nations by baptizing them and teaching them. When Jesus commissioned his disciples to baptize he transformed the baptism administered by John in two very significant ways. First he directed the Apostles to baptize in the name of the Father and of the Son and of the Holy Spirit. By baptizing in the name of the Father, the Apostles made it clear that those baptized have been adopted as children of the Father. By baptizing in the name of the Son, the Apostles made it clear that those baptized were to be joined to Christ in his death and in his resurrection. By baptizing in the name of the Holy Spirit, they made it clear that baptism in water is a prophetic sign of being baptized in the Holy Spirit. Secondly Jesus directed that they were to baptize not only the children of Israel but all nations. In doing this Jesus opened up the kingdom of God to all peoples. John the Baptist had been sent to Israel; the Apostles to the whole world. Here is one of the most essential differences between the old kingdom of Israel and the new kingdom of God; the new kingdom of God was open to all the peoples of the earth. This was something very new, yet it was also something very old. When God first gave the Covenant to Abraham, he provided that in the seed of Abraham all the nations of the earth should be blessed. The New Covenant had been promised in the Old Covenant.

On the day of Pentecost, the Apostles began to carry out the commission which Jesus had given them. Peter preached to the people of Jerusalem that the Jesus who so recently had been crucified, God had raised up. God had appointed him the Lord of the kingdom which the prophets had so long promised. With the proclamation of the new kingdom came the proclamation of a New Covenant, "Repent and be baptized every one of you in the name of Jesus Christ for the forgiveness of your sins; and you shall receive the gift of the Holy Spirit. For the promise is to you and your children and to all that are far off" (Acts 2:39). In this sermon Peter proclaimed the New Covenant. This New Covenant was like the Old Covenant in that God promised himself to his people, "I will walk among you, and you shall be my people" (Lev. 26:12). Even in the form that the Covenant was given to Abraham and sealed by circumcision it was a Covenant of grace. The Old Covenant promised the gift of the land and the establishment of descendants as numerous as the stars of the sky. The New Covenant on the other hand promised the pouring out of God's Spirit, salvation by grace, the putting away of sins, and everlasting life. Baptism was a sign of this New Covenant just as circumcision had been a sign of the Old Covenant. On the day of Pentecost three thousand people were baptized into the church. By receiving the covenant sign of baptism, they became participants in the New Covenant, children of the kingdom and members of the church.

As the story of the earliest church unfolds through the book of Acts we read of a number of different baptisms. We should notice how the baptisms are at first baptisms of Jews in Jerusalem, and then as we read on we hear of the baptism of an Ethiopian, then the baptism of a Greek lady, Lydia, and the baptism of the Philippian jailer and his whole house. In these baptisms the Apostles were doing just what Jesus had directed them to do; they were making disciples of all nations. The New Covenant was being opened up to the Gentiles. We notice that the Apostles baptized very quickly. Three thousand were baptized on the very day of Pentecost, the Ethiopian eunuch was baptized on the same day he heard the gospel and the Philippian jailer and his family were baptized as soon as they cared for Paul's wounds. In the earliest Christian church baptism stood at the beginning of the Christian life.

The Apostle Paul tells us that in baptism we are joined to Christ in his death and resurrection (Rom. 6:1–11; Col. 2:11–13). There are two possible ways of understanding this. First, one could understand this from the standpoint of the ancient Greek mystery religions. Understood as a Greek mystery, baptism would be a dramatic rite portraying the death and resurrection of Christ. When one went through such a rite, then, it was believed, that which had been dramatized would become a reality in the life of the one going through the rite. The chances are Paul did not understand baptism in terms of the Greek mystery religions. He was far too Jewish for that. A second explanation of these words of the Apostle reaches back to the Hebrew concept of covenant. It understands baptism as a covenant sign given by Christ to his disciples. This covenant sign promises to us that our Lord will share with us the spiritual benefits, or consequences, of his death and resurrection. A covenant is an alliance or a bond which joins a community together. Once that community has been banded together then the members have a share in the spiritual endowments of the community. The church is a covenant community and the greatest endowments or treasures of this community are freedom from sin, victory over death, and eternal life. Entering Christ's church by baptism, we share in his death to sin and his resurrection to new and eternal life. The fact that our union with Christ is to be understood as a covenantal union is made particularly clear by the strong emphasis which the passage puts on the effects of receiving the covenant sign. The sign of baptism is not magic; it is a means of grace. God uses the sign to strengthen our faith; that we might "believe that we shall also live with him." God uses the sign to produce in us holiness of life; that "we too might walk in newness of life." (Rom. 6:4).

The New Testament tells us very little about how baptism was administered. We are often told that baptism was given by someone in the name of Jesus to someone else. We never hear of one baptizing oneself. Sometimes we hear of sermons preceding a baptism or of prayers following the baptisms. We are not told what method of baptism was used, whether it was by total immersion, or by some form of pouring or sprinkling. Probably each of these was used at one time or another depending on the circumstances. Sometimes we hear of some manifestations of the presence of the Holy Spirit, but not always (Matt. 3:16; Acts 2:3; 8:39; 9:17–18; 10:47–48). One thing is clear from numerous passages of the New Testament; baptism was understood primarily as a sign of washing (Acts 22:16; 1 Cor. 6:11; Eph. 5:26; Titus 3:5; Heb. 10:22). There are of course a number of things which baptism means; for example, that we are joined to Christ in his death and resurrection, that we are born again from above, and that our hearts have been illumined by the Word of Truth, but the primary import of the sign of baptism is not these things. Baptism signifies above all the washing away of sin. This is the reason the word baptism was used. While in classical Greek baptism may have originally meant to submerge or sink, in the popular Greek of New Testament times it meant to wash (Mark 7:4; Luke 11:38). One gets the impression that this baptismal washing was carried out in a very simple and straightforward manner. That at least is the case with the New Testament and with such very early Christian documents as the *Didache* and the *Apology* of Justin Martyr, which reflect the practice of the late first century and early second century.

It is another matter when one gets to the last half of the fourth century. By then the Christian sacrament of baptism had become an elaborate liturgical drama rivaling the initiation rites of the Greek mystery religions. The convert to Christianity was no longer baptized immediately as had been the case of the New Testament, but was expected to go through as much as three years of preparation, instruction, and scrutiny before receiving baptism. We have several documents which tell us in considerable detail how baptism was celebrated at the end of the fourth century. First there is a series of sermons *On the Sacraments* by Ambrose of Milan. Then there are a number of sermons by Augustine of Hippo which give us glimpses of how baptism was celebrated in North Africa. Most interesting of all is the *Mystagogical Catechism* of Cyril of Jerusalem. From these documents we find that several weeks before Easter those who were ready for baptism were solemnly enrolled. Each day they went to the church for special prayers, for instruction in the basic Christian beliefs, and for exorcism. A few days before Easter they were given the creed to be learned by heart, and probably the Lord's Prayer as well. On Saturday before Easter they returned to the church to make their profession of faith. Later that evening they returned to the church for the Easter vigil, a service which lasted all night. The baptism itself took place in the baptistry, a special building reserved for that purpose. With elaborate ceremony the baptismal font was blessed. In the baptistry those to be baptized removed their clothes. As a sort of final exorcism they were anointed with oil. Then they were immersed three times, in the name of the Father and of the Son and of the Holy Spirit. After this they were taken to the bishop who laid hands on them and anointed them with chrism. Now they were dressed in white robes and led back into the church. All this had been timed in such a way that as the newly baptized re-entered the church to receive their first communion the light of Easter day was beginning to break. Surely one would easily admit that this was all quite splendid as liturgical drama, but then one also has to admit that it was far removed from the sort of baptismal services held by the Apostles. It no longer stood at the beginning of the Christian life. In fact we frequently hear that baptism was delayed until late in life until such a time as one could be sure one could successfully lead a completely Christian life. Essentially, in that day one had to have already become Christian before one could qualify for baptism. Baptism had become a sign of salvation by works rather than salvation by grace.

By the beginning of the fifth century things began to change. Such church leaders as Augustine of Hippo (354–430) in the West and John Chrysostom (347–407) in the East began to urge Christians not to delay their baptism. Augustine, involved in a controversy with a very moralistic British monk named Pelagius (died after 418), argued that because baptism was a sacrament of grace it should be received at the beginning of the Christian life. Augustine claimed that ever since the days of the Apostles it had been the practice to baptize the infant children of Christians. The baptism of infants, Augustine felt, demonstrated that salvation is a gracious gift of God. Furthermore Augustine pointed to the fact that baptism was a divine work and without that divine work no human work would avail for our salvation. In baptism as Augustine understood it the Christian is consecrated to serve God and equipped to do good works. From the time of Augustine on, the church began to emphasize the absolute necessity of baptism for salvation. Under the influence of Augustine, instead of delaying baptism to the end of life, it became increasingly frequent for the children of Christians to be baptized shortly after birth.

For the next thousand years baptism began to lose its importance in the worship of the church. More and more it became a semiprivate religious rite which celebrated the birth of children. The rite became overburdened with exorcisms and anointings as though the main point of baptism were to chase out the devil. It became almost an act of magic by which one was automatically saved rather than a sacrament or covenant sign. The absolute necessity of baptism for salvation had been so strongly insisted upon that children were often baptized by the midwife immediately after birth rather than risk the possibility that the child die unbaptized. Baptism was no longer preceded or followed with any kind of introductory instruction. The whole teaching ministry of the church declined seriously. By the time of the Protestant Reformation the rite of baptism was in serious need of reform.

In 1523 Martin Luther (1483–1546) published his *German Baptismal Book*. This was the first attempt to translate a liturgical form. It was primarily a German translation of the old Latin rite yet several steps were taken to reform the rite itself. Within the next few months several Reformers published baptismal rites. In Zurich, Leo Jud (1482–1542) published a much more radical attempt at reforming the rite. In Nuremberg, Andreas Osiander (1498–1552) took another approach to the reform of the baptismal rite. He translated the text, but otherwise stuck closely to the old Latin rite. The Reformers of Strasbourg published a German baptismal service early in 1524 which might best be regarded as a rather timid attempt at reform, but within a year their reforms had become much bolder. The baptismal rite found in the *Strasbourg Psalter* of 1525 represents a thoroughgoing attempt to reform the rite.

In December of 1524 the Reformers of Strasbourg published one of the most significant documents in the history of Reformed worship, *Grund und Ursach der Erneuerung*. We might freely translate the title of this work as "Fundamental Principles for the Reform of Worship." As the Reformers of Strasbourg saw it the first thing necessary was to clear away from the rite all the extraneous exorcisms, anointings, consecrations, and other ceremonies which obscured the basic sign of washing. The Reformers were well aware that many of these ceremonies were very old, even if they did not go back to the days of the Apostles. The problem was that these auxiliary rites confused the basic meaning of baptism. This was particularly the case with the exorcisms. One did not need to assume that the children of Christians were demon-possessed. Likewise the anointing with chrism after the baptism tended to imply that while baptism with water was a sign of the washing away of sins something else was needed before the baptized receive the gift of the Holy Spirit. For the Reformers baptism was a sign of both the washing away of sins and the pouring out of the Holy Spirit. They insisted that there was but one baptism, that the outward washing of water was a sign of the inward work of the Holy Spirit. It is because the Reformers saw in the simple sign of washing such rich biblical meaning that they wanted to make this basic sign a prominent part of their worship.

Let us take a brief look at the way baptism was celebrated in the Reformed Church of Strasbourg at the end of the 1520s. Baptism was to be celebrated at the regular service of worship on the Lord's Day. After the sermon the parents and the child to be baptized met the minister at the baptismal font. There was first the Baptismal Exhortation. Here the minister set forth the promises of Scripture which are sealed in baptism. This was to be done in the form of short commentary on one of the classic baptismal texts. A list of about a dozen is given. This is followed by the Baptismal Invocation in which God is asked to send forth the Holy Spirit that what is signified in the sign might become an inward reality in the life of the one baptized. The parents are admonished to bring up the child in the nurture and admonition of the Lord. An important part of this admonition deals with the importance of the child receiving catechetical instruction when he or she comes to the appropriate age. The child is then baptized by pouring water on the head three times, "in the name of the Father and of the Son and of the Holy Spirit." The impressive thing about this rite is the way the baptismal washing itself has been emphasized. The use of triune pouring rather than a single immersion underlines the fact that it is washing which is primarily signified. One is struck by the fact that this rite has no catechetical instruction in it, no confession of sin or act of repentance and no profession of faith. Nevertheless, we can be quite certain that the Reformers considered all of these essential to baptism. What has happened is this: these parts of the rite have been postponed. When the child gets to be ten or twelve years old the child will be expected to learn the catechism and having learned the catechism to make a profession of faith. When one looks at the catechism which was used it becomes particularly clear. It is indeed an elaborate confession of faith in which the Apostles Creed is learned, explained, and confessed. Quite clearly those baptized are baptized unto repentance, unto the learning of all that Christ commanded, unto faith and the profession of faith; clearly baptism stands at the beginning of the Christian life as a sign of what the Christian life is to be.

Martin Bucer (1491–1551), the leading Reformer of Strasbourg, was particularly concerned that baptism be performed as part of the regular worship of the Christian congregation rather than as a sort of private service conducted for the family. The reason for this was that Bucer understood baptism as the sacrament of our incorporation into the church, the body of Christ. If indeed this was the case, then the church should be assembled when baptism was celebrated. Bucer and other Reformers tried to get parents to wait until the Sunday service to have their children baptized so that the sacrament of baptism might be a "Word made visible," to use the phrase of Augustine, reminding those present of the meaning of their own baptism. The logic of Bucer's teaching was quickly received by the other Reformers and the early

Reformed church quickly restored baptism to the regular worship of the church.

Ulrich Zwingli (1484–1531), one of the most nimble-witted young scholars of his day, wrote a series of works on baptism in which he began to develop a very new approach to the understanding of baptism. Zwingli found it hard to believe that by sprinkling a few drops of water on the head of an infant, that child was automatically assured of eternal salvation. Zwingli reached back behind the theology of the Schoolmen and drew on the ideas of Tertullian, a North African theologian who wrote in about the year 200. It was Tertullian who really coined the word *sacrament*. In the Latin language the word *sacramentum* was used to speak of the oath of allegiance which was given by a soldier on entering military service. Zwingli, well trained by some of the outstanding literary scholars of the Renaissance, knew a great deal about how the earliest Christians used language. He could see how over the centuries the meaning of the word *sacrament* had changed. Zwingli began to understand that a sacrament was not a ritual that conferred salvation upon someone, but rather a sign or emblem which distinguished the members of a community. For Zwingli the ecclesial aspect of baptism was of greatest importance. Zwingli's successors would deepen his insights considerably, but Zwingli's basic insight is important. Baptism is a sign of our entrance into the church.

Certainly one of the Reformers' cardinal concerns in the reform of the sacrament of baptism was to find a way of understanding baptism which did not make it seem like a magical way of saving people by means of putting them through some sort of religious rite. For the Reformation it was very clear, "by grace you have been saved through faith" (Eph. 2:8). The ancient Greek and Roman mystery religions had taught that one would achieve salvation by going through their initiation rites and it was natural and easy for the Christians of the third and fourth centuries to try to explain baptism in terms of these pagan mysteries or liturgical dramas. The Reformers soon found a much more biblical way of explaining baptism. The South German Reformers, particularly, were accomplished Old Testament scholars and they soon discovered in the Old Testament concept of covenant a much better way of explaining the sacraments. They found that the New Testament used the language of Covenant theology to speak of the sacraments. They found evidences that the Church Fathers had also used covenant terms to speak of baptism and the Lord's Supper. It is probably to Zwingli, the Reformer of Zurich, that credit should go for first developing this line of thought. (Quite possibly equal credit should go to John Oecolampadius [1482–1531], the Reformer of the Swiss City of Basel.) Zwingli, being very unhappy with the attempt of Scholastic theology to explain baptism in terms of form and matter suggested that baptism like circumcision should be understood as a sign of the Covenant (Gen.17:11). From this point on Covenant theology became the Reformed sacramental theology.

Both Zwingli and Oecolampadius died in 1531, early in the Reformation, and so it was left to Zwingli's successor, Henry Bullinger, to develop what today we call Covenant theology. Henry Bullinger (1504–75), being an excellent biblical philologist and having a remarkable mastery of the ancient languages, carefully studied the biblical concepts of sign, symbol, mystery, and particularly how these concepts are related to the concept of covenant. Bullinger showed that all the way through the Bible God made known his will through prophetic signs. These signs were visual evidences of God's promises. For example, after the Great Flood God promised never again to destroy the earth by a flood; seed time and harvest, summer and winter, day and night would never again disappear. Then God gave a rainbow as a sign of that covenant promise (Gen. 9:13). The story of Gideon's fleece is an example of how God gave a sign to strengthen and confirm the faith of his people. God had promised Gideon victory. The sign of the fleece gave Gideon confidence that God would fulfill his promise (Judg. 6:36–40). The signs of the Covenant in Scripture were God's way of making very clear to his people what he was about to do in their lives and thereby inspiring in them faith in himself. In the same way the signs which Jesus performed announced and demonstrated the kingdom which was at hand. This particularly was the case with the signs reported in the Gospel of John. When Jesus turned the water into wine at the wedding of Cana, he demonstrated that he was the true bridegroom who had come to claim the bride. We read, "This, the first of his signs, Jesus did at Cana in Galilee, and manifested his glory; and his disciples believed in him" (John 2:11). The sign inspired the faith of the disciples. By explaining the sacraments in terms of the biblical concept of covenant signs the Reformers were able to show how the sacraments were means of grace, that is, they were able to show the importance of the sacraments to saving faith. The function of the sacrament is to inspire, strengthen, and confirm faith.

For the Reformed understanding of baptism, the doctrine of the Holy Spirit is fundamental. Beginning in about the fifth or sixth century, the sacrament of baptism began to split up into two sacraments. Baptism proper was understood as the washing away of sins while the sacrament of confirmation was understood to confer the gift of the Holy Spirit. The Reformers were very much opposed to any understanding of baptism in which baptism with water was thought of as being one thing and baptism of the Holy Spirit as something else. Using Augustinian terms they saw baptism with water as the outward sign of baptism with the Holy Spirit which was the inward grace. It was not the physical washing with water which saved those who were baptized but rather it was the work of the Holy Spirit in the hearts of the baptized which gave them faith and thereby cleansed them from their sins. For the Reformers it became very important, then, that at the time of baptism the church should pray that the Holy Spirit accomplish inwardly the purification and sanctification that the outward sign of baptismal washing promised.

In 1523 when Martin Luther published his first German baptismal service he had put a great emphasis on the prayers which accompanied the rite of baptism. As Luther saw it these baptismal prayers should set the example of the prayer of the church. When someone is received into the church by baptism, it is the responsibility of the church continually to support that one in prayer. Bucer took up this thought of Luther's showing that baptismal prayer is a type of prayer which is a continual experience of the Christian throughout life. The Christian should continually pray to be cleansed from sin and filled with the new life of the Holy Spirit. From Luther on, the Baptismal Epiclesis or Baptismal Invocation has been an important part of the rite. In fact, without understanding the epicletic nature of baptism one would miss one of the major facets of the Protestant understanding of the sacrament. It is the epicletic nature of the sacraments which distinguishes them from magic.

Still another reform which the earliest Protestants were intent on making in the church's practice of baptism was the revival of some sort of catechetical instruction. They remembered that Jesus had sent out the

Apostles to make disciples by baptizing them and by teaching them. Baptism they believed entailed teaching. The Reformers very much admired the institution of the catechumenate which had so flourished in the fourth century. They tried to find some way of recovering something like the catechetical instruction of that period, taking into account the fact they were baptizing infants. The Reformers were amazingly successful in establishing regular catechetical instruction for children. By 1525, a few short years after the beginning of the Reformation, the churches of Zurich and Basel had regular religious instruction for children. In Strasbourg the pastors conducted weekly catechetical services for children in each parish. In 1527 Strasbourg's Wolfgang Capito (1478–1541) published a catechism. It must have been about the same time that Oecolampadius published his first catechism in Basel. In 1528 Konrad Sam in Ulm published a catechism as well. Luther's shorter catechism of 1529 was the classic Protestant catechism. In fact, with the Reformation the ministry of Christian teaching prospered generally. At the time children were presented for baptism their parents were asked to promise that their children would receive the regular catechetical instruction which all the early Reformed churches instituted for that purpose. After the children had received this instruction then they were asked to make a profession of faith before the whole congregation and they were admitted to communion.

By 1525 the Reformed churches of the Upper Rhineland were just beginning to bring into effect their reforms of the rite of baptism. It was at this point that they became aware of the position of the Anabaptists. The Anabaptists had a very different approach to the reform of the rite of baptism. They urged that only those be baptized who had undergone a conversion experience, had a conscious faith, and led a truly Christian life. They understood baptism primarily as a symbolic confession of faith on the part of one who was already a Christian. To be baptized was a visual confession of faith that one had already been cleansed from sin. The Anabaptists claimed that in New Testament times the Apostles had not baptized children and that it was only in later centuries that infants began to be baptized. At first several of the Reformers of classical Protestantism were somewhat swayed by the position of the Anabaptists but within a short time they began to see that the Anabaptist position was inconsistent with the Reformers' theology of grace. The Reformers were not convinced that the Apostles had not baptized children, pointing to several passages of the New Testament which indicated that whole families had been baptized (Acts 16:25–34; 18:8; 1 Cor. 1:16). John Oecolampadius, who had a profound knowledge of the literature of the ancient church pointed to passages in the writings of Tertullian, Origen, and Cyprian which indicated that the church had baptized the infant children of Christians from earliest times. These documents taken as a whole indicate that at the beginning of the second century it was taken for granted that the practice of baptizing the infant children of Christians went back to apostolic times. In defending infant baptism, once again the Reformers turned to the biblical concept of covenant to show that in the Scriptures children participated with their parents in the Covenant. They belonged to the people of God just as surely as their parents. It was Henry Bullinger who most fully worked out the ideas first developed by Zwingli and Oecolampadius. Bullinger pointed to the continuity between the Old Covenant and the New Covenant. As Bullinger put it, in the end there is but one Covenant, the eternal Covenant. The New Covenant is a fulfilling and opening up of the Old Covenant. If the Old Covenant included children, how much more should the New Covenant include children.

One of the strengths of Covenant theology is that it does full justice to the biblical concept of the unity of the family. Just as it was possible for Joshua to say "as for me and my house we will serve the Lord," so it was possible that Paul could say to the Philippian jailer, "Believe in the Lord Jesus, and you will be saved, you and your household" (Acts 16:31). It was very important for biblical peoples that God bless not only them but that the divine blessing should be passed on to their children and grandchildren. When God first gave the Covenant to Abraham, an essential aspect of that Covenant was the blessing of the future generation of Abraham's seed. This is no less true in the New Testament than in the Old. When Peter proclaimed the New Covenant in his sermon on the day of Pentecost he made it clear, "the promise is to you and to your children" (Acts 2:38–39).

Equally important in Covenant theology is its recognition of the importance of baptismal typology. For the theologians of the New Testament church, typology was a significant way of understanding spiritual truths. While typology may not be in vogue today, one only need read the epistle to the Hebrews to see how important typology was to the earliest Christians. In the first epistle of Peter baptism is understood in terms of the story of Noah and the flood (1 Peter 3:20–21). The Apostle Paul sees in the passage through the Red Sea a type of baptism and in circumcision a shadow of things to come (1 Cor. 10:1–2; Col. 2:11–12, 17). During the patristic period the explanation of the sacraments by means of the Old Testament types was exceedingly popular. Tertullian, Ambrose of Milan (339–97), Hilary of Poitiers (315–67), and Cyril of Alexandria (–444) have left us elaborate explanations of the baptismal typology. In fact one could say that the classic way of explaining baptism is by recounting the Old Testament types of baptism. As early as the beginning of the third century we know that it was customary to read the Old Testament types of baptism at the baptismal service. Even the baptismal prayers drew heavily on the imagery of Noah and the flood, the crossing of the Red Sea, going over the Jordan, the story of Jonah and the whale and the three young men in the fiery furnace. Martin Luther in writing prayers for his first German baptismal rite did full justice to the baptismal types. Luther's lead in this matter was followed by both Leo Jud and Ulrich Zwingli.

Among the most important types of baptism should be reckoned circumcision. In the seventeenth chapter of Genesis, which tells us of the institution of circumcision, we read that circumcision is a sign of the Covenant which God made to Abraham. For the South German Reformers the type of circumcision was of particular value in understanding baptism. The Scriptures are very clear that Abraham was justified by faith, "Abraham believed God, and it was reckoned to him as righteousness" (Gen. 15:6; Rom. 4:1–6). Further, the Apostle Paul tells us that Abraham "received circumcision as a sign or seal of the righteousness which he had by faith while he was still uncircumcised" (Rom. 4:11). The Reformers saw the possibility of explaining baptism the same way, namely that while we are justified by faith the sacrament is given as a sign or seal of a righteousness which was to be had by faith alone. This cleared up for the Reformers the problem of the relation of faith and sacrament but it did more. It also showed the Reformers how they could understand the baptism of infants. God had specifically directed Abraham to circumcise his male descendants as infants. That is, while Abraham received circumcision as a seal of a faith which he already had, his descendants were to receive that same sign as a sign of a faith and a righteousness they were yet to have. For Abraham and his descendants, that rite of circumcision became the divinely given sign and seal of the covenant promises.

More and more the Reformers came to understand baptism in terms not only of the covenant signs found in Scripture but also in terms of the prophetic signs of Scripture. They identified a whole series of prophetic signs which they found in both the Old and New Testament. When Jacob laid hands on the two sons of Joseph it was clearly a prophetic act. Jeremiah took the potter's vessel and broke it as a prophetic act signaling the destruction of Jerusalem. Jesus' act of cleansing the Temple was a prophetic sign. Perhaps the prophetic sign most clearly analogous to the baptism of children is the story of Samuel anointing David to be king while David was still a shepherd boy. It would be many years before that prophetic act would be fulfilled. Surely David understood very little of what Samuel did to him. It was only as the years went by that the meaning of that act unfolded. Yet that act was there, it was there quite indelibly nurturing the faith of David. David believed God would be faithful to the promise and indeed God was. The sign was given to awaken faith and nurture faith.

The question of infant baptism had been debated for more than ten years before John Calvin began to exercise theological leadership in the Reformed Churches. He too gave great attention to the question of the baptism of infants. It cannot be said as some have recently tried to say that the Reformers only baptized infants because it was the common custom of the time and the Reformers never got around to thinking through the question. In the chapter of his *Institutes of the Christian Religion* which he devotes to the question of infant baptism, Calvin summarizes the argument from Covenant theology. Baptism when it is administered to children is a particularly clear sign that God out of his grace has taken the initiative for our salvation. If the classical Reformers of sixteenth-century Protestantism continued the practice of administering baptism to infants it was because they had a very strong theology of grace. While the Reformers were strongly Augustinian, their opponents were openly Pelagian! The Anabaptists believed in decisional regeneration. That is, they believed one is saved by making a decision for Christ. There is a big difference between decisional regen-

eration and justification by faith. While the baptism of infants was perfectly consistent with a strong doctrine of grace and with the doctrine of
justification by faith it was not consistent with any kind of theology
which makes salvation a matter of human decisions.

When Calvin published the *Genevan Psalter* of 1545 the Reformers
of classical Protestantism had thought over the Anabaptist challenge
very carefully for almost twenty years. The Reformers had thought out
their baptismal rite both over against the old Latin rites and over against
the Anabaptist teaching. This had the effect of making the rite very well
balanced. Let us look at this Genevan baptismal rite.

The rubrics at the beginning of the rite specify that children are to be
presented for baptism at a regular service of worship, for baptism is a
solemn reception into the church and therefore should be celebrated in
the presence of the congregation. After the sermon the children are to be
presented and the minister is to begin the service, "Our help is in the
name of the Lord who made heaven and earth. Amen." Then the minister is to ask, "Do you present this child to be baptized?" The parents
answer that they do. The minister gives the Baptismal Exhortation much
in the same way as at Strasbourg. Next follows the Baptismal Invocation. The prayer begins with an anamnesis of God's covenant with
Abraham, "Lord God, Father eternal and almighty, since by your infi-
nite mercy, you have promised to be not only our God, but the God and
Father of our children as well . . . " (Calvin, *Opera Selecta* II, 30–38
[author's translation]). The prayer continues asking the forgiveness of
sins, the gift of faith, the sanctification of God's Spirit. It concludes
with the saying of the Lord's Prayer. The prayers being finished, the
parents are asked to promise that the child receive catechetical instruction and that the child be brought up in the nurture and admonition of
the Lord. It is important to notice that these promises are made by the
parents not the god-parents. The reason is to be found in Covenant
theology. The children are baptized because of the faith of their parents
not because god-parents have vicariously confessed faith for them. Such
promises having been made, the parents are asked to name the child. It
is quite clear that in the Genevan baptismal rite the child is given a
Christian name. This was not done in the German-speaking Reformed
churches of the Rhineland. Even before the Reformation it seems to
have been a peculiarly French custom. Nevertheless the Reformers had

noted that according to the Gospel of Luke it was at circumcision that names were given to children (Luke 1:59–60; 2:21). When one sees how important the Reformers considered the relationship between circumcision and baptism, then one is not at all surprised to discover that the Reformers encouraged the practice of giving Christian names at baptism. The parents give the name to the child and the minister baptizes the child, "in the name of the Father, and of the Son, and of the Holy Spirit." The baptism is performed by a single sprinkling. This done the minister gives a benediction to the child as well as to the parents.

Again we notice as we noticed with the Reformed baptismal rite of Strasbourg, the rite contains neither catechetical instruction nor a profession of faith. Catechetical instruction was postponed until later years. The Church of Geneva provided very thorough catechetical instruction for children from ten to twelve years old. Having received that instruction the children made their profession of faith and were admitted to communion. It should be noted that there was no thought that the baptism was incomplete until the catechetical instruction had been received and the profession of faith made. It was more that the Reformers understood that baptism entailed these things. The sign of washing was complete in itself, but its meaning would be unfolded through the whole of life.

In the Reformed understanding of baptism, baptism is a prophetic sign at the beginning of the Christian life the fulfillment of which continues to unfold throughout the whole of life. The sign of baptism claims for us the washing away of sins and calls us to newness of life. The sign of baptism calls us to repentance and to the profession of Christian faith. Whenever we confess our sins in prayers of confession or profess our faith by saying the Apostles Creed we are living out our baptism. Baptism is not something which is done once and then is finished and over. It is something which shapes the whole of the Christian life, from the very beginning to the very end. Baptism is a means of grace. It is the work of the Holy Spirit in our lives which brings about and fulfills what the sign of baptism had promised. That inward working of the Holy Spirit takes place through the whole of life until at last we die in Christ and are raised in Christ.

In the seventeenth century the Puritans developed this theme at considerable length. The *Westminster Larger Catechism* taught the importance of "improving our baptism." By this the Westminster Divines meant that Christians should "make good use of" their baptisms. This was to be done all through life, especially in times of trial and temptation. By a serious and thankful consideration of the divine promises made to us in our baptism our faith is strengthened. Our assurance of God's grace and favor is refreshed. Matthew Henry (1662–1714), the great Bible commentator, wrote a treatise on baptism about the year 1700. Henry had been brought up and nourished by the practical Puritan piety of the Westminster Assembly. His writings are a good reflection of Reformed spirituality at the beginning of the eighteenth century. How much of this work is devoted to the question of "improving one's baptism"! It is clear that for Matthew Henry the fact of his baptism as an infant determined the whole course of his life. He understood by this that from earliest childhood he had been called to the service of God and that he had been empowered by the gifts of God's Spirit to carry out that service. Baptism was the sign under which the whole of his life was lived.

Baptism is the presupposition and basis of all Christian worship. Not only does baptism call us to holiness of life, it consecrates us to the priestly service of prayer and praise (1 Peter 2:4–10; Rev. 1:5–6). In baptism we are set apart to God's service. At the center of that service is the service of worship. Baptism is a sign at the beginning of the Christian life that to serve God we must turn away from all other forms of service to the gods of this world. It is a sign that to serve God in truth we must be anointed by God's Spirit. It is God's Spirit who fits us and empowers us for his service. True worship is God's work within us and we serve him best when we give ourselves to him and allow ourselves to become the members of his body. It is when our hands and our tongues are moved by the Spirit of Christ that we do the work of Christ in this world to the glory of the Father who is in heaven.

III

The Lord's Day

Concern for the observance of the Lord's Day has always been a strong feature of Reformed worship. One notices that the *Westminster Directory* devotes a whole chapter to the subject of the observance or sanctification of the Lord's Day. Let us look carefully at the commandment to remember the Sabbath and its Christian interpretation.

The Sabbath Day was first of all a day in which God commanded his people to "remember." This word, "remember," is a very rich word in the biblical vocabulary. It means much more than as though the text read "Don't forget today is the Sabbath." The commandment has in mind far more than a mere mental noting of the fact that it is the Sabbath Day when it rolls around each week. It has much more the meaning of "Hold a service of memorial on the Sabbath." This becomes very clear when one compares the version of the Ten Commandments found in Exodus with the version in Deuteronomy. In Deuteronomy we find that the fourth commandment begins, "Observe the Sabbath Day" (Deut. 5:12). To remember the Sabbath Day means to observe the day, to celebrate the religious rites appropriate to the day.

What then was to be celebrated on this day? The Sabbath was a day in which a memorial was held celebrating God's works of creation and redemption. The celebrating of this memorial had the function of transmitting the witness to God's mighty acts, the creation of light out of darkness, the creation of heaven and earth, Adam and Eve, the call of Abraham, the deliverance of the children of Israel from Egypt and the gift of the law and the promised land. When Jesus at the Passover shared the bread and the cup with his disciples, he told them that from now on they were to do this in remembrance of him. The sharing of bread and wine was the new memorial. To be sure it was a memorial of the first creation, just as the old Sabbath had been, but it was more, it was a memorial of the new creation in Christ. It was a memorial of the new creation of which the first creation was a type and a promise. To be sure the sharing of bread and wine was a memorial of the deliverance from Egypt, just as the old Passover had been, but even more it was a memorial of the deliverance from sin and death accomplished in the fulfillment of the paschal mystery by Jesus. The new memorial celebrated Christ's passage from death to life, "out of this world to the Father" (John 13:1).

The Old Testament Sabbath was not only a day of remembrance; it was also a day of rest. "Remember the sabbath day, to keep it holy . . . . in it you shall not do any work"(Exod. 20:8–10). The two are intimately related to each other. In order to celebrate God's work, we refrain from our human works. John Calvin (1509–1564) in his passage in the *Institutes* on the fourth commandment makes a great point of this. ". . . under the repose of the seventh day the heavenly Lawgiver meant to represent to the people of Israel spiritual rest, in which believers ought to lay aside their own works to allow God to work in them" (Calvin, *Institutes* II: viii, 28).

Let us look for a moment at the divine works of which the Old Testament Sabbath was a memorial. The creation story at the very beginning of Genesis explains the creation in terms of the six days of creation and the seventh day of rest: here we see very clearly that the Sabbath Day is a memorial of creation. The Scriptures are no less clear that the Sabbath was a memorial of deliverance from Egypt. In the version of the Ten Commandments found in Deuteronomy we read, "Observe the sabbath day . . . in it you shall not do any work, you, or your son, or your daughter, or your manservant. . . . You shall remember that you were a servant in the land of Egypt, and the LORD your God brought you out thence with a mighty hand and an outstretched arm; therefore the LORD your God commanded you to keep the sabbath day" (Deut. 5:12–15). Here the diaconal aspect of worship is clearly underlined. By releasing laborers and servants from servile work on the Sabbath, one celebrated release from slavery in Egypt.

The memorial, however, is not only a celebration of the past but a promise of the future as well. The consummation of history was understood as a Sabbath rest (Ps. 95:11). Jewish thinkers in ancient times often explained that just as there were seven days of creation so there would be seven ages of history and finally seven ages of consummation. Particularly the Jewish apocalyptic writers of the two centuries immediately before Jesus developed these themes in a great variety of ways. During this time the Jewish messianic hopes and expectations became closely associated with speculations about the Sabbath and its implications for the future. We find some of this sabbatarian speculation concerning the ages to come in the book of Daniel. In the book of Revelation it is even more highly developed. The basic idea behind all this was that just as there were seven days of creation at the beginning, so there would be seven days of consummation at the end. The last day was thought of as a Sabbath of Sabbaths, a year of release, and this final Sabbath was to be brought in by the Messiah, who was the bringer of the new Sabbath. It is in the light of this Jewish eschatological sabbatarianism that many of the sayings of Jesus about the Sabbath are to be understood. Let us now turn to consider how Jesus understood the Sabbath and its observance.

First of all we should notice how often the Gospels specifically tell us that Jesus healed people on the Sabbath (Mark 3:1ff.; Luke 13:10–13; 14:1–4; John 5:1–10; 9:1–8). The frequency of healings might even suggest that Jesus very purposely chose to heal on the Sabbath. He did this not to shock people, not to break the law, not to show that the law was worn out and old-fashioned, but rather as a sign that the day of release had come. When Jesus healed the woman with the crooked back he explains, ''And ought not this woman, a daughter of Abraham whom Satan bound for eighteen years, be loosed from this bond on the sabbath day?''(Luke 13:16). The Sabbath which the Messiah brought in was a day of release from the bondage of Satan. Healing is not a human work but a divine work. The work of Jesus in releasing the woman did not hinder the Sabbath rest but rather established a deeper quality of Sabbath rest. The old Sabbath rest was in fact a sign or type of the deeper Sabbath rest which Jesus would bring. The Sabbath rest remembered the release from the bondage of Egypt but promised, as a sort of prophetic sign, release from the bondage of Satan.

The meaning of all this becomes even more clear, however, when we consider what great importance the New Testament gives to the fact that the resurrection took place on the first day of the week. All the Gospels are very clear and very explicit about this. The first day of the week was the day of the resurrection, the day when Jesus came to his disciples and broke bread with them. It was Jesus who took the initiative of making this the day of Christian worship, the day of remembrance, the day on which, with the breaking of the bread and the sharing of the cup, the church celebrated the memorial of Christ's passage from death to life. It was on this day that the risen Jesus again and again came to his disciples as they broke bread. The story of Jesus coming to two of his disciples on the road to Emmaus, on the first day of the week, first explaining to them the Scriptures and then breaking bread with them, is the prototype of the Christian Lord's Day service. The earliest Christians worshiped on the first day of the week because this was the day the risen Jesus came to them. This was the first day of a new age, the eighth day of the old age. This was the new Sabbath, brought in by the Messiah, the new Sabbath of release from the bondage of Satan which Jesus fulfilled by appearing to his disciples and eating with them.

The question is, did Jesus or did someone else change the Sabbath from Saturday to Sunday and make of the first day of the week the Christian Sabbath? The New Testament gives us no clear statement as to what happened or how it happened. All we know is that already in New Testament times Christians celebrated worship on the first day of the week and that they called it "the Lord's Day" (Acts 20:7; 1 Cor. 16:2; Rev. 1:10). It is hard to imagine how any Jew would tamper with something so sacred as the Sabbath. Certainly the disciples would never have done it on their own. One can only imagine Jesus himself doing it and then only if he had a profound sense of his having divine authority. Could we possibly imagine that Lord's Day worship was something which gradually evolved because someone thought it was a meaningful idea and after a while it gradually caught on? Never! The Sabbath had been established by divine authority and only by divine authority could it have been changed. The old Sabbath would only come to an end when the anointed Son of God brought in the final Sabbath of the last day, the Day of the Lord. If the first Christians worshiped on the Lord's Day it was because they believed that Jesus, by his resurrection, had brought in the final age. The Lord's Day took the place of the old Sabbath because it was on that day when Jesus came to his disciples and celebrated with them the memorial of his entry into the new age, his passage from death to life. This was the mighty act of redemption toward which all the others had pointed and it was this which was celebrated when the first Christians broke bread and shared the cup in remembrance of Jesus. It is in a very real sense Jesus himself who, fulfilling the old Sabbath, established the Lord's Day. But did Jesus give us a specific word or a concrete act by which he instituted the Lord's Day? This he did when he commanded his disciples to "Do this in remembrance of me," when he rose on the first day of the week and when he came to his disciples and ate with them on that day which was from then on his day.

Let us look a bit more closely at some examples of Lord's Day worship in the primitive Christian church. It was on the Day of Pentecost, the fiftieth day, the first day of the week after seven weeks, that the Holy Spirit descended upon the church and the first believers were baptized. Had it already after only a few weeks become customary for all the Christians to gather together on the morning of the first day of the week? It is very important to notice that it was on the Lord's Day that our Lord poured out his Holy Spirit. The first day of the week was not only the day of resurrection but the day of giving the Spirit as well. Later on we read that in Ephesus the Christians were gathered together to break bread on the first day of the week (Acts 20:7–11). Here the text does seem to imply that it was the regular procedure to meet on the first day of the week and break bread. Again, it was probably because the first day of the week was already the day of Christian worship that Paul tells the Corinthians to make their collection for the saints of Jerusalem on that day (1 Cor. 16:2).

It is in the book of Revelation, however, that we find the most elaborate development of the theme of the Lord's Day of which all Sabbaths and Sabbaths of Sabbaths are the prophetic type. It is the day of rest, the day of consummation, the day of never-ceasing praise and glory. The book of Revelation makes abundant use of the sabbatarian speculations of the Jewish apocalyptic writers. From the book of Revelation we discover what a rich theology of the Lord's Day the New Testament church had developed.

Following the history of Christian worship down through the centuries we discover that the earliest documents make a considerable point of the fact that Christian worship is held on the first day of the week. In the description of Christian worship given by the Roman writer Pliny in A.D. 110, it is specifically noted that it takes place on the first day of the week. Justin Martyr, writing about A.D. 160, says, "On the day which is called Sunday, all who live in the cities or in the countryside gather together in one place . . . " In another one of Justin's works, *Dialogue with Trypho*, we find a roughly developed theology of Lord's Day observance. It was not, however, until the first Christian emperors, in the fourth century, that Sunday became a public holiday and a day of rest for pagan and Christian alike. There was nothing illegitimate about this development. It was only natural and proper that the day of worship should be the day of rest. Only with the Christian emperors was it possible for the day of worship to become a public day of rest.

Starting in the third and fourth century the church began to develop an elaborate liturgical calendar of annual feasts and fast days. While the Christian observance of Easter and Pentecost may well have gone back to the first century, Christmas and Epiphany developed much later. Christmas we know to have been the remodeling of the pagan celebration of the sun god. Lent started out not as a time of remembering our Lord's Passion but as a time of penitential preparation for baptism at the Easter vigil. Advent and Lent became increasingly important as the whole of Christian devotion became obsessed with penance. Asceticism set the foundation of much in the liturgical calendar. Advent and Lent were above all seasons of fasting. By the end of the Middle Ages the season of Advent was cultivated but the twelve days of Christmas were of considerably less concern. Particularly in the West the penitential season of Lent called forth the most lush devotional practices, while the joyful seven weeks of Easter remained secondary. Advent and Lent, rather than the seasons of Christmas and Easter, became the religious seasons of the year. The development of the calendar of the saints goes back much further but it was only toward the beginning of the fifth century that the Marian feasts developed.

In the course of the Middle Ages, the liturgical calendar showed great vitality and developed with flamboyant complexity. The multiplication of feasts and saints days tended to obscure the celebration of the Lord's Day. Penitential purple was even allowed to veil the Easter glory of Sunday. By the beginning of the sixteenth century the trimming of the calendar had an obvious place on the agenda of church reform. Different Reformers had different approaches to calendar reforms. The Lutherans emphasized the liturgical seasons giving great importance to the penitential seasons of Advent and Lent. The Lutherans also celebrated most of the major feasts of the Christian year: Christmas, Circumcision, Epiphany, Good Friday, Easter, Ascension, and Pentecost. They also observed those saints days which commemorated saints mentioned in the New Testament. The Lutheran calendar represented a moderate reform. Its strong point was that it provided a Christocentric celebration of the calendar which emphasized the central acts of redemption: the incarnation, the passion, the resurrection and the glorification of Christ.

The South German churches took a much more incisive look at the problem and began to delve into the deeper meaning of the biblical sign of the Sabbath. They had no more begun their reform than some of the Anabaptists proposed going back to observing the Jewish Sabbath claiming that Sunday worship was the invention of the Emperor Constantine. The Strasbourg Reformer, Wolfgang Capito (1478–1541), a colleague of Martin Bucer, studied the matter very carefully and his work had great influence on the practice of Reformed churches. Capito was uniquely qualified to study this matter. Not only was he one of the pioneering Old Testament scholars of the day, he was trained in the history of the law, having a doctorate in law as well as in theology. Not only did he study the Old Testament concept of Sabbath but he was able to study the development of the Lord's Day observance in Roman law during the period of the Christian emperors. As Capito and the Strasbourg Reformers understood it, the question was basically one of the relation of the Old Testament to the New Testament. Capito in a typically Augustinian manner found a strong continuity between the two testaments. He stressed the position that the Old Testament prefigured and promised the New. With an appeal to the fourth chapter of Hebrews, Capito claimed that the old Sabbath was a sign of the rest and salvation that would begin with the resurrection of Christ. The old Sabbath was a promise of a day of rest that the Jews under the law had not yet experienced (Heb. 4:8). While that day of rest was the final day of consummation at the end of history, it is, even in this life, already experienced in the Lord's Day, the day of resurrection, which clearly, according to the Gospels, is the first day of the week. Ever since this basic study of Wolfgang Capito, Reformed churches have given special attention to the liturgical implications of the Lord's Day.

In the early 1530s there was considerable discussion in the Reformed Church of Strasbourg as to whether other feast days should be observed in addition to the Lord's Day. Capito, good patristic scholar that he was, turned his attention to the quartodeciman controversy in the second century because much of the earliest thinking of Christians regarding the calendar came to light in the course of that discussion. The Church of Strasbourg observed Easter and Pentecost from the beginning of the Reformation. About the celebration of Christmas there was considerable reservation, because the Reformers knew from patristic sources that it had not been observed until the fourth century. Within a few years the Reformed Church calendar was fairly well established. The heart of it was the weekly observance of the resurrection on the Lord's Day. Instead of liturgical seasons being observed, "the five evangelical feast days" were observed: Christmas, Good Friday, Easter, Ascension, and Pentecost. These were chosen because they were understood to mark the essential stages in the history of salvation. Lent and Advent were not observed because of their basically ascetic and penitential orientation. Saints days were not observed at all except insofar as it seemed appropriate on weekdays to mention the witness of the martyrs and the example of holy men and women who had gone before. John Oecolampadius (1481–1531), the Reformer of Basel and one of the leading patristic scholars of his day, was concerned that the church should maintain a remembrance of the great Christians of the past, particularly the martyrs. He recommended that this be done during the weekday services through sermon illustrations. We find much the same sentiments echoed by the English Puritan Richard Baxter (1615–1691). If the Reformed Church did not want a calendar of saints, it had no intention of forgetting about great Christians of the past.

In England, the Anglican party opted for what was essentially the Lutheran approach. The calendar reform became a major point of tension between the Anglican party and the Puritan party. The so-called "High Churchmen" put a greater and greater emphasis on the feasts and the liturgical seasons while the more radical Puritans underlined Sabbath observance to the point of tedium. When under Cromwell the more radical Puritans gained control of Parliament, they tried to suppress all the feasts and even the observance of Christmas. Sunday alone, as they saw it, was to be observed. In those Anglo-Saxon churches which to one degree or another share the Reformed tradition, whether Congregational, Methodist, Disciples, Baptist, or Presbyterian, there runs a strong current of Puritanism. This is particularly to be seen in the case of the calendar. Even a hundred years ago few Presbyterian, Congregational, or Disciples congregations would have held a service on Christmas Eve or even have noted that Pentecost Sunday had rolled around again. It should be noted, however, that in regard to the calendar, the Anglo-Saxon Puritan tradition was definitely different from the Continental Reformed usage.

Among the more moderate Puritans, a very rich theology of the Lord's Day was developed. A good example of this is found in a work by Thomas Shephard (1605–1649), one of the first American Reformed theologians. He was the first pastor of the Church of Christ in Cambridge, Massachusetts, and one of the founders of Harvard University. In a manner typical of Reformed theology, Shephard finds the worship of the church already instituted in the law. Christians are to observe the Sabbath, according to Shephard, on the first day of the week, because that is the day on which Jesus rose from the dead. Jesus taught his disciples to worship on the first day of the week. Although this is not recorded in the Bible, we can be sure that it took place, because, the learned Puritan tells us, we find in the Bible that the primitive Christian church did this. Shephard presents the Sabbath as a sign of man's eternal rest, "that so his perfect blessedness to come might be foretasted every Sabbath day, and so has begun here." Any attempt at recovering a Reformed spirituality would do well carefully to study the best of the Puritan literature on the observance of the Lord's Day.

IV

The Ministry
of Praise

The beginnings of Christian praise go back at least as far as King David and the worship of Solomon's Temple. Let us look then at the Temple praises to discover what they really were. There were two major places in the Temple worship where hymns of praise were sung. The first was on entering the Temple; the second was during the immolation of the sacrifice.

When pilgrims went up to Jerusalem they sang as they went. Psalms 121 and 122 were probably first written for pilgrims going off to the Temple:

> I was glad when they said to me,
>   "Let us go to the house of the LORD!" . . .
> Jerusalem, built as a city
>   which is bound firmly together,
> to which the tribes go up,
>   the tribes of the LORD,
> as was decreed for Israel,
>   to give thanks to the name of the LORD.
>
>   (Psalm 122:1–4)

In Psalm 84 we get a vivid picture of the pilgrims going up to Jerusalem.

> How lovely is thy dwelling place,
>   O LORD of Hosts!
> My soul longs, yea, faints
>   for the courts of the LORD . . .

> Blessed are the men whose strength is in thee,
>   in whose heart are the highways to Zion.
> As they go through the valley of Baca
>   they make it a place of springs . . .
> They go from strength to strength;
>   the God of gods will be seen in Zion.
>
> (Psalm 84:1–7)

When David brought the ark of the Covenant to Jerusalem the ark was accompanied by hymns of praise (2 Sam. 6:1–15; Ps. 131). In fact the usual way to approach Zion was with hymns of praise. Psalm 100 tells us,

> Make a joyful noise to the LORD, all the lands!
>   Serve the LORD with gladness!
>   Come into his presence with singing! . . .
> Enter his gates with thanksgiving,
>   and his courts with praise!
> Give thanks to him, bless his name!
>
> (Psalm 100:1–4)

Praise can be defined as the sense of awe and wonder which we have when we enter the presence of God. So, then, that is why the entering of the Temple is with hymns of praise.

When the pilgrims approached the gates of the Temple there were evidently particular rites for opening the gates. At least two psalms come from these rites, Psalms 15 and 24. When we add these psalms to the seventh chapter of Jeremiah we get a fairly clear picture of what happened during the ceremonial opening of the gates at a great feast. The people approached the gates singing a hymn of praise, "This is the temple of the Lord, the temple of the Lord" or as we have it in Psalm 24, "The earth is the LORD'S and the fullness thereof, the world and those who dwell therein." This opening hymn of praise might chant God's glory and power or it might greet or acclaim Mount Zion or the Temple itself. Having arrived at the Temple gates, one of the Temple prophets, Jeremiah, for example, preached a penitential sermon designed to lead the people to examine their lives, confess their sin, and so to enter the Temple.

> Who shall ascend the hill of the LORD?
> And who shall stand in his holy place?

He who has clean hands and a pure heart,
who does not lift up his soul to what is false,
and does not swear deceitfully.

(Psalm 24:3-4)

After the people had confessed their sin the prophet was supposed to intercede for the people (cf. Jer. 7:16; 14:7-9). Then the prophet bestowed on them a benediction or assurance of pardon. At last the people cry out, "Lift up your heads, O ye gates, and be lifted up ye everlasting doors." The gates were opened, the hymns began again, and the people entered the Temple.

It should be noticed here first of all that the beginning of worship is always praise, but second, it should be noticed that praise and the confession of our sin go hand in hand. Just as Isaiah when he was confronted by the presence of God in the Temple was first caught up by the Seraphic song, "Holy, holy, holy is the LORD of Hosts" and then prostrated himself on the ground with his humble confession, "Woe is me! . . . for I am a man of unclean lips, and I dwell in the midst of a people of unclean lips" (Isa. 6:5), so we approach God in both praise and confession.

It was during the actual immolation or burning of the sacrifice that the singing of the psalms played its primary role. While the sacrifice was being burned on the altar a psalm of praise and thanksgiving was sung by the Levites as the one who offered the sacrifice circumambulated the altar (Pss. 25—26). That is, the worshipers walked around the altar, usually seven times, by which rite they "owned" the sacrifice, identifying it with themselves as the smoke of the sacrifice ascended to heaven. God was praised and thanked for works of creation and providence. The story of God's saving acts toward Israel was recounted. Often the story of the election of the patriarchs, the deliverance of the children of Israel from Egypt, their trials in the wilderness, and their possession of the promised land was recounted. At other times more personal acts of deliverance were described. In such cases the psalm was the personal witness of the worshiper. The psalm told what God had done in the worshiper's life. Such a psalm was a confession of faith but it was also a confession in the sense that it admitted to the obligation which the worshiper now bore by virtue of having received the deliverance and gracious bounty of God.

In later times, that is, in the days of the Second Temple, a psalm was sung at the very end of the service. Seven particular psalms were used at that point, one for each day of the week. Starting with Sunday these psalms were: 24, 48, 82, 94, 81, 93, and 92 for the Sabbath. The Temple worship was understood to end with praise just as it had begun with praise.

When the Temple of Solomon was destroyed and the Jews were deported to Babylon, the normal place of worship came to be the synagogue. This involved far more than just a change in architectural setting. It involved two very different liturgies and two very different approaches to worship. While the Temple service centered on the sacrifices, the synagogue service centered on the study of law and on the saying of the daily prayers. The synagogue service never took over the sacrifices. They were performed exclusively in the Temple, but the synagogue did take over from the Temple the psalms that had accompanied the sacrifices. Just when these psalms began to be used in the synagogue service and just which psalms were used is not clear. When the psalms were used in the synagogue, however, they were sung without the elaborate instrumental accompaniment used in the Temple.

From Psalm 137 we perhaps find a hint that the first Babylonian exiles did in fact sing the psalms, the songs of Zion, when they gathered together for worship even though it was with heavy hearts.

> By the waters of Babylon,
>   there we sat down and wept,
>   when we remembered Zion.
> On the willows there
>   we hung up our lyres.
> For there our captors
>   required of us songs,
> and our tormentors, mirth, saying,
>   "Sing us one of the songs of Zion!"
>
> (Psalm 137:1–3)

At least by the time of Jesus we know that the synagogue service included the singing of psalms. Rabbinical sources from that time indicate that the synagogue worship began with psalmody. On weekdays Psalms 145—150 were sung and on the Sabbath Psalms 95—100 were sung. Again, although the sources are rather late, we learn that the seven psalms that were sung at the end of the Temple service were also sung at the end of the synagogue service. It is quite possible nevertheless, that this usage went back long before the first Christian century. To begin and end the service of worship with psalms of praise was a very natural thing to do in synagogue worship just as it had been very natural in the Temple.

The first Christians took over many of the worship traditions of the synagogue. They did not take over the rich and sumptuous ceremonial of the Temple, but rather the simpler synagogue service, with its Scripture reading, its sermon, its prayers, and its psalmody. We find many evidences of this in the New Testament. In Acts 4:23–31 we read of Christians gathering for prayer. Their prayer service began with the whole congregation singing psalms. Several times the Apostle Paul tells Christians to sing psalms. In 1 Corinthians 14:26 Paul tells the church that when they are gathered together for worship among other things they are to sing psalms. The text actually reads, "When you come together, each one has a hymn, a revelation." This probably means that the whole congregation is to sing a psalm, but it may indicate that the first Christians had cantors like the synagogue. The cantor would sing the text while the congregation answered by singing "Hallelujah" after each verse. It surely did not mean that everyone was supposed to get up and sing a solo.

Both in Paul's letters to the Ephesians and to the Colossians we read of singing, "psalms, hymns and spiritual songs." The Psalms of the Old Testament were considered perfectly acceptable for Christian worship. They were the songs of the Holy Spirit. The first Christians were particularly conscious of the presence of the Holy Spirit in their worship. It was the Spirit who inspired their worship. Their preaching and their interpretation of the Scriptures was the work of God's Spirit crying out within them. It was the Spirit within them who bore witness that Jesus was the Christ, the Lord's anointed. It was the same Holy Spirit who moved them to praise. It is interesting how often the mention of singing psalms and hymns in the New Testament is accompanied by references to the Holy Spirit. For example, Paul admonishes the Ephesians to be filled with the Holy Spirit, to sing psalms and spiritual songs, making melody in their hearts (Eph. 5:18–20). In the fourth chapter of Acts we find another example. We read that the congregation, "lifted their voices together." Then a line from Psalm 146 is quoted and after that several lines from Psalm 2. What is of particular interest is that Psalm 2 is introduced by a benediction very similar in literary form to the benediction used to introduce the psalmody in the synagogue, ". . . the mouth of our father David, thy servant, didst say by the Holy Spirit . . . " (Acts 4:25). Quite obviously for the first Christians this was an important consideration. When they sang the Psalms the Holy Spirit was praising the Father within their hearts.

The Psalms formed the core of the praises of the New Testament church; nevertheless the earliest Christians sang praises other than the one hundred fifty canonical psalms and the occasional psalms or canticles found elsewhere in Scripture. In the first place we find a number of Christian psalms such as the Song of Mary (Luke 1:46–55), the Song of Zechariah (Luke 1:68–79), and the Song of Simeon (Luke 2:29–32). These are clearly Christian psalms written in the literary genre of the Hebrew votive thanksgiving psalms. There is a sense in which these Christian psalms complete the Old Testament Psalms. So many of the Psalms contained prophetic oracles which intimated the reign of the Christ. Now that the Christ had indeed come, surely the people of God should sing the votive thanksgiving psalms. In Covenant theology the thanksgiving hymn filled a most significant role. It confessed the obligation which God's people owed to their Redeemer. They had cried to God; God heard their cry and saved them; now they owed to God their lives in obedient service. Even more than that the thanksgiving hymn was a thankful confession before the world of the covenant faithfulness of God to his people. The Old Testament Psalms had for generations cried out for the Lord's anointed; now the New Testament psalms confessed that the cry had been heard and the promise fulfilled.

The canticles in the Gospel of Luke are the core of Christian praise. From these Christian psalms Christian hymns rapidly developed. Yet these Christian hymns went beyond the Hebrew literary forms and took on Greek poetic features more familiar to the new Gentile congregations which were springing up over the whole Mediterranean world. In the epistles of Paul we find two hymns to Christ which many scholars feel reflect the hymnody of the Greek speaking congregations. The so-called Christological hymn of Philippians is the leading example:

> Christ Jesus, who, though he was in the form of God, did not count
> equality with God a thing to be grasped, but emptied himself, taking
> the form of a servant, being born in the likeness of men.
> And being found in human form he humbled himself and became obedi-
> ent unto death, even death on a cross.

Therefore God has highly exalted him and bestowed on him the name which is above every name, that at the name of Jesus every knee should bow, in heaven and on earth and under the earth, and every tongue confess that Jesus Christ is Lord, to the glory of God the Father.

(Philippians 2:5–11)

A similar hymn-like passage is found in Colossians:

He is the image of the invisible God, the first-born of all creation; for in him all things were created, in heaven and on earth, visible and invisible, whether thrones or dominions or principalities or authorities—all things were created through him and for him.
He is before all things, and in him all things hold together.
He is the head of the body, the church; he is the beginning, the first-born from the dead, that in everything he might be preeminent. For in him all the fulness of God was pleased to dwell, and through him to reconcile to himself all things, whether on earth or in heaven, making peace by the blood of his cross.

(Colossians 1:15–20)

There is little question but what the first Christians did write hymns to Christ and sing them in their worship side by side with the psalms which they sang as fulfilled prophecies of the coming Messiah. In fact very shortly after New Testament times we read in one of the letters of the Roman governor Pliny to the Emperor Trajan a short description of a Christian worship service. It clearly says that the Christians sang hymns to Christ.

There is another kind of singing which we find in the New Testament. In the pages of the New Testament we often hear the worship of heaven. In the Gospel of Luke we hear the song of the angels, "Glory to God in the highest, and on earth peace, goodwill toward men." In the Revelation we hear the angels worshiping God, "Holy, holy, holy, is the Lord God Almighty." It is said that the angels never cease to sing this hymn. They sing it over and over again as they sing Hallelujah again and again. But perhaps the most interesting thing we read about this heavenly hymnody is that in heaven the saints sing "The Song of Moses and the Lamb." The Song of Moses is the hymn we find in Exodus 15:

I will sing to the LORD, for he has triumphed gloriously;
the horse and his rider he has thrown into the sea.

(Exodus 15:1)

This song of Moses was regularly sung in the Temple in New Testament times. Was "The Song of Moses and the Lamb" a Christian version of Exodus 15 or was it an entirely new composition based on the Song of Moses? Perhaps it is a hymn like the one John hears.

> "To him who sits upon the throne and to the Lamb be blessing and honor and glory and might for ever and ever!"
>
> (Revelation 5:13)

We cannot say exactly. The hymns of the book of Revelation surely reflect the praises of the earliest Christians. Scholars have often said this and it is no doubt true. Scholars have also pointed to the fact that the hymns of Revelation are very closely patterned on the Temple hymnody. They are a Christian reworking of the seraphic hymn of Isaiah, the Song of Moses, and the Psalms. That at any rate is the way some scholars would put it. The way the early church understood it, however, would have been more like this: just as the architectural structure of the Temple followed the patterns of the heavenly sanctuary, so the hymns of the Temple followed the pattern of the angelic worship. It is the hymns of Revelation which are more nearly like the heavenly worship. John heard the heavenly worship more clearly than either David or Isaiah. He understood that the Song of Moses was in reality the song of the Lamb. It is for this reason that the canticles, reworked in a Christian manner, became increasingly important in the worship of the church.

But now the question is, did the first Christians understand their hymns, the hymns they wrote, to be the hymns of the Holy Spirit in the same way they understood the Psalms to be the hymns of the Holy Spirit or the canticles to be the reflection of the heavenly worship? When Paul spoke of "spiritual songs" did he mean songs inspired by the Holy Spirit, which were a Christian counterpart of the Old Testament Psalms? Probably not. The reason is that all these early Christian hymns disappeared. The New Testament never included a collection of Christian psalms to go with the Gospels and Epistles. In the course of the second century the Gnostics wrote lots of "spirit-inspired hymns." But the orthodox became more and more of the opinion that there was something much more inspired in the psalms and canticles than in the "spiritual hymns" which appeared in the worship of the early church. It seems much more likely that the earliest Christians understood their hymnody as a sort of elaboration, a sort of drawing out, commentary, or perhaps a sort of meditation on the canonical psalms and canticles traditionally used in the worship of the Temple and the synagogue.

Not too long after the close of the New Testament period we know that the church began to cultivate psalmody as the preferred expression of Christian praise. More and more the orthodox became weary of new hymns supposedly inspired by the Holy Spirit. In the Eastern churches the writing of Christian hymns enjoyed some popularity in orthodox circles but it was more characteristic of various Gnostic sects. In the West the church sang psalms and canticles almost exclusively until the time of St. Ambrose of Milan toward the end of the fourth century. The hymns of St. Ambrose were so popular that other Christian poets began to try their hand at writing hymns. We find hymns by Prudentius (348–410), Venantius Fortunatus (530–610), and Gregory the Great (540–604). These hymns however never replaced the psalms during the patristic period either in cathedral churches or in monasteries. Both hymnody and psalmody continued to be cultivated. Gregory the Great did much to develop both hymnody and psalmody with the music which today we call Gregorian Chant.

With Gregory the Great we begin to enter the Middle Ages. More and more it was the monks who were charged with the praise of the church, particularly in the monasteries, but also it was the monks who as members of the *schola cantorum* provided music for the cathedrals. It was only at the beginning of the ninth century that the church began to use organs. Up until that time there was no instrumental music in Christian worship. As the Middle Ages progressed church music became more and more elaborate. It is to the credit of the monks that they did so much to develop Christian praise during the period. They had both the leisure and the culture and they used it well. It is really the church of the Middle Ages which developed the choral and instrumental music of the church which today we take so much for granted.

With the Reformation the praises of the church took a very different direction. The Reformers wanted the whole congregation to sing the praises of the church. They wanted the people to sing in their own language and in music simple enough for the people to learn. This meant, quite practically speaking, the production of a wholly new church music. One could not really expect the whole congregation to sing what the trained monastic choirs had been singing, nor could one simply translate the Latin texts into German or French and sing the new text to the old music. Besides that, taste in music was changing rapidly. The average Renaissance musician regarded the liturgical music of the late Middle Ages with disdain. Even the sophisticated Erasmus would rather hear no music in church than hear the music of the monks. This often happens to even the best of music; people simply get tired of it. Those who sing it get tired of it and those who hear it get tired of it. It was not that the music was bad as much as it was stale. The Reformation was amazingly successful in refreshing the praises of the church.

The contribution of Martin Luther to the history of Christian praise and even to the history of music in general is enormous. He wrote music himself and wrote hymns which are still immensely popular. Of the more than thirty hymns of Luther's which have come down to us we have German versions of Psalms 12, 14, 46, 67, 124, 128, and 130. Luther did as much as anyone to revive and popularize psalm singing in the sixteenth century. Luther also produced a number of festal hymns, that is, hymns for the feasts of Christmas, Easter, and Pentecost. Luther's contributions to church music are well known, but Luther was only one Reformer among many, particularly in this respect. It was because there was a whole host of hymn writers traveling the same road as Luther that within a generation the churches which received the reform had developed a rich tradition of doxology.

It is to the Reformed Church of Strasbourg that we must first turn. The city was well known for its poets and musicians and with the reform of worship they quickly set to work producing psalms and hymns in the German language. In the early days it was the psalms which received the greatest attention. Just a few years before the beginning of the Reformation, Johann Reuchlin (1455–1522), the great Christian Humanist who did so much to revive the study of biblical Hebrew, published a Latin translation of a little book by Athanasius on the praying of the psalms. Athanasius (c. 296–373), one of the greatest of the Church Fathers, had been patriarch of Alexandria at the beginning of the fourth century. This little book gives us a good idea of how important the psalms were to the prayer life of the ancient church. From Athanasius the Reformers of Strasbourg got the inspiration of developing a popular psalmody for the church of their own day. Originally the developing of a popular psalmody was thought of in terms of the singing of the daily office, the daily prayer services, which with the coming of the Reformation were held each morning and evening in the cathedral as well as in the neighborhood churches of the city of Strasbourg. The *Strasbourg German Service Book* of 1525, the first attempt at a "Reformed" service of worship, appeared with a number of metrical psalms to be sung by the congregation. Metrical psalmody was part of Reformed worship from the very beginning. Two psalms of Luther's are included; there are several psalm versions by Matthew Greiter, the director of music at the cathedral, and Wolfgang Dachstein, one of the most renowned organists of the day. Ludwig Oehler began a systematic translation of the psalter and his versions of the first eight psalms are included. With each succeeding edition of the *Strasbourg Psalter* the number of psalms is augmented.

As these psalm versions were being produced, Martin Bucer (1491–1551) was busy producing his remarkable commentary on the Hebrew text of the Psalms. For a thousand years Christian biblical scholars had neglected the original Hebrew text of the Psalms. Bucer on the other hand returned to the original text. The Strasbourg Reformer made himself thoroughly familiar not only with the commentaries of the Church Fathers but with the standard rabbinical commentaries as well. In this commentary Bucer took pains to make the original meaning of the Hebrew text quite clear, but Bucer also recognized the legitimacy of the Christian interpretation of the Psalms. It is the New Testament itself, Bucer recognized, which again and again gives us the Christian interpretation of the Psalms. For Bucer, just as for the New Testament church, the Psalms were the songs of the Holy Spirit and were therefore most appropriate for Christian prayer. The biblical research of Bucer gave theological substance to the revival of psalmody in the Church of Strasbourg.

In the meantime another notable collection of praises was being developed by the Reformed Church of Constance. Constance, famous as the seat of an ecumenical council a century before the Reformation, had been led into the Reformation by Johannes Zwick (1496–1542) and the brothers, Ambrosius and Thomas Blarer (1492–1564 and 1499–1570). All three of these men wrote hymns which even today are included in the standard Swiss and German hymnals. They produced festal hymns for the feasts of Christmas, Easter, Ascension, and Pentecost. They left us hymns for both morning and evening prayer, and of particular interest they provided a collection of catechetical hymns for children. These included versions of the Lord's Prayer, the Creed, the Ten Commandments, and the Beatitudes. Johannes Zwick was particularly dedicated to the Christian education of children. Zwick was a man of diverse talents. Having studied law in Italy he became professor of jurisprudence in Basel. He had already won a good reputation in the legal profession when he was called into the ministry of his native city. There he distinguished himself as a preacher, but even more as a teacher of children. His catechism is regarded as one of the best produced in the sixteenth century. He wrote these catechetical hymns for the Sunday afternoon children's services in order that praise and prayer might be an integral part of catechetical instruction.

The *Constance Hymn Book* of 1540 deserves to be recognized as one of the most significant monuments in the history of Reformed worship. There must have been an edition of the *Constance Hymn Book* at least as early as 1533 but the first edition which has come down to us is the edition of 1540. The preface written by Johannes Zwick is a notable defense of the new Protestant approach to the use of popular psalmody and hymnody. The volume contains more than 150 pieces, half of which are metrical psalms. While a good portion of the hymns were produced by local authors and composers, we also find hymns by the Reformers of Wittenberg, Johann Agricola, Justus Jonas, and of course Luther. The psalmodists of Strasbourg, Ludwig Oehler, Johannes Englisch, Heinrich Vogtherr, Matthew Greiter, and Wolfgang Dachstein are represented by a significant number of works. We also find works by Hans Sachs, the almost legendary meistersinger of Nuremberg, and by Augsburg's Jakob Dachser and Zurich's Leo Jud. This hymnbook testifies to the vitality of Protestant hymnody in the early sixteenth century.

In the meantime the *Strasbourg Psalter* had been growing rapidly. Each new edition increased the number of psalms and canticles available. With the *Strasbourg Psalter* of 1537 there was a major revision of the liturgy of the Reformed Church of Strasbourg. This revision was the result of discussions with other Reformed churches in the Upper Rhineland. In regard to the ministry of praise the Strasbourgers had initially been inclined toward the singing of the biblical psalms and canticles alone, but with the *Strasbourg Psalter* of 1537 they have obviously yielded to the lead of their colleagues in Constance. The new edition of the psalter added the festal hymns of Johannes Zwick and the Blarer brothers as well as their morning and evening hymns and even their catechetical hymns. The 1537 edition of the *Strasbourg Psalter* is a magnificent liturgical book, containing the standard liturgical texts for the Lord's Day, matins, vespers, baptism, and the marriage service. But one thing this psalter makes very clear is that the psalms and hymns themselves are to be counted among the basic liturgical texts of Protestantism. These texts are the prayers of the people. From now on it is the psalter which is the fundamental liturgical book of Reformed Protestantism.

It was the year following the publication of this epoch-making edition of the psalter that John Calvin became pastor of the congregation of French exiles which had taken refuge in Strasbourg. Calvin set about developing a similar collection of psalms and prayers in the French language. The collection included thirteen psalms by Clément Marot. Calvin tried his hand at five psalms, but withdrew them in succeeding editions. Marot's metrical psalms were magnificent! Clément Marot was the leading French lyric poet of the sixteenth century. The metrical psalms of Marot represent French lyrical poetry at its best. He used a great variety of meters and rhythm structures. We are not too sure how Calvin and Marot first got together but in 1542 Calvin was able to publish another psalter with additional psalm versions by Marot. In addition to the new psalms the *Genevan Psalter* of 1542 contained some canticles and catechetical hymns. As the years went by Calvin was able to secure the service of some very fine poets and musicians. Louis Bourgeois and Claude Goudimel provided excellent music and Theodore Beza provided some fine texts. When the *Genevan Psalter*, or as it is more popularly called, the *Huguenot Psalter,* was finally finished it was a classic, providing the prototype of Reformed psalmody for generations to come.

Unfortunately Calvin did not follow the lead of Strasbourg and Constance in maintaining a balance between psalmody and hymnody. The *Genevan Psalter*, while it contained a few gospel canticles and catechetical pieces, settled for virtually exclusive psalmody. In the preface to the *Genevan Psalter* Calvin gives us his reasons for this. "The psalms incite us to praise God, to pray to Him, to meditate on His works to the end that we love Him, fear, honor and glorify Him. What St. Augustine says is quite true, one can not sing anything more worthy of God than that which we have received from Him." It is for this reason, Calvin continues,that no matter where we search we will not find better or more appropriate songs for our worship than the psalms of David. For after all, these songs come from the Holy Spirit. When we sing them it is God himself who is putting the words in our mouths so that it is he himself who sings within us, exalting his glory. It is for this reason, Calvin tells us, that Chrysostom exhorts men, women, and children regularly to sing the psalms that in this way they might join themselves to the company of the angels. One notices that Calvin does not appeal to the authority of Scripture in this matter. In defending his preference for psalmody Calvin appeals not to Scripture but to John Chrysostom and Augustine. This being the case one can be sure that Calvin had no objection if in other churches hymns other than psalms were sung. His use of exclusive psalmody was a matter of preference.

As Bucer before him, Calvin began work on a commentary on the Hebrew text of the Psalms. Today this four volume work is considered by some Calvin's greatest biblical commentary. The commentary gives considerable attention to the nature of prayer as revealed in the Psalms. Calvin begins his commentary by developing one of the themes set forth by Athanasius in his essay on the devotional use of the psalms. The book of Psalms is an anatomy of all the parts of the soul. Every emotion that we experience is reflected in the book of Psalms as in a mirror. Here the Holy Spirit has revealed all the griefs, sorrows, fears, doubts, hopes, and confusions with which our minds are apt to be disturbed. The Spirit has uttered these prayers in our own utterance that we might the better grasp them. In the psalms we are drawn to examine ourselves and discover our true need; for, as Calvin never tires of saying, true prayer proceeds first from a sense of our need and next from faith in the promises of God. Calvin sees the use of psalms in meditation and self examination as an important function of the psalms in worship. He has in mind particularly the many psalms of lamentation which are found in the psalter.

Psalmody also has a didactic function for Calvin. We use the psalms in worship because in the psalms we learn God's Word. In the psalms we meditate on the law. Calvin is fond of that text from Psalm 1 which tells of the delight which the righteous have in meditating on the law day and night. That the study of the law should be something of such joy may be difficult for us to fathom, but surely this is one of the clearest characteristics of a Calvinist spirituality. There is a joy in learning the law of the Lord!

For Calvin the chief function of psalmody in the worship of the church is doxological. The psalms lead us in the right manner of offering the sacrifice of praise to God. Calvin is fond of saying that in praying the psalms we are exercised in praise. When the whole congregation sings a psalm of praise together then all are stirred up to more and more genuine devotion to God. It is in this sense that Calvin speaks of the praying of the psalms as an exercise. In the psalms we hear of God's mighty acts of creation, providence, and redemption. We hear of one deliverance after another and hearing all this we are encouraged to direct our hopes to this same Almighty God. When the church thus grows in its praise then God is magnified.

Even with Wittenberg, Constance, and Strasbourg taking the lead for a generous supplementing of the psalms with Christian hymnody, the preference of Geneva for exclusive psalmody prevailed in Reformed churches for the next two hundred years. In England a psalter was gotten together as early as 1547 by Thomas Sternhold. Before his death in 1549 he was able to compose thirty-seven psalms. The work was taken over successively by John Hopkins and John Day. The complete edition was printed in 1562 and commonly known as the *Sternhold and Hopkins Psalter*. The *Sternhold and Hopkins Psalter* enjoyed tremendous popularity for the remainder of the sixteenth century, although it drew criticism from many quarters. The High Church party disdained the metrical psalms because they lacked the artistic finesse of monastic psalmody. With a sneer Queen Elizabeth I dismissed them as "Geneva jigs." On the other side they were criticized because they did not stick closely enough to the original text of the Hebrew Psalms. A certain legalism set in at this point. More and more the work of the poet was hampered by the demand for very literal translations. This literalism tended to ossify the tradition. A number of other attempts were made to come up with better psalters. The most memorable of these were the *Scottish Psalter* (1635), the *Bay Psalter* (1640), and Nahum Tate and Nicholas Brady's *New Version of the Psalms* (1696). The *Bay Psalter* had the distinction of being the first book printed in America. The psalms were put into meter by Richard Mather, Nathaniel Ward, and Thomas Shephard, leading ministers of the Massachusetts Bay Colony. To accompany this psalter Thomas Shephard wrote a work on psalmody, *Singing of Psalms, a Gospel Ordinance*, which gives us a good insight into the liturgical theology of early New England. In 1643, Francis Rous (1579–1659) published *Psalms Translated into English Meter*. Rous had studied both at Oxford and Leyden. For more than thirty years, from the reign of Charles I through the great days of the Commonwealth, Rous sat in Parliament. He never took ordination but he was a respected amateur theologian. His version of the psalms was approved by the Westminster Assembly and authorized by Parliament. Many of his psalms found their way, in revised form, into the *Scottish Psalter* and are still in use today. Unfortunately none of the versions ever attained anything like the poetic or musical quality of the *Huguenot Psalter*.

At the beginning of the eighteenth century, the psalmody and hymnody of the English-speaking Reformed churches experienced a substantial revival under the leadership of Isaac Watts (1674–1748). Isaac Watts was an English Congregational minister who because of ill health had had to retire from his London pastorate. Watts wrote both Christian hymns and metrical psalms. He translated the psalms into English meter with a free hand never shrinking from finding Christ in the psalter. For example his version of Psalm 72 begins

> Jesus shall reign where'er the sun
> Does his successive journeys run;
> His Kingdom stretch from shore to shore,
> Till moons shall wax and wane no more.

In fact there were those who complained that his versions were not metrical psalms so much as psalm paraphrases. Nevertheless the Watts psalms were extremely popular and surely one of the reasons for this is that he allowed himself such a free hand in rendering the psalms into metrical versions. Isaac Watts' version of Psalm 90:

> O God, our Help in ages past,
> Our Hope for years to come,
> Our Shelter from the stormy blast,
> And our eternal Home.

is surely one of the most beloved hymns in the English language. Again Watts' version of Psalm 98, "Joy to the World!", is indeed a very free rendering of the psalm, yet it is a very fine and sensitive Christian interpretation of that psalm.

The remarkable thing about Isaac Watts' hymns and spiritual songs is the way they take on the character of Christian psalms. In a way not unlike the Christian psalms of the New Testament, the hymns which Watts wrote were elaborations and meditations on the canonical psalms. One of Watts' hymns which gives the impression of being an imitation of a psalm is

> I sing the mighty power of God,
>   That made the mountains rise;
> That spread the flowing seas abroad,
>   And built the lofty skies.
> I sing the Wisdom that ordained
>   The sun to rule the day;
> The moon shines full at His command,
>   And all the stars obey.

The devotional quality of Watts' hymns is unsurpassed. Perhaps his best remembered hymn is, "When I Survey the Wondrous Cross," a meditation on Christ's Passion. Such hymns paved the way for a far greater acceptance of Christian hymnody. Watts was followed by a whole host of hymn writers, such as Philip Doddridge, Charles Wesley, John Newton, and William Cowper.

The work of Isaac Watts exemplifies the Reformed doxological tradition at its best. We find in his work a balance between psalmody and hymnody. The hymnody springs from the psalmody; it is inspired by the psalmody. Watts' hymnody comments on, interprets, and continues the psalmody. While one would not want to return to a legalistic insistence on exclusive psalmody, one can certainly see great benefit in an attempt to recover psalm prayer for our day. The church has not always through its long history kept a balance between psalmody and hymnody. Pendulum-like the Christian devotional tradition has regularly swung from one extreme to another. For a while we seem to rely on psalms alone and then for a while "hymns of human composure" seem to monopolize our liturgical life. It is when there is a dynamic relation between the two that Christian doxology is best served.

V

The Ministry
of the Word

One often reads of preaching in the Scriptures but one does not often read in the Scriptures of preaching in a service of worship, or at least in such a way that we can determine much about how it was done. There are a few exceptions. One of these is the sermon which Jeremiah preached at the Feast of Tabernacles (Jer. 7:1–15). From the rather brief report which we have of that sermon, it would appear that it was a sermon on the Ten Commandments. The prophet goes over the Commandments one by one and then exhorts the people to live by them. The giving of such a penitential sermon surely belonged to the liturgy of the Feast of Tabernacles. We have evidence of this in Psalm 24 as well as other entrance psalms. Perhaps sermons of other prophets besides those of Jeremiah had their liturgical setting in the Feast of Tabernacles.

Surely preaching and teaching were an integral part of the worship of the Temple. We know, for example, that the regular reading through of the Book of the Covenant was an essential part of the rites of the renewal of the Covenant (Deut. 31:10–13). It was no doubt the Temple ministry of the prophets to proclaim the Word of God when the people gathered as a holy assembly. That Jeremiah preached in the Temple was surely nothing exceptional. That Amos preached in the king's sanctuary was extraordinary only because he was neither a prophet nor a prophet's son. Ordinarily one expected prophets to preach in the Temple. In the days of Jesus the great rabbis and teachers of the law taught daily in the courts of the Temple. One might even say that it was in the courts of the

Temple that the classes of the theological seminary of Jerusalem were held. This custom must have stemmed from much older traditions of sacred learning which went far back into history. Even from earliest times the priests also must have had a ministry of the word. They were ministers of the Word as well as ministers of the altar.

In the eighth chapter of Nehemiah we read of a solemn reading of Scripture which tells us much about the origins of liturgical Scripture reading in both synagogue and church. About 445 B.C. the Persian Emperor, Xerxes, sent Ezra to re-establish the Jerusalem Temple and its customary services. Ezra initiated the newly regularized worship by calling a solemn assembly. At this solemn assembly he had read the entire book of the law. A special wooden platform was built for the occasion. Ezra, escorted by the leading elders of the nation, ascended the pulpit. They lifted up the scroll of the law so that it could be seen by all, then unrolled it over the wooden pulpit. As a mark of respect the whole assembly rose to its feet, a prayer was said before beginning the reading and the people concluded the prayer by saying "Amen, Amen." Ezra began to read and after he had read a section one of the Levites stepped forward and explained the passage which had just been read. Then another passage was read and it, too, was explained. So, it continued all morning long each day for an entire week until the whole of the law of Moses had been read. Several particular points should be noticed.

First, it occurs on the first day of the seventh month. The usual day for the beginning of the Feast of Tabernacles was the fifteenth day of the seventh month. The tenth day was the Feast of the Atonement and the first day a solemn assembly according to Numbers 29. The reading was a sort of preface to the solemnities of the seventh month. That this should be done is already mentioned in Deuteronomy, but Deuteronomy sees it taking place only in the year of Jubilee. How the Scripture reading changed from the Sabbath month of the Sabbath year to each weekly Sabbath is not at all clear. It may well have been one of Ezra's reforms.

Second, Ezra is described as a scribe although Ezra was himself of priestly lineage. He had been sent by Xerxes to supervise the restoration of the Temple and its worship, but he was not acting primarily as a royal official but as a scribe as the text tells us. The ministry of Ezra is conceived of primarily as a ministry of the Word. Ezra was a scholar, devoted to the study of Scripture. What seems to be behind this is that during the Exile the study of Scripture had become increasingly important. It was because of the neglect of the law and an overemphasis on the sacrificial ceremonial that God had turned the Israelites over to the rod of their enemies. The prophets had warned that this would happen and so under the chastening of captivity the Jews turned to an intense study of the law. The reading and preaching of the Scripture became a primary element in their worship. The member of the house of Aaron became a scribe; the performer of sacrifices became a student of the Scriptures; the priest became a preacher.

Third, it was an act of public worship. It was done with great solemnity and reverence. It was a public event, not merely the private teaching of a particular rabbi. The presence on the platform of the leading elders of the religious community gave it an official character. It was an act of the whole religious community.

Fourth, it was this rite which was taken over by the synagogue when each Sabbath the Scriptures were publicly read and explained in the synagogue service. All the elements of the synagogue service are clearly recognizable: the lifting up of the scroll of the law, the introductory prayer, the pulpit, the standing of the people, the presence of a number of readers, and the explaining of the passage that was read.

Fifth, it is clearly said that the whole book of the law was read during the seven day feast. This public reading of the whole of the law in the course of seven full mornings was not taken over by the synagogue but rather rearranged so that a portion of the law was read each Sabbath. In the course of a year, or perhaps three years, the whole of the law was read. It was read in what today is called a *lectio continua*, that is, the reading took up each Sabbath where it had left off the Sabbath before.

Sixth, before the Scriptures were read there was a prayer or benediction accompanied by the usual gestures of prayer. After the benediction the people said "Amen." That the reading of the Scripture was already prefaced at this time by a prayer is significant. The fact shows clearly that the reading is considered an act of worship.

Finally, we are told that the passage was explained. This is the origin of our sermon. From the very beginning the sermon was supposed to be an explanation of the Scripture reading. To what extent this was necessary because the congregation found it hard to understand the more classical Hebrew is not clear. At any rate one point is quite clear: a sermon is not just a lecture on some religious subject, it is rather an explanation of a passage of Scripture.

A second passage of Scripture which tells us how the Scriptures were read and preached in the synagogue is found in the Gospel of Luke. It is the familiar story of Jesus preaching in the synagogue of Nazareth. We can assume that the service began with the traditional psalmody and the traditional prayers. We can also assume that the law was read in the manner which by then was traditional. Jesus was called to the platform. It was already an old custom that a visiting rabbi should be invited to read a passage of Scripture and then to comment on it. Jesus was handed the book of the prophet Isaiah, and he opened it to the place he had in mind. He stood at the pulpit and read the passage. The book was closed and handed to an attendant who replaced it in the Ark, a great cupboard-like chest where the copies of sacred Scriptures were kept. While this was being done a psalm may well have been sung and Jesus sat down in the seat of Moses, a great thronelike chair behind the pulpit, and began to preach.

In this passage from the Gospel of Luke we have the oldest historical record of the second lesson. The synagogue service had first a lesson from the law and a second lesson from the prophets. Each Sabbath had its assigned lesson from the law. In Palestine the lessons were divided up so that in the course of three years the whole law was read through. The beginning and ending were uniformly established so that every synagogue in Palestine had the same lesson from the law on the same Sabbath. The second lesson, however, the lesson from the prophets, was left to the discretion of the preacher who chose a passage from the prophets which would explain the passage from the law. The sermon then showed how the one passage explained the other. Already the principle was at work that Scripture was to be explained by Scripture.

Luke tells us that it was the custom of Jesus to go to the synagogue on the Sabbath. Not only was it the custom of Jesus but the custom of his disciples as well, and they continued in their custom well after the day of Pentecost. With Paul and presumably other early Christian missionary preachers, the synagogue custom of inviting visitors who were well versed in the Scriptures to read a lesson and preach on it afforded an excellent missionary strategy (Acts 13:14–43). When Paul went to a new city he started his work by going to the synagogue and claiming his right to preach. When controversy over Jesus began to divide the synagogues, Christians established their own synagogues (James 2:2). In these Christian synagogues many of the traditional forms of worship were continued much as they had been previously observed in the Jewish synagogues. Certainly one of these traditions was the reading of the Old Testament Scriptures. Paul tells Timothy to see to the public reading of the Scriptures in the same way that he instructs him in conducting public prayers (1 Tim. 4:13). Paul's admonition obviously concerns the reading of the law and the prophets, not the New Testament books, which were probably not yet considered Holy Scripture.

There is another passage of Scripture which reports for us even more clearly the homiletical methods of Jesus. It is the sermon on the bread of life in the sixth chapter of the Gospel of John. John presents the material in the form of a discourse; nevertheless the material he gives us perfectly fulfills the form of the synagogue sermon. Indeed, at the end of the discourse we read, "This he said in the synagogue, as he taught at Capernaum" (John 6:59). Surely this statement encourages us to find here a fully liturgical sermon.

The text from the law is quoted, "He gave them bread from heaven to eat." This text comes from the story of the manna in the book of Exodus (Exod. 16:4ff.). Since John specifically tells us that "The Feast of Passover was at hand," we have every reason to believe that we are dealing with the lesson normally read on the Sabbath before Passover. The sermon has a second lesson, a lesson from the prophets, "And they shall all be taught by God" (Isa. 54:13). It is with the aid of the text from Isaiah that Jesus interprets the text from Exodus. "Scripture is to be interpreted by Scripture." This homiletical maxim Jesus himself honored. More importantly, however, Jesus demonstrates for us in this sermon the dynamic relation of the two lessons. This liturgical form flowered in the time of Jesus and the sermon in John 6 proves Jesus to be a master craftsman of this liturgical form.

As we study this sermon we find that Jesus takes four phrases from the text and explains each phrase in turn. First he takes the phrase, "He gave" and explains that it was not Moses who gave the manna but, "my Father gives you the true bread from heaven." Next Jesus explains what is meant by bread. He tells them "I am the bread of life." Then Jesus explains what is meant by the bread being from heaven. He tells them that he is the living bread which comes down from heaven. Here he applies the text from Isaiah "And they shall all be taught by God." Jesus presents himself as fulfilling this prophecy. In Jesus' teaching God himself is teaching his people. Finally Jesus explains the word, "to eat," by telling his listeners, "he who eats my flesh and drinks my blood has eternal life." From the text which Jesus took from the law he developed a four point sermon. From the standpoint of homiletical method it is a good rabbinical sermon conforming perfectly to the liturgical forms of the synagogue, but even more it is the prototype of the Christian sermon because it announces that the law and the prophets are now fulfilled. In this sermon Jesus moves from the promises of the Old Testament to their fulfillment in himself.

Let us now turn our attention to the historical development of Christian worship from the time after the end of the New Testament period. The earliest source documents for the history of Christian worship indicate that in the worship of the church, just as in the worship of the synagogue, the reading and preaching of the Scriptures was an essential element. Justin Martyr, writing in the middle of the second century, tells us that at the ordinary Sunday service there were readings from the "Memoirs of the Apostles or the Writings of the Prophets." Then when the reader was finished, the one presiding gave a discourse encouraging the people to practice these examples of virtue. From this it is clear that by this time there were Old Testament readings as there had been in the synagogue and New Testament readings as well. Already the writings of the Apostles, both Gospels and Epistles, were being read as New Testament Scripture. There was as yet no fixed lectionary, for Justin tells us that these writings were read, "as long as there is time." Unlike the synagogue there seems to be a single reader and a single preacher. The preacher was the one who presided over the service.

In the fourth century we begin to find a liturgy which is considerably more fixed. The *Apostolic Constitutions* which represents the worship customs of Antioch shows us that there were at each service four Scripture lessons, a reading from the law followed by a reading from the prophets, just as there had been in the synagogue, and then a reading from the Epistles and a reading from the Gospels as a sort of New

Testament counterpart to the double lesson from the Old Testament. This usage may well go back much further into history. Between the lessons, psalms or parts of psalms might be sung. Following the lessons there was a sermon.

Christian preaching flourished from the middle of the fourth century until well into the fifth century. Let us look at a few of the greatest preachers of the patristic period.

John Chrysostom crowns his age. While still a presbyter of his native Antioch he preached daily at the patriarchal cathedral for some twelve years from 385–397 winning a great reputation as a preacher. John Chrysostom mastered classical rhetoric and perfected the arts of public speaking. This he combined with great skill as an interpreter of Scripture. Even today he instructs us with his sober Antiochene exegesis, always respecting the simple grammatical sense of the text. John Chrysostom was a great ethical preacher who always sharpened the text so as to thrust it deeply into the heart of a moral issue. His excellence we appreciate today from an exegetical point of view, from an ethical point of view, and from a literary point of view.

The preaching of this master centers in his series of exegetical sermons on individual books of the Bible. John Chrysostom preached through most of the books of the New Testament. We have eighty-nine sermons on the Gospel of Matthew. When we look at these sermons we discover that he proceeds through the whole of the Gospel explaining the text verse by verse. He begins his sermon with exegetical remarks on the text, and having done this at some length he then makes his application. He applies the text to the practical problems of the Christian life and in moving oratory urges the Christian to live according to the Word of God. He preached through the Gospel of John in the same way leaving us ninety sermons. His series on the Acts of the Apostles counts some forty-four sermons, and his series on the Pauline epistles more than two hundred fifty sermons. He has also left us several series on the books of the Old Testament: sixty-seven sermons on Genesis, a long series on the Psalms, and another on Isaiah. Few preachers in the history of the church have piled up such a treasury of expository sermons.

While John Chrysostom's expository preaching forms the center of his ministry we also have hagiographical sermons on the martyrs of the church of Antioch which were preached at services remembering the anniversary of their witness. For the feast days of Christmas, Epiphany, Easter, and Ascension, he composed special sermons. Both in Antioch and Constantinople this fearless preacher regularly addressed the issues of the day. Intrigues at court he exposed, members of the imperial household he called to repentance, and the conscience of the general populace he rallied in times of civil emergency. While the heart of his preaching was expository, he was perfectly capable of using other homiletical forms. Nevertheless his great authority as a preacher rested in his faithfulness to Scripture. When he preached there was never any question but that it was the Word of God which he preached.

In the West, Ambrose of Milan was a renowned preacher. He preached in Milan, the capital of the Western Empire, at the same time John Chrysostom filled the pulpit in Antioch. Ambrose fascinated his congregation with his expositions of the Old Testament. Unfortunately Ambrose reworked these expository sermons as treatises before publishing them so that we no longer have his actual sermons. Nevertheless we can deduce a great deal about his work as a biblical preacher. He was greatly influenced by Alexandrian exegesis. Alexandrian exegesis, unlike the Antiochene exegesis championed by John Chrysostom, quickly left the literal meaning of the text of Scripture, preferring allegory to the grammatical, historical method of understanding the text. His treatises on Genesis draw much from Philo, and his long series of sermons on the Gospel of Luke depends heavily on Origen. For us today this Alexandrian allegorizing of the text holds little interest although it delighted his listeners at the time. Like John Chrysostom, Ambrose was a preacher to the court and exercised his Christian political responsibility well. His sermons, although remaining primarily expository sermons, frequently responded to the social and political issues of the day. Unlike John Chrysostom, Ambrose had led a very successful career as a high state official before being called into the ministry and he knew well how to exercise his influence in civil affairs. He was more apt to exert his influence on the court through his letters and his pastoral work than through his actual preaching.

The catechetical sermons of Ambrose claim our particular attention. Each year before Easter he prepared those to be baptized by preaching to them daily, carefully explaining the basic teaching of the Christian faith. He would always treat in turn the Apostle's Creed, the Lord's Prayer, and give a detailed explanation of the sacraments of baptism and communion. This procedure remained the schema for classical catechetical preaching for generations. The Protestant Reformers of the sixteenth century revived this same design when they wrote their catechisms and preached their catechetical sermons. Indeed one might even regard Ambrose as the father of catechetical preaching.

Augustine of Hippo (354–430) might well be regarded as the disciple of Ambrose. He was the greatest Latin theologian of antiquity. After being baptized in Milan he returned to his native North Africa and became a very popular preacher. He was a master of classical oratory. Like John Chrysostom and Ambrose of Milan, Augustine was a great expository preacher. Several of his courses of sermons on various books of the Bible have come down to us either in sermon form or slightly reworked into commentaries. We have a long series on the Sermon on the Mount. We have one hundred twenty-four sermons on the Gospel of John. His commentary on 1 John is really a course of sermons preached to the newly baptized just after Easter in the year 413. His very lengthy commentary on the Psalms is compiled from his sermons over a period of several years. Besides these longer series of sermons we have a collection of perhaps three hundred separate sermons of that most profound of thinkers.

Ordinarily Augustine preached a *lectio continua* as did John Chrysostom and Ambrose, but in the preaching of Augustine we begin to find evidence for the evolution of a different principle of selecting the Scripture passages to be read during worship. This is the principle of the *lectio selecta*. According to this principle special lessons were selected for special days. Augustine tells us for instance that it was the custom to read the resurrection story from the Gospel of John on Easter Sunday morning. In Augustine's day the Christian year was developing rapidly and as the Christian year developed so the custom proliferated of choosing appropriate lessons for the feast days and fast days of the newly developing religious calendar. For Augustine, to be sure, only a small portion of the year was involved. At the beginning of the fifth century only the feasts of Easter, Pentecost, and Christmas, a few fast days, especially those before Easter, and a limited number of saints days were about all that would merit a special lesson. Things changed. Within a few centuries this principle of the *lectio selecta* would almost entirely supplant the *lectio continua*.

The sermons of Augustine are remarkable in that we find in these sermons one of the greatest intellects of history trying to make his profound teaching so clear and simple that the ordinary people of a small provincial city might hear with enjoyment and profit. Today we respect Augustine for his works on philosophy; we highly honor him as one of the four doctors of the Western Church, a theologian without parallel. His reputation rests on the *City of God,* a profound work on the philosophy of history. It rests as well on his *Confessions,* a work which treats the deep themes of how the individual soul comes to faith. It is a classic in the field of religious psychology and a turning point in the science of epistemology. The sermons are very different. They show how a lofty mind grasped as well the simple basics. If the biblical expositions of John Chrysostom most often instruct the faithful in matters of Christian conduct, the opening of the Scriptures was used by Augustine to teach Christian doctrine. Augustine was a great doctrinal preacher and yet he simplified doctrine in his sermons. He used rhetoric to clothe the most complex philosophical ideas in similes and figures of speech. His artful allegorical interpretations delight, amuse, and cajole us into discovering the truth even today.

Augustine wrote a manual on preaching, *De doctrine christiana,* "On Christian Teaching," which is worthy of careful study by the preacher of our own day. Much of what the great rhetor has to say about method is still quite valid. He talks about the value of studying the text in the original languages, the great value of literary studies to preaching, and the importance of mastering the use of language. He gives us a classic statement on using Scripture to interpret Scripture and much else; however, the purest gold to be mined from this work is what he has to say about the spiritual tools of exegesis. For Augustine the understanding of Scripture is a spiritual discipline to be undertaken with prayer and carried out in faith, in hope, and in love.

Leo the Great was the bishop of Rome from 440 to 461. In these years, the eternal city suffered political collapse and more than any other person he saved his people from utter destruction. Through his personal mediation he was able to win important concessions for the city even to the point of persuading Attila the Hun to leave Italy. His preaching ministry comes clearly to light in ninety-six sermons which have come down to us. They are remarkable for their brevity, simplicity, and clarity of style. These sermons also interest us because they reflect the growth of the liturgical year. His preaching is not primarily a systematic attempt to interpret Scripture but rather a series of sermons based on the lectionary. The *lectio selecta* has developed rapidly since the days of Augustine and Leo's sermons are based on the *lectio selecta*. His sermons are not intended to explain the Scripture lessons which have been read so much as to present the liturgical theme of the day. They are liturgical homilies rather than expositions of Scripture. The great majority of Leo's sermons were preached for one of the two great liturgical cycles of the year. First, attention is given to the paschal cycle which begins with Lent, Holy Week, and Easter and which concludes with the feasts of Ascension and Pentecost. Second, there was the Christmas cycle, which began with Advent and ended with Epiphany. Today liturgists study these sermons with great delight because they are the prototype of "preaching the lectionary."

The golden age of patristic preaching all too quickly ran to its end. With the barbarian invasions and the disruption of regular education, the study of Scripture and the cultivation of preaching began to be neglected. The great preachers of the fourth and fifth centuries, John Chrysostom, Theodore of Mopsuestia, Ambrose of Milan, Augustine, Basil of Caesarea, Gregory of Nazianzus, Cyril of Jerusalem, Leo the Great, and finally Gregory the Great, all disappeared with the eventide of classical civilization.

In the West, there was a revival of preaching in the high Middle Ages. Norbert (1080–1134), founder of the Praemonstratensian order, demonstrated the effectiveness of preaching in combating the heresies which had become so rife in that day. Bernard of Clairvaux (1090–1153) became one of the most inspiring and effective preachers the church has ever known. Dominic (1170–1221) and Francis of Assisi (1181–1226) founded orders which emphasized preaching, but this preaching tended to be occasional rather than an integral part of the mass. Nevertheless, this revival of preaching went hand in hand with the revival of learning. Preachers understood the need to cultivate the use of language and literary studies were important to them. They admired a clear and precise use of language. They also understood the importance of developing a literate congregation. As the level of education rose, interest in preaching rose.

With the sixteenth-century Reformation, biblical preaching once again took a prominent place in the regular worship of the church. People were eager to learn and eagerly sat under the pulpits of preachers who could expound to them the Holy Scriptures.

Martin Luther (1483–1546), professor of Scripture at the University of Wittenberg, was one of those bright young men who took most seriously the job of explaining the Scriptures from his classroom lectern, but he also took just as seriously the ministry of preaching from the pulpit of the Castle Church in Wittenberg. For the most part Luther preached the Gospels and Epistles of the Roman lectionary. He had plenty of criticisms of the lectionary but nevertheless he stuck to it whenever he preached on Sunday morning to the faithful who came to hear mass. For him it was a sufficient reform to explain the text of the traditional pericopes of the lectionary. This he did with new insight and considerable fervor. While Luther was primarily a preacher of the lectionary, he did do several series on individual books of the Bible or major portions of those books. We have series of sermons on the Gospels of Matthew and John, a series on the Psalms and a series on both Genesis and Exodus. Apparently however these series were not given in the context of worship even though they still maintained the form of the homily. Luther, whether preaching from the lectionary or preaching in course, normally went through the selected passage verse by verse, first explaining the text and then applying it. For Luther the essential matter was to present the clear message of the passage before him.

Ulrich Zwingli (1484–1531) blazed for preaching a much more thoroughgoing path of reform. After his studies at the University of Basel the young Christian Humanist scholar hid himself away in a valley of the Swiss Alps as parish priest of the little town of Glarus. With an extraordinary personal library of biblical and patristic literature he worked away in his study for more than a dozen years. He mastered the literary disciplines of the Renaissance during those years and assiduously applied them to his study of the sacred writings. The Reformation had just begun when in 1519 he was called to Zurich to begin his ministry of preaching. He started out by taking the Gospel of Matthew and preaching through it verse by verse, day after day for a whole year.

Every man, woman, and child who could possibly get there crammed into Zurich's Great Minster to hear him. Zwingli began his reform with a return to the classical practice of systematic expository preaching. The interesting thing is, one of his most important guides in this enterprise was the great preacher of the fourth century, John Chrysostom, the patriarch of Constantinople. Zwingli, true to the ideals of the Christian Humanism which had trained him was not interested in religious revolution but rather restoration. The motto of the Christian Humanists was "ad fontes," that is, "to the sources" or "Let us drink from the clear springs of classical Christianity." We should not be surprised that Zwingli studied the classical sermons of Christian antiquity. Like a Christian Ezra, he based his reform on preaching through the law of Christ. Like a Swiss John Chrysostom he preached through the Bible, verse by verse, one book at a time.

On the threshold of the Age of Reform the Upper Rhineland could boast a high level of the preaching art. Johannes Heynlin von Stein (1430–1496), former rector of the University of Paris had retired to Basel's Chartreusian Monastery. While there Heynlin became a regular preacher at the cathedral. The distinguished Johann Ulrich Surgant (1450–1503) was preaching at the Church of St. Theodore in one of the suburbs. Down the Rhine in Strasbourg, Johann Geiler von Kayserberg (1445–1510), who is reckoned as one of the outstanding preachers in Christian history, filled the cathedral pulpit. Most of the South German and Rhenish cities had one or more handsomely endowed pulpits. These endowed pulpits were a feature of the church life of the day. Monasteries, parish churches, or cathedrals might have such endowed pulpits. Learned preachers were in demand for these positions. Often these preachers were required to have a university doctorate. While their appointment sometimes rested with the bishop, abbot, or cathedral chapter they were often appointed by the city council or even the syndics of a guild. The demand for learned and literary preaching was well supported and good preachers were enthusiastically received.

In 1518 John Oecolampadius (1482–1531), a Christian Humanist scholar who had mastered both Greek and Hebrew, was called to fill just such an endowed pulpit at the Cathedral of Augsburg, only a few months after Luther had posted his ninety-five theses on the door of the Wittenberg church. With all the literary tools of the new learning he began his work. While in Augsburg, he carefully studied the classic sermons of Gregory of Nazianzus and Basil of Caesarea; then he discovered John Chrysostom. He began to translate the sermons of the great Church Father from Greek into Latin, making much of this treasury of expository preaching available to the Western world for the first time. Returning to Basel he became preacher at St. Mark's Church where he set to work preaching, just as John Chrysostom had done, through one book of the Bible after another. From the very beginning of his ministry he gave special attention to the Old Testament prophets. In 1523 he was invited by the city council to preach to them on Isaiah. Preaching on the Hebrew text, as he did, was a startling innovation in that day. Only very rarely in the Middle Ages had a Christian theologian been able to study the Bible in Greek, let alone in Hebrew. The scholarly preaching of John Oecolampadius so completely won the city that a few years later in 1529 Basel officially embraced the Reformation.

Strasbourg, like Basel, fairly bubbled up and overflowed with excitement for the new learning of the Christian Renaissance. In that imperial free city lived many of the great thinkers of the day. One only need mention the names of Sebastian Brandt, the great German folk poet, or Johann Gutenberg, who a generation before had invented the printing press. At the beginning of the sixteenth century, Strasbourg, as Basel, was one of the centers of the printing industry. In 1518, Matthew Zell (1477–1548), the rector of the University of Freiburg, was called to fill the distinguished pulpit of Johann Geiler von Kayserberg. He began his ministry by preaching through the four Gospels in a popular manner designed to appeal to the burghers of that very free and independent city. His presentation of Jesus was fresh and human, very moral and practical. Although Zell was a scholar he had an ability to speak to the guild members and craftsmen of the city. Early in his ministry he declared for Luther and the Reformation.

Zell was soon joined by Wolfgang Capito (1478–1541), a distinguished Renaissance scholar who had earned doctorates in law, medicine, and theology and who, like his friend Oecolampadius, was distinguished by a mastery of both Greek and Hebrew. When the Reformation broke loose, Capito held the endowed pulpit in the Cathedral of Basel where his preaching won for him the admiration and friendship of Erasmus, the prince of Renaissance scholars. In 1523 he was called to be probst of Strasbourg's famous Thomas Stift. He was the paradigm of the gentleman scholar, devoting much time to his personal correspondence with Erasmus, Luther, and Zwingli. For Wolfgang Capito, who preached regularly at the Church of St. Peter the Younger, preaching went step by step with a careful exegesis of the text of Holy Scripture. Capito's remarkable study of the prophet Hosea gave an insight into the message of an Old Testament prophet who up to this time had been all but unknown to Christendom. Capito as a preacher was irenic and moderate, allowing the carefully explained biblical text to speak for itself. Having family connections with the flourishing printing industry of Strasbourg, Capito saw to the publishing of the commentaries of his good friend Oecolampadius. This scholarly work, to be sure, bore fruit in his pulpit as Capito preached through Isaiah, Jeremiah, and Ezekiel following the commentaries of his colleague in Basel. The gentle reasonableness and kindly intelligence of this man did much to win the leading thinkers of his day for the Reformation. His life and his teaching were of one piece. The preaching of such a man was true worship because it bore a sincere witness to the glory of God.

Martin Bucer (1491–1551), the best known of the Strasbourg Reformers, arrived in the city in 1523 and was soon given charge of the Church of St. Aurelius, the most proletarian congregation in Strasbourg. There his preaching won a devoted following. He frequently preached in the cathedral, and was invited to lecture on the interpretation of Scripture in the home of Capito and then later in the Dominican priory. Unfortunately less than a dozen sermons of Bucer have come down to us and all of these can be classified as occasional sermons. What we discover even in these occasional sermons is that Bucer chose a passage of the Bible appropriate to the occasion and carefully explained the text and then applied it to the matter at hand. It was Bucer's long series of expository sermons which formed the heart of his preaching ministry. We know that he did a long series of sermons on the Gospel of Matthew, the Gospel of John, the first epistle of Peter and the book of Psalms. Bucer wrote commentaries on the Pauline epistles of Romans and Ephesians and we can assume that this exegetical work reflected his preaching.

From the early editions of the *Strasbourg Psalter* we learn much about the preaching ministry of Bucer and his colleagues. For the Sun-

day morning celebration of communion the passage of Scripture selected was taken from one of the Gospels. This was done in such a way
that each Gospel was preached through on the principle of the *lectio
continua*. The Gospels and Epistles of the Roman calendar were set
aside because they were considered inadequate for fully presenting the
message of the biblical writers. The pericopes are disparagingly called
"scraps and remnants" or "bits and pieces" of Scripture. If the Gospels were preached through in course on Sunday morning, then the New
Testament Epistles were preached through either later on Sunday, at
vespers perhaps, or else at the daily preaching services. It was the same
with the Old Testament books. Strasbourg had a wealth of capable
preachers and biblical scholars and they were all involved in the work of
daily expounding the word of truth. Even today one would be hard
pressed to find a theological seminary where more learned biblical exposition takes place in the course of a week than took place in the city of
Strasbourg in the age of the Reformation.

Catechetical preaching was a major concern of the Strasbourg Reformation. Each Sunday afternoon the catechism was preached. In Strasbourg this meant that each year the Creed, the Lord's Prayer, the Ten
Commandments, and the sacraments of baptism and communion were
explained in detail. One immediately recognizes the schema of the catechetical sermons of the patristic age, especially Cyril of Jerusalem and
Ambrose of Milan. Just as the Reformers had been inspired by the
expository preaching of the patristic age, so they were inspired by the
catechetical preaching of the patristic age. Although the catechetical
preaching of Strasbourg was probably the most intensive of the early
sixteenth century, much the same thing was being done in Wittenberg,
Zurich, Basel, and, above all, in Constance, where the catechetical
work of Johannes Zwick won great renown.

For his day, Bucer pioneered much that in our day seems more than
obvious. He has left us a short work on his hermeneutical principles
which was originally written in a letter to the Waldensian pastor, Fortunatus Andronicus. The Latin title might be translated, "An Instruction on How the Sacred Scriptures Are to Be Handled in Sermon." The
work is rich in its insights and practical advice. Bucer defines the purpose of preaching as to offer to individuals the grace of Christ in such a
way that it be laid hold of by faith and realized in a life of Christian

love. He emphasizes that since all Christian teaching is in the end the work of the Holy Spirit the sermon must be prepared through prayer and that the preacher must pray that the Holy Spirit grant to the preacher the right words and to the hearers the right frame of mind to hear the Word of God. He gives great attention to the selection of the text, going into detail about how he understands the use of the *lectio continua*. First the Gospels and the Acts of the Apostles should be preached. This is because they are most easily understood. Then one should preach the easier Pauline epistles, the Pastorals, and the letters to the Colossians, Philippians, and Corinthians. Romans and Galatians are to be preached to a more mature congregation. Only when this foundation is well established should one proceed to the law and the prophets of the Old Testament. The parts of Exodus, Leviticus, and Numbers which regard the ceremonial law and such things can well be left on the side as well as the apocalyptic visions of Ezekiel and Zechariah. One should above all have regard for the capacity of one's hearers. As Bucer saw it, it was one thing to preach on some of the more difficult Old Testament books to advanced theological students at the Thomas Stift on Sunday afternoon and something quite different to preach to the normal congregation at the cathedral on Sunday morning. For Bucer the sermon is not the place for the speculative, the controversial, and the obscure. He comes out strongly against the allegorical interpretation of Scripture. The sermon should not be used by the preacher to display cleverness and ingenuity. Elaborate attempts to harmonize the apparent contradictions of Scripture should be avoided. The sermon should be a witness to Christ as Lord and should make clear to Christians the path of life. The preacher should have uppermost in his mind "these things are written that you might believe . . . and that believing you might have life" (John 20:31).

Zwingli, Oecolampadius, and Bucer did not rediscover preaching, as though it had been neglected for a thousand years. They were brought up under the pulpits of great preachers. It was far more that their reform of preaching consisted in establishing regular and systematic expository preaching. It was this approach to preaching which Calvin introduced to Geneva and which the Marian Exiles took with them when they returned to England and Scotland. The exposition of Scripture in course became one of the biggest planks in their platform of Christian revival. To them it was an essential component of a Christian worship that was according to Scripture and after the example of the ancient church. To these Reformers the sermon was an act of worship. It was the fruit of prayer, a work of God's Spirit in the body of Christ; it was the doxological witness to the grace of God in Christ. It was set in the praise and prayer of the worshiping congregation. It called Christians to communion with God and sent them out into a life of Christian service.

When Calvin began his ministry in Geneva, William Farel (1489–1565) had already established in that French-speaking city republic many of the liturgical reforms which had by then become familiar in the Rhineland. The service book which Farel published in 1533 had directed in regard to preaching that the minister should first read the Scriptures and then preach a sermon explaining the text which had been read. This, Farel reminds us, is what Jesus had done in Nazareth. In the same way, following the example of Ezra, the minister was to preface the preaching of the Scriptures with a prayer that the Holy Spirit would make clear the true meaning of the Word in such a way that it would bear fruit in the lives of the people. Calvin closely followed this pattern. He had the same devotion to expository preaching, and to preaching books of the Bible through in course that his Rhenish predecessors had. Calvin regarded the lectionary of the Christian year as cutting up the Bible into unrelated scraps. It imposed an arbitrary arrangement on Scripture. As Calvin saw it, the pericopes of the lectionary often separated a text from its natural context. The texts of Scripture should be heard within the total message of a particular biblical author. A lectionary could not help but encourage over the years a stereotyped interpretation. Part of the pastoral responsibility of the faithful minister of the Word was to select those passages of Scripture which were most needed for the nourishment and upbuilding of the church at any particular time.

Fortunately a great amount of Calvin's sermons have been preserved. For well over ten years (1549–1560) at the height of Calvin's ministry provision was made for a stenographer to record Calvin's sermons. Over two thousand sermons were taken down. From 1542, when he returned from his exile, Calvin was the ordinary preacher at the Cathedral of St. Pierre. Sunday morning Calvin normally preached through the Gospels or the Acts of the Apostles. At Sunday vespers he would preach through the Psalms or perhaps a New Testament epistle.

On weekday mornings he preached through Old Testament books. Other preachers were responsible for weekday evening sermons, and they preached through New Testament books. One notices that the Reformer has reserved the Gospels for Sunday morning when he could count on the greatest number of hearers.

Calvin preached through most of the books of the Bible and he preached his way slowly through each book. Normally, he took three to six verses at a time. This system produced, for example, 123 sermons on Genesis, 200 sermons on Deuteronomy, 159 sermons on Job, 176 sermons on 1 and 2 Corinthians, and 43 sermons on Galatians. In more than twenty years as preacher at Geneva, Calvin must have preached through almost the entire Bible. He seems to have missed only a few books. He preached through most of the historical books. First and Second Chronicles, Ezra, Nehemiah, and Esther he never reached, having finished 2 Kings shortly before his death. He probably did not think it necessary to preach through those passages of Exodus, Leviticus, and Numbers which treated in detail the interpretation of the law. Calvin did, nevertheless, write a commentary on these passages. He preached on all of the prophets, both major and minor. He does not seem to have treated Proverbs, Ecclesiastes, or the Song of Solomon. He did not preach on the Revelation. He did preach a long series on the Synoptic Gospels, on Acts, and the Pauline epistles. Sermons have not come down to us on the Gospel of John or the catholic epistles, but we can assume that Calvin preached through these books early in his ministry before the stenographer was made available. In all probability he preached through the Gospels, certain Pauline epistles, and the Psalms more than once. Taken as a whole, however, his life's work was to preach through the whole Bible. What a life's work that was!

Calvin's purpose in preaching was to present the message of the text in a simple and straightforward manner and then to apply the text to the lives of his hearers. What surprises the modern reader of Calvin's sermons is the simplicity of his sermons. We find no engaging introductions, no illustrative stories nor anecdotes, no quotations from great authors, no stirring conclusions. Although Calvin was one of the most literate men of his age, and although he was a master in the use of language, his sermons depend not at all on literary elegance. The forcefulness of his sermons is to be found in the clarity of his analysis of the text. Calvin seems to have no fear that the Scriptures will be boring or irrelevant unless the preacher spices them up. In fact, Calvin seems to have a horror of decorating the Word of God. Scripture does not need to be painted with artists' colors! So confident is the Reformer that God will make his Word alive in the hearts of his people, that Calvin simply explains the text and draws out its implication. The simplicity and directness of his style is based in his confidence that what he is preaching is indeed the Word of God. This simplicity is an expression of reverence.

This does not mean that Calvin was unaware of rhetoric. He was a master of it! He knew Aristotle, Cicero, and Quintillian well. He had carefully schooled himself in John Chrysostom and Augustine, both accomplished in the art of rhetoric. As is often said of very great artists, he had mastered his art so completely he knew how to hide it. Calvin was well aware of all the classical rhetorical forms. As Professor Rudolphe Peter has recently shown, Calvin, in his commentaries on Scripture, never tires of pointing out the use of various rhetorical forms. He is forever admiring striking similes, effective metaphors, an audacious hyperbole, or a clever pun. His sermons often use similes, metaphors, epithets, synechdoche, and antithesis. One often finds the use of climax, apostrophe, prosopopoeia, epiphonomia, and anaphora in his sermons. Yet when Calvin uses these rhetorical forms they are never studied, artificial, or contrived; they flow naturally.

The most important method Calvin used to explain a text was to bring to it a parallel text. A single sermon will often quote a dozen or more passages from other parts of the Bible. As Augustine, he believed Scripture is best interpreted by Scripture. It is rather strange that Calvin did not use a second Scripture lesson, but then he probably figured that was best done in the course of the sermon. Another method which Calvin frequently used was to paraphrase the text. How often he will say something like, "It is as though Jeremiah had said . . . ." Sometimes he engages the prophets or Apostles in conversation. He frequently delves into the reasons behind the biblical characters' actions or thoughts, "why then did the shepherds go to Bethlehem?" All these methods Calvin found used in most exemplary fashion in the sermons of John Chrysostom.

As T. H. L. Parker has put it, "The predominate mark of Calvin's style is his clarity of thought and expression." Compared to Luther, Calvin is bland and colorless. One has to say the Reformer of Geneva lacks imagination, the flair for the dramatic, and the emotional appeal. He seems to be concerned about one thing alone, presenting the Word of God simply and directly. This he does with great ability!

In Scotland the Reformed tradition of preaching bloomed with vigor. The expository preaching of books of the Bible in course became a continuing feature of the Scottish pulpit. Early in the Reformation, George Wishart (1513–1546) began a typical Reformed preaching ministry. Graduating from Kings College in Aberdeen he traveled in Germany and Switzerland in 1539 and 1540. While on the continent he fully informed himself of the Reformers' preaching method. Returning to Scotland in 1544 he began a remarkable preaching ministry. While in Dundee he preached through Paul's epistle to the Romans. In addition to this he is known to have preached in Montrose, Perth, Edinburgh, Leith, and Haddington. His ministry though brilliant was unfortunately short. In 1546 George Wishart was burned at the stake at St. Andrews.

It was John Knox (1505–1572), won for the Reformation by Wishart, who took up his master's torch almost, as it were, from the flames of his martyrdom. Right there in St. Andrews, Knox began to preach the Reformation. Soon Knox was arrested for his preaching and sentenced to the galley ships. Nevertheless during that short ministry he must have won a good reputation for as soon as he was released he was called to England by Archbishop Cranmer, named Chaplain to King Edward VI, and sent about England to preach the Reformation. In the course of the next five years he became one of the best known of English preachers. He was even offered a bishopric in the Church of England! With the accession of Queen Mary to the throne of England, Knox, as other leading Protestants, went into exile on the Continent. Knox settled in Geneva as pastor of the English-speaking congregation. He spent several peaceful years there. The peaceful years in Geneva gave him time to study Greek and Hebrew, and the opportunity to sit under the pulpit of Calvin.

Soon the respite came to an end. The cause of the Reformation was gathering strength in his native Scotland and Knox returned to lead the nation in those most critical years. With the official adoption of reform in 1560, Knox became preacher at St. Giles Cathedral in Edinburgh. There he exercised as dramatic and powerful a preaching ministry as any preacher in the history of Christendom. It was concerning his preaching at St. Giles that the English ambassador wrote to Lord Cecil, "I assure you the voice of one man is able, in an hour, to put more life in us, than six hundred trumpets." It was from the pulpit that Knox exercised his tremendous influence on the history of Scotland. Fearlessly he attacked the easy morality of the court. With all the audacity of a John Chrysostom denouncing the Byzantine empress, Knox opposed the religious policies and politics of Mary, Queen of Scots. Even in the presence of the Queen's consort, Lord Darnley, he preached against his vacillating opportunism. And he did this in the course of expository preaching never departing from the text of Scripture. His hearers knew he was preaching the Word of God. Fearing no one, he exhorted Scotland to be obedient to God and God alone. As John Knox understood it even the queen had authority only insofar as she bowed to God's authority. The same principle was behind his own authority as a minister of the Word of God. As a minister he had authority only to the extent that he faithfully expounded Scripture. Amazingly, Scotland recognized the authority behind the preaching of Knox and in a generation Scotland was a changed nation.

Knox had been influenced by John Calvin. But Knox had something as a preacher Calvin never had. One of Knox's greatest sermons was preached in St. Giles at the funeral of the Earl of Murray, the murdered regent of Scotland. He preached on the text, "Blessed are the dead which die in the Lord." Thomas M'Crie tells us, "Three thousand persons were dissolved in tears before him, while he described the regent's virtues, and bewailed his loss" (Thomas M'Crie, *Life of John Knox*, 239). The "Thundering Scot" could move the hearts of a congregation. While Calvin's appeal was to the mind, Knox's appeal was to the heart. That does not mean that Knox was simply an emotional rabble-rouser as some people have presented him. Knox was far more. As Calvin, Knox was a studying preacher. He knew how to search out the meaning of the text and make it speak to the problems of the day. For Knox a careful exposition of the text was essential to a sermon. It was for this reason that Knox could awaken the conscience in a way that a simple emotional appeal could never do.

If Knox followed in a great tradition he also founded a great tradition. Ever since Knox Scotland has abounded in great preachers. One of his successors in the pulpit of St. Giles was Robert Bruce. Born to one of Scotland's noble families he attended St. Andrews University in the day George Buchanan and Andrew Melville had brought the university to its zenith. He mastered the new learning of the Renaissance, applying himself particularly to the study of Greek and Hebrew. He gave careful attention to the study of the Fathers, particularly Augustine and Irenaeus. Bruce is remembered especially for two series of sermons. The first series was preached during the threatened invasion of the Spanish Armada in 1588. Professor Thomas Torrance has called these sermons an outstanding example of how great preaching can strengthen a nation in time of crisis. The second, frequently reprinted even to this day is his series of catechetical sermons on the sacraments.

In England during the reign of Queen Elizabeth I, it was William Perkins (1558–1602) who was the most notable exponent of the Reformed approach to preaching. While today Perkins' fame has faded, he was one of the most notable English theologians of his day. His theological treatises were translated into numerous other languages and in Germany, Holland, and Switzerland he was clearly the most widely read of English theologians. He was particularly well known for his defense of Calvinism against the attacks of Arminianism. In England he was highly regarded as a preacher. It was as a preacher to prisoners in the Cambridge jail that he began his ministry; nevertheless in 1585, he was appointed rector of St. Andrew's Church in Cambridge, giving him the opportunity to preach to one of the intellectual centers of the nation. Many of Perkins' publications were a reworking of his sermons. His commentaries on the Sermon on the Mount, Paul's epistle to the Galatians, Hebrews, Jude, and Revelation reflect his ministry of expository preaching. In the same way his catechetical preaching is reflected in his works on the Lord's Prayer, the Ten Commandments, and the Apostles Creed. A good number of his other treatises reflect occasional sermons. For example, *The Calling of the Ministerie,* was originally a series of sermons designed to encourage Cambridge students to enter the pastorate.

Perkins was particularly concerned with the cultivation of good preaching. In 1592 he published a short work on preaching, *The Art of*

Prophesying. In this work he tells us that prophecy is a public and solemn speech of the prophet, pertaining to the worship of God and the salvation of our neighbor. He tells us there are two parts to prophecy, "the preaching of the Word and the conceiving of prayers." According to Perkins the prophet is the voice of God when he preaches and the voice of the people when he prays. He goes on to define the preaching of the Word as "prophesying in the name and room of Christ, whereby men are called to the state of grace and conserved in it." What is fascinating about this essay on preaching is the way it reaches back to the Old Testament concept of prophet and defines the preacher in terms of the prophetic ministry. Nevertheless Perkins' concept is thoroughly Christian. He has obviously been influenced by what the Apostle Paul has to say about preaching and the gift of prophecy in the fourteenth chapter of 1 Corinthians. When Perkins tells us that the Christian minister prophesies "in the name and room of Christ," he clearly means that the ministry of the Word continues the prophetic ministry of Christ.

Perkins underlines the importance of the minister being diligent in his private study. As preparation for his ministry the preacher needs a solid education in the liberal arts, in philosophy, and very particularly in literature. Then he needs to study the Scriptures using all the tools of grammatical, rhetorical, and logical analysis. He should study the great theologians both ancient and modern. Perkins, as the Puritans who followed him, gave a high value to a "learned ministry." It is most clear that by this is meant particularly a literate ministry. In order to understand the written word the minister must study great literature and pursue literary studies. After all, how can one be a minister of the Word without being skilled in the use of words.

True to the Reformed tradition, learning and godliness are understood to be equally necessary for the preacher. As Perkins understood it, speech is gracious when it comes from a grace-filled heart. The minister must have a good conscience or else he would not dare to preach. Without integrity the minister cannot be a sound preacher. He must have "an inward feeling of the doctrine to be delivered. . . . he must be godly affected himself who would stir up godly affections in other men." The preacher must have a sense of "the fear of God, whereby being thoroughly stricken with a reverent regard of God's majesty, he speaketh soberly and moderately." Again we recognize the influence of

Augustine who gave such great importance to faith, hope, and love as the spiritual tools of exegesis. A preacher must have a love of the people. That this might come about Perkins admonishes the would-be preacher to be fervent in prayer for the people of God. What comes through with particular clarity in this work of Perkins is this balance between learning and piety. Nothing could be more characteristic of a truly Reformed spirituality.

With the seventeenth century the number of truly great preachers became astounding. Among the Puritans particularly the quality of preaching rose. One should mention among the leading preachers during the next two centuries at least the following: John Preston (1587–1628), the great preacher at Trinity Church in Cambridge; Stephen Charnock (1628–1680), another one of the Cambridge Presbyterians, so distinguished for his works on systematic theology, who won an outstanding reputation as a preacher in Dublin; and Dr. James Ussher (1581–1656), the Calvinist Archbishop of Armagh, universally recognized for his learning. One should mention Edmund Calamy (1600–1666), one of the Fathers of the Westminster Assembly. It was Dr. Calamy who was commonly regarded as the greatest of the Puritan preachers. Thomas Watson (c. 1620–1690) was highly regarded as a preacher. His 176 catechetical sermons based on the *Westminster Shorter Catechism*, as well as his catechetical sermons on the Lord's Prayer and the Ten Commandments are particularly valued. Richard Baxter (1615–1691) was surely one of the most able preachers of the century. In New England right from the beginning there were outstanding preachers, Richard Mather (1596–1669), Thomas Shephard (1605–1649), and above all, Jonathan Edwards (1703–1758).

By the middle of the seventeenth century when the Westminster Assembly produced its directory for worship there was considerable departure from the approach of the Continental Reformers. We notice for instance, that the *Westminster Directory* has separate chapters for the "Publick Reading of the Holy Scriptures" and "The Preaching of the Word." It is obvious that the two are thought of as separate parts of the worship service. The public reading of the Scriptures in the congregation is one of the means which God has appointed for the edification of his people. Such reading is worship, the *Directory* tells us, because we thereby acknowledge our dependence on God. The *Direc-*

tory further teaches us that normally a whole chapter from the Old Testament and a whole chapter from the New Testament should be read at each service but the exact length of the lesson is left to the wisdom of the minister. "All the canonical books are to be read over in order, that the people may be better acquainted with the whole body of the Scriptures; and ordinarily, where the reading in either Testament endeth on one Lord's day, it is to begin the next." On the other hand we read that those portions of the Scriptures which the minister considers, "best for the edification of his hearers," are to be read more frequently. This reading is not necessarily the passage on which the sermon is to be preached, for we read, "When the minister who readeth shall judge it necessary to expound any part of what is read, let it not be done until the whole chapter . . . be ended." The sermon comes later in the service. Clearly the Westminster Divines saw a value in the public reading of the Scriptures aside from simply reading out the passage on which the sermon was based.

In its chapter on preaching the *Westminster Directory* weakened the stand of the Continental Reformers.

> Ordinarily, the subject of his sermon is to be some text of Scripture, holding forth some principle or head of religion, or suitable to some special occasion emergent; or he may go on in some chapter, psalm, or book of the holy scripture, as he shall see fit.

What the Fathers of the Westminster Assembly obviously envision is primarily textual preaching on various topics or occasions and only secondarily the expository preaching of books of the Bible in course. Nevertheless, the *Westminster Directory* does have in mind that a sermon is to be a careful and learned interpretation of Scripture. In time the Puritans became masters of the occasional sermon. They preached at all kinds of occasions, in addition to the usual Sunday morning and Sunday evening sermon. There were sermons for special days of fasting and repentance, for special days of rejoicing and thanksgiving. Sermons were preached at weddings and at funerals, or any other public occasion. In New England there were election day sermons. It must be admitted, however, that there is a dark side to this growth of the occasional sermon. The occasional sermon tended to go adrift from the liturgy. It is unfortunate that the Puritans lost the unity between word, prayer, and sacrament which the Continental and Scottish Reformers had tried to recover. In England the old medieval separation between preaching and the communion liturgy on one hand and between preaching and the order for morning and evening prayer on the other hand, was not healed by the Reformation. It is therefore not at all surprising that in the *Westminster Directory* preaching has lost much of its liturgical character.

An outstanding example of the preaching ministry of a Puritan Divine is found in the work of Dr. Thomas Manton (1620–1677). More than many of the Puritans, Dr. Manton followed the tradition of the Continental Reformers. Manton was brought up in a devout family, having a minister for father and having ministers for grandfathers on both sides of the family. After his studies in Oxford he quickly won a reputation as a learned preacher. Manton had read widely in the literature of the ancient church and in the Continental Reformers, and possessed a large private library which was greatly admired by his colleagues. He was particularly well known for his knowledge of the Scholastic theologians. From 1653 until 1662 he was pastor of St. Paul's Covent Garden, the most prominent Puritan pulpit in London. Although not a member of the Westminster Assembly, he was chosen to write the preface to the Assembly's Confession of Faith. He was one of those Presbyterians who supported the restoration of Charles II, but who refused to go along with episcopacy and was therefore under the Act of Uniformity denied the right to preach. Manton was a prolific writer. Twenty-two volumes of his works, a large part of which are sermons, have come down to us.

The great bulk of Manton's sermons is made up of his *lectio continua* preaching. One notices however that with Manton the *lectio continua* has slowed down to such a pace that he is no longer preaching through individual books but rather through chapters. We find for example:

27 sermons on Matthew 25
45 sermons on John 17
24 sermons on Romans 6
47 sermons on Romans 8
40 sermons on 2 Corinthians 5

65 sermons on Hebrews 11
32 sermons on Ephesians 5
16 sermons on 2 Thessalonians 1
18 sermons on 2 Thessalonians 2
190 sermons on Psalm 119

One can surely object that when the *lectio continua* is preached so slowly one of the advantages of this approach to preaching is lost. One does not get the whole message of a particular biblical writer. This approach did nevertheless produce a remarkable faithfulness to Scripture and in the pulpit of Thomas Manton it made for great preaching.

The series of sermons on Psalm 119 is indeed famous in the history of preaching. It is remarkable for the fact that Dr. Manton was able to go through the 176 verses of the psalm in 190 sermons without becoming tedious or repetitious. Only a man of tremendous intellectual vitality could have preached such a series and yet maintain the interest of his congregation. These sermons were delivered in the course of a bit more than a year. Two sermons were preached on the Lord's Day and one during the middle of the week.

In addition to these sermons we find a number of sermons for funerals and weddings. As England became better supplied with preachers we find that funerals and weddings were more and more considered appropriate occasions for sermons. At one wedding service Manton chose a text from Genesis 2:22, "And [God] brought her to the man." Dr. Manton developed the text in such a way that the providence of God in choosing a husband or wife is recognized. Christians should receive their life partner from the hand of God. He reminds us of the story of Isaac and Rebecca. He quotes from Proverbs 19:14 "Riches and honours are an inheritance from our fathers: but a good wife is from the Lord." Manton tells us that when the Christian sees God's hand in this relationship he will be more diligent and patient in seeking God's blessing in it. The *Westminster Directory for Worship* in its chapter "The Solemnization of Marriage," had explicitly taught that an exhortation from the Word of God was a legitimate part of the wedding service, ". . . because such as marry are to marry in the Lord, and . . . have special need of instruction, direction, and exhortation, from the word of God, at their entering into such a new condition, . . . we judge it expe-

dient that marriage be solemnized by a lawful minister of the word."
This sermon is clearly addressed to the whole congregation. The unmar-
ried are instructed on how they are to seek a husband or wife. The
married are admonished to acknowledge God's providence that they
might recognize God's blessing. The sermon even has words of comfort
for those who have lost a husband or wife. Manton has clearly recognized the pastoral opportunity provided by preaching at a wedding.

In much the same way, funerals were considered appropriate times
to witness to the Christian belief in the resurrection of the body and the
life everlasting. At the funeral of Mistress Jane Blackwell, the wife of a
fellow minister, Dr. Manton selected the text, "Blessed are the dead
who die in the Lord," and developed from it a three point sermon. First
he tells us what it is to die in the Lord, second he tells us what the
blessedness is of those who die in the Lord, and third he tells us how the
Christian comes to be blessed with dying in the Lord. This sermon as all
of Manton's sermons is marked by a straightforward analysis of the text
of Scripture. Here we have a perfect example of what the Puritans
meant by a "plain style of preaching." The beauty of the sermon is the
clarity with which he draws from the Bible the Christian teaching on the
hope of eternal life. There is in the whole sermon a remarkable pastoral
tone of a minister who recognizes what the Christian needs to know
when faced by death.

As a preacher Thomas Manton is distinguished by his profound
insight into the meaning of the text of Scripture. It is simply in his
mastery of the Scriptures that Manton surpasses other preachers. How
often one is amazed at his resourcefulness in bringing parallel passages
to the illumination of his text. His sermons are great because he was a
most able interpreter of Scripture. The greatest example of his ability as
an expositor is his commentary on the epistle of James. This commentary is an adaptation of a series of sermons which he delivered on weekday mornings at Stoke Newington. We find in it a perfect balance between a clear analysis of the text and practical application to the
Christian life. Today, almost 350 years later, this commentary can be
bought in two or three different editions. It remains unsurpassed, the
great classic commentary on the epistle of James. Surely the preaching
ministry of Thomas Manton proves to us once again that the greatest
preaching is that which most clearly sets forth Scripture.

VI

The Ministry
of Prayer

One of the most informative passages of Scripture on the subject of corporate prayer is Solomon's prayer for the dedication of the Temple (1 Kings 8:23–53). In the course of this long prayer he outlines the uses for which the Temple had been set apart. It is clear that Solomon dedicates the Temple as a house of prayer. This primary purpose of the Temple is affirmed again and again. Jesus himself understood the Temple as "a house of prayer for all the nations" (Mark 11:17). Let us look at this prayer for a picture of the ministry of prayer as it was carried out in the Temple.

Solomon begins the prayer by remembering at length the covenant promises of God. God is above all one who keeps covenant and shows steadfast love, or, to use the Hebrew word, *hesed*, which means God's covenant faithfulness with his people. Solomon remembers God's covenant with the house of David and the promises that were given him concerning a Temple where God would make his name to dwell. That is, the Temple was built in obedience to the Word of God and with the expectation that when the Temple was so built, God would honor the prayer that was offered in the Temple. What is abundantly clear at this point is that the theological foundation of prayer is the doctrine of the Covenant.

Having remembered before God the covenant promises, Solomon mentions seven instances for prayer in the Temple. Particularly important among these are prayers in time of drought, pestilence, or military defeat. It is assumed that such things come about because the people have sinned and so if the people "turn again to thee, and acknowledge thy name, and pray and make supplication to thee in this house; then hear thou in heaven, and forgive the sin of thy people Israel" (1 Kings 8:33–34). What is in question here is public sin, public confession, and the forgiveness of the whole people. What Solomon seems to envision is holding fast days, days of public repentance.

Several other places in Scripture enliven our picture of this public penitential prayer which took place in the Temple. The lamentations in the book of Joel exemplify the sort of prayers offered in the Temple when some national catastrophe occurred. The calamity which fell upon Israel on that occasion was the destruction of the land by a plague of locusts. Trumpets were blown, the priests cried and wailed before God wearing sackcloth and besmearing themselves with ashes. The book of Jeremiah, in chapter 14, records for us the prayers that were offered in the Temple on the occasion of a drought. A certain order is to be noted in these prayers. First there is the song of lamentation:

> "Judah mourns
>   and her gates languish;
> her people lament on the ground,
>   and the cry of Jerusalem goes up.
> Her nobles send their servants for water;
>   they come to the cisterns,
> they find no water,
>   they return with their vessels empty;
> they are ashamed and confounded
>   and cover their heads.
> Because of the ground which is dismayed,
>   since there is no rain on the land,
> the farmers are ashamed,
>   they cover their heads.
> Even the hind in the field forsakes her newborn calf
>   because there is no grass.
> The wild asses stand on the bare heights,
>   they pant for air like jackals;
> their eyes fail
>   because there is no herbage."
>
> (Jeremiah 14:2–6)

This is followed by a penitential prayer which acknowledges the sin of the people and asks God's mercy. The prayer pleads the covenant relation which Israel has with God who is addressed as the "hope of Israel."

> "Though our iniquities testify against us,
>   act, O LORD, for thy name's sake;
> for our backslidings are many,
>   we have sinned against thee.
> O thou hope of Israel,
>   its savior in time of trouble . . ."

(Jeremiah 14:7-8)

After this prayer of confession and supplication, the people awaited an oracle from one of the Temple prophets. Doubtless in many cases there was an oracle which was an assurance of pardon and forgiveness, but in this case (Jer. 14:10), the prophet was bound to announce there was no forgiveness.

A less ,vivid although happier example of this liturgy of penitential prayer we find in Psalm 12. In the first two verses we hear the lamentation, in the second two verses the supplication for mercy and in the fifth verse the prophetic oracle in which God promises justice to the afflicted, " 'Because the poor are despoiled, because the needy groan, I will now arise,' says the LORD; 'I will place him in the safety for which he longs.' " The liturgy achieves completion then in a hymn of thanksgiving, "The promises of the Lord are promises that are pure." The liturgy has these four parts: (1) song of lamentation in which the people cry to the Lord, (2) prayer of confession and supplication for mercy, (3) the divine oracle of forgiveness and assurance of redemption, and (4) the hymn of thanksgiving. This four part prayer liturgy as well as individual parts of it, we discover in a good number of the prayers of the book of Psalms.

As we have seen, Solomon's prayer of dedication has particularly in mind the prayer of the whole nation in time of national emergencies but Solomon also has in mind the prayer of "any man . . . each knowing the affliction of his own heart" (1 Kings 8:38). Every day many Israelites must have come to the Temple as private individuals with a great variety of very personal troubles about which they wanted to pray. The priests stood in attendance to assist such people in their prayers; they led them in prayer, and offered sacrifices in their name and surely on occasion delivered to them a word of promise from God. The prayer of the

Temple served not only public concerns but the personal and private needs of anyone who sought the Lord.

A particularly moving example of this is the story of Hannah's prayer for the gift of a son (1 Sam. 1:1—2:11). To be sure, the story unfolds in the sanctuary of Shiloh rather than in the Temple of Jerusalem, but we can be well assured that much the same thing would have happened in Jerusalem. First we hear of how Hannah wept bitterly before the Lord. This lamentation is a natural part of prayer and we find prayers of lamentation throughout Scripture. Then she made a vow that if God would give her a son she would dedicate him to God's service. She mentioned her lamentation deep in her heart. All this was done before Eli the priest, who, finally, in a conversation with her discovered the deep tribulation of her heart. Eli gave her a benediction or prophetic oracle, "Go in peace, and the God of Israel grant your petition." Hannah returned home and in due time, the child for which she had prayed was born. Then, when the child grew old enough to be taken to the Temple, Hannah led her son, whom she had named Samuel, up to the sanctuary at Shiloh. With her she brought a bull to be presented for sacrifice. Then in fulfillment of her vow she delivered the child to Eli the priest and gave her witness that God had answered her prayer. She sang the votive thanksgiving psalm which is recorded at the beginning of chapter 2. (Votive, it should be explained, means in regard to a vow. A votive sacrifice was a sacrifice made in fulfillment of a vow. The votive thanksgiving psalm was sung when the votive sacrifice was presented.)

In reading this votive thanksgiving psalm, one is somewhat surprised to find that it is not particularly appropriate to the occasion. It is a stereotyped prayer which would be appropriate to many different kinds of people who came to the Temple to make a votive sacrifice. Doubtless this prayer was a standard votive thanksgiving prayer, rather than a prayer composed for Hannah. The Temple must have had a collection of prayers of lamentation and a collection of votive thanksgiving psalms which were used on ordinary occasions. Surely special occasions would from time to time demand a new composition, but in most cases the standard prayers must have been used. In this way, the private prayers of individuals were inserted into the prayer of Israel. Private prayer became public prayer.

This sort of thing must have happened frequently in the Temple.

Relatives must have come to the Temple to pray for the members of their family who were ill. Farmers surely came to pray for good crops, as well as any number of others in a multitude of different needs. The vows did not have to be made in the Temple, as the story of Jonah makes clear. The vows could be made anywhere and then when the suppliant was delivered from danger, he or she would make a pilgrimage to Jerusalem and there pay the vows. In Psalm 107 we have a sort of corporate votive thanksgiving psalm. This psalm must have been used at one of the great annual festivals when there were numbers of people who all wanted to pay their vows at the same time. They wanted to witness to how God had heard their prayers when they were lost in the desert, in trouble at sea, suffering in prison, and a number of other calamities. All these individual prayers and private concerns mingle together in a single hymn of thanksgiving to God who is the savior of his people and "whose mercy endureth forever." All the personal concerns like little streams finally join into a great river of corporate prayer.

The relation between private prayer and corporate prayer in the worship of the Temple needs to be looked at carefully. When one studies the prayers in the book of Psalms one notices that it is not always clear whether the prayer is intended for individual use or for corporate use. There is good reason for this. The fact that one came to the Temple to pray meant that one was appealing to the whole community for support in one's prayer. It is a most natural thing for people facing very individual and personal problems to ask the support of others in their prayers. When as Christians today we assemble together for prayer, we appeal to the whole Christian community to support us in our prayer.

Personal prayer relates to corporate prayer in still another way. One notices in the book of Psalms that there are a number of prayers which are centered around the person of the king. Some of these are coronation prayers or prayers for military success. There is even a royal wedding psalm. Scholars speculate much about these royal psalms but one thing is quite clear, prayers for the king and his well-being were in fact intercessions for the whole nation. It has often been suggested that many of the prayers which appear in personal and individual terms are really intended for the king. David was among other things a champion of prayer. Those who would learn to pray have only to follow his example. The prayers of David are the "type" of the prayers of the people. The life of prayer becomes an imitation of the life of David. David prayed for Israel and Israel prayed for David; even more Israel prayed in David. That is why so many of the psalms have superscriptions telling us about the situation in the life of David which gave rise to the prayer. In the book of Acts we see how the primitive Christian church developed this idea. Since David was understood as the type of Christ, the prayers of David, the prayers for David, and the prayers for David's kingdom were adopted as the prayers of Christ and his church (Acts 4:23–31). The Christian prays in the name of Jesus. Christ prays for the church and the church prays in Christ. One thing this means is that the Christian inserts his or her own prayers into the prayer of Christ. Another thing it means is that the Christian appropriates the prayer of Christ. The ascended Christ at the right hand of the Father intercedes for the church and presents our individual prayers at the throne of grace, as part of his own prayers. Our prayer mingles with the sweet incense of his prayer.

The prayer of the synagogue developed in a very different way from the prayer of the Temple. The central prayer of the synagogue was the *Amida,* or as it is sometimes called, the Prayer of the Eighteen Benedictions. The prayer was fairly well formulated by the first Christian century and we can be fairly certain that Jesus and the Apostles followed this form of prayer. At that time, the *Amida* was a form of prayer rather than a formula. The exact text was not set. The arrangement and themes of each of the eighteen parts of the prayer were clearly established. When a well-known rabbi or a particularly venerated holy man led the prayer it was expected, however, that he would extemporize on the various themes. The prayer began with three benedictions of praise and thanksgiving. In the center of the prayer were six supplications or petitions of a more personal nature followed by six intercessions for the well-being of the nation of Israel. The final three benedictions concluded the prayer with praise and thanksgiving and introduced the giving of the Aaronic Benediction.

Characteristic of this prayer is the way its supplications and intercessions are couched in praise and thanksgiving and the way each supplication or intercession is concluded with a benediction or thanksgiving. For example, the sixth benediction is a supplication for mercy:

> Forgive us, our Father, for we have sinned; pardon us, our King, for we have transgressed, for thou art good and forgiving. Blessed be thou, O Lord, who art gracious and dost abundantly forgive.
>
> (Hedegard, *Seder R. Amron Gaon,* 88)

The eleventh benediction is an intercession for the Jewish Civil Authority:

> Restore our judges as at first, and our councillors as at the beginning and reign thou over us, O Lord, above in grace and mercy and righteousness and judgment. Blessed be thou, O Lord, the King who lovest righteousness and judgment.

> (Hedegard, *Seder R. Amron Gaon,* 92)

The concluding sentence is, properly speaking, the benediction, "Blessed be thou, O Lord, the King who lovest righteousness and judgment." The subject of the benediction matches the subject of intercession. The prayer asks for the establishment of a just civil authority and at the same time blesses God for his love of justice. When the Apostle Paul told the Philippians to make their prayers and supplications to God with thanksgiving (Phil. 4:6), it must have been something quite similar to this prayer which he had in mind.

Now let us turn to the prayer of the New Testament church. When one has a clear picture of how this prayer of the Eighteen Benedictions was prayed, one begins to see many indications or hints in the New Testament of how the infant church exercised the ministry of prayer. The prayer of the primitive Christian church bears the marks of the liturgical mold of the synagogue. First let us look at the teaching of Jesus regarding prayer in light of what we have learned about the *Amida*. The Sermon on the Mount preserves for us a number of Jesus' teachings about prayer. Jesus, in criticizing the Jewish practice of prayer, very specifically has in mind the way his fellow Jews prayed the *Amida*, for we read, "for they love to stand and pray in the synagogues and at the street corners" (Matt. 6:5). *Amida* means "standing," that is, it is the prayer which is said standing. The point of Jesus' criticism is that the truly devout should not make a show of their praying, but aside from that Jesus probably had in mind that the prayers which were said would not differ so very much from the traditional *Amida*. For the *Amida* itself, as a form of prayer, there is no criticism. Jesus will add to the content, as we shall see, but the basic form will pass into the prayer of the church. One detail that can perhaps be noted here is that the practice of standing for prayer would be maintained in the church for many centuries.

Jesus goes on then to teach a specific form of prayer. This form we call the Lord's Prayer. The Lord's Prayer has many similarities to the

Amida both in terms of form and content. Like the *Amida*, it begins with praise, "Our Father who art in heaven, hallowed be thy name." If the traditional doxology, "For thine is the kingdom and the power and the glory, for ever," is indeed original, then the Lord's Prayer, like the *Amida*, ends with praise and thanksgiving. The central portion is made up of two intercessions and three supplications. From the standpoint of form, the Lord's Prayer might be called a very short Christian version of the *Amida*.

With the basic form of the *Amida* in mind, some of the teachings of Jesus on prayer become much more striking. Jesus particularly taught his disciples to pray for their enemies and for those who persecuted them. He exemplified this when he prayed on the cross, "Father, forgive them." In the Sermon on the Mount he taught, "For if you forgive men their trespasses, your heavenly Father also will forgive you." The Prayer of the Eighteen Benedictions had no prayer for the Gentiles or for the persecutors of Israel; it prayed for the salvation of Israel alone. Jesus very specifically taught his disciples otherwise.

The intercessory prayer of Jesus in John 17 is very interesting in this respect. This prayer is also a list of intercessions. Jesus prays for the church which his disciples are to gather out of the world. He prays for the unity of the church, the continuity of the church, and the holiness of the church. Jesus teaches us here that the prayers of his disciples should embrace a much broader concern than the traditional nationalistic concerns of the *Amida*. Jesus wanted his disciples to pray for the coming of his kingdom among all nations and the doing of his Father's will over all the earth as it is in heaven.

Now let us look at several passages in the letters of the Apostle Paul. Of first importance is the passage in 1 Timothy in which the Apostle instructs his young assistant.

> First of all, then, I urge that supplications, prayers, intercessions, and thanksgivings be made for all men, for kings and all who are in high positions, that we may lead a quiet and peaceable life, godly and respectful in every way. This is good, and it is acceptable in the sight of God our Savior, who desires all men to be saved and to come to the knowledge of the truth . . . .
> I desire then that in every place the men should pray.
>
> (1 Timothy 2:1–4, 8)

Having seen this concern of Jesus that the ministry of intercession reach out beyond the confines of Israel, the instructions of Paul to Timothy take on much greater clarity. Paul instructs Timothy to see that the prayers of the church include prayers for all men, even for the Gentile rulers of the world. Paul underlines this by stressing that God's will is for the salvation of all peoples and therefore we should pray to this end. The *Amida* never included prayers of this scope and so Paul instructs Timothy in this way lest the prayers of the church follow too closely the prayers of the synagogue.

Paul frequently requests his churches to include particular intercessions in their common prayer. He asks the church at Ephesus to pray for all the saints and also to pray for him as a minister of the gospel (Eph. 6:18–19). He asks the Colossians to support him and his fellow workers in their ministry, "that God may open to us a door for the word, to declare the mystery of Christ" (Col. 4:2–3).

A number of passages in the epistles of Paul indicate how the Apostle was accustomed to pray. Frequently in the very beginning of his letters he begins by telling the church to which he is writing that he regularly makes mention of them in his prayers. Paul writes to the Philippians, "I thank God in all my remembrance of you, always in every prayer of mine for you all making my prayer with joy, thankful for your partnership in the gospel" (Phil. 1:3–6). To the Thessalonians we find very similar words, "We give thanks to God always for you all, constantly mentioning you in our prayers, remembering before our God and Father your work of faith and labor of love and steadfastness of hope" (1 Thess. 1:2–3). In both examples we find that Paul's regular intercessions for his churches were combined with thanksgiving. We gather that when Paul and those who were with him offered their prayers, the specific churches were remembered particularly. The passage in 1 Thessalonians would indicate that the prayers in question were common prayers not just personal private devotions. For Paul, these intercessions were a duty, a ministry of prayer which he felt he and his colleagues were "bound" to perform (2 Thess. 1:3).

At the beginning of the letter to the Ephesians, the introductory prayer is particularly festive.

> Blessed be the God and Father of our Lord Jesus Christ, who has blessed us in Christ with every spiritual blessing in the heavenly places,

> even as he chose us in him before the foundation of the world. . . .
> I do not cease to give thanks for you, remembering you in my prayers,
> that the God of our Lord Jesus Christ, the Father of glory, may give you
> a spirit of wisdom and of revelation in the knowledge of him.
>
> (Ephesians 1:3–4, 16–17)

Here we undoubtedly have the wording of the Apostle's customary prayer. It is clearly in the tradition of the Prayer of the Eighteen Benedictions. It is a benediction worthy of the school of Gamaliel.

Having given a picture of the ministry of prayer in the earliest Christian church, the church of the New Testament period, let us turn now to finding how this ministry developed in the centuries that followed.

All things considered, we have a fairly good amount of documentation for the second and third Christian centuries, at least for this aspect of the history of Christian worship. The epistle of Clement, written in Rome about the year 90 concludes with a prayer that undoubtedly reflects the liturgical prayer of that church. It is, like the *Amida*, a prayer of supplication and intercession beginning and ending with praise and thanksgiving. It may well be that what we have in this letter has been abbreviated to some extent and perhaps somewhat adapted to the more specific concerns of the letter, but the general liturgical form is nevertheless clear. The opening words of the prayer seem to be missing but the first paragraph of what has been preserved for us is a solemn prayer of praise to the source of all creation, who in wisdom and justice governs the affairs of all men and nations, and who has chosen from out of all the peoples of the earth a people to serve him. Then follows a list of intercessions for the afflicted, the fallen, the needy, the sick, the wandering, prisoners, and the salvation of all nations. Again meditating on God's mercy and faithfulness to his people, the prayer asks for mercy to those who have sinned and peace "for us and to all that dwell on the earth." The next paragraph blesses God as sovereign ruler of the world and then intercedes for those to whom God has entrusted the government of this world. It is an intercession for the civil authority as well as the leaders of the church. The prayer ends with a doxology praising God through Jesus Christ, the high priest and guardian of our souls. After a few other matters are mentioned regarding the delivery of the letter, there is an elaborate benediction, which, like the ascriptions of praise and benedictions at the end of the New Testament Epistles, may well reflect the benediction which concluded the prayer of the synagogue as well as the prayer of the church.

In the writings of the Church Fathers of the second and third centuries we find a number of remarks about the church prayers. From Justin Martyr (100–165) we learn that one of the cardinal components of the worship of the church on the Lord's Day was a Prayer of Intercession, not only for the spiritual growth of Christians but for all people everywhere. Justin clearly indicates that this general prayer comes after the sermon and before the communion service. This prayer like the *Amida* of the synagogue is given with the congregation standing. It is clearly a different prayer from the Prayer of Thanksgiving said at the communion service. Then we notice with particular interest that having finished his description of the Sunday worship, Justin speaks of the ministry of the deacons, the giving of alms, and the care of the poor. This, too, obviously belongs to the worship of the Lord's Day.

By the middle of the fourth century we begin to get a much clearer picture of Christian worship. We even begin to get the complete text of some of the prayers. The Prayer of the Faithful or the Great Prayer of Intercession is a regular feature of the liturgy. The *Apostolic Constitutions,* dating from the end of the fourth century provides us with a complete text of the liturgy of the church of Antioch. In this liturgy we find a fully developed intercessory prayer for the whole church throughout the world, the local church of Antioch, prayers for the ministry, the local bishop, for presbyters, deacons, and other church leaders. There are prayers for married people, for the celibate, for women expecting children, the sick, the exiled, and those in prison. There are prayers for enemies and those who persecute the church and those who are outside the church. Finally there are prayers for those who are present and for the preservation in grace of every Christian soul. One finds in this prayer the influence of both the old Jewish Prayer of the Eighteen Benedictions and the specific concerns of Jesus and the Apostles flowing together in such a way that the prayer is a comprehensive prayer for the salvation of all peoples.

Having flowered into a very full and comprehensive prayer of intercession, the Prayer of the Faithful began to fade as the Middle Ages progressed. This is the case in the West at least. By the end of the Middle Ages the Prayer of the Faithful had all but disappeared from the

Roman mass. Certain of the intercessions were to be found in the canon of the mass, but the Latin mass of the Middle Ages had lost a separate general prayer of intercession. In a vestigial form it was still found in the prayers of Good Friday, to be sure, but during the rest of the year these intercessions were missing.

With the coming of the Reformation there was a radical reform of public prayer. The disciplines of prayer which had developed during the Middle Ages had broken down. This often happens with methods of prayer. They are developed with a great deal of fervor by one generation but then after a few generations the old prayer forms grow moribund and calcified and inevitably break down. The Reformers gave themselves to an intensive study of the prayers of Holy Scripture to discover what the prayer which is according to Scripture should be. It took some time for the new Evangelical forms of prayer to evolve. At first many of the old Latin prayers were simply translated. In Strasbourg, for instance, when it was decided to reform the daily prayer services, the old daily collects were gone over and those which were found suitable were translated into German. Some of the collects were not found suitable and so new prayers were written to take their place. At first these new collects were in form quite similar to the old collects, but within a few years the Reformers' approach to prayer had so completely changed that even the collect form was largely bypassed.

Over the course of a dozen years or so the Reformed Church of Strasbourg developed two basic prayers for common worship, the General Confession and the Prayer of Intercession. The General Confession started out as a sort of Protestant *Confiteor*. The *Confiteor* of the Roman mass, so heavy with the intercession of the saints, was expurgated so that it was a rather simple confession of sin. In time the prayer began to be influenced by the psalms of lamentation, particularly Psalms 25 and 26. When we meet the General Confession in the *Strasbourg Psalter* of 1537 it has become a comprehensive prayer of confession and supplication. It has followed very closely the pattern we found in the Temple. First there is the lamentation and confession of sin, then a supplication for forgiveness, an assurance of pardon spoken by the minister, and finally a psalm sung by the congregation.

The recovery of a comprehensive Prayer of Intercession became an important feature of the regular worship of the Church of Strasbourg.

Here, it was above all Martin Bucer (1491–1551) who was responsible for the writing of the liturgical texts. In Bucer's final form of the liturgy of the Reformed Church of Strasbourg we find a long Prayer of Intercession which resembles the intercessory prayers of the patristic age. First there is a prayer for the civil authority, then a prayer for the ministry of the gospel, a prayer for the conversion of all mankind, a prayer for the perfection of the saints, and finally a prayer for the afflicted. Bucer phrases the text of his prayers in such a way that we recognize quite clearly that he has built the prayer on those admonitions of Jesus and the Apostles which direct Christians to include specific concerns in their prayer. The influence of Paul's instructions to Timothy (1 Tim. 2:1–8) shines through unmistakably. Likewise Ephesians 6:18–19, James 5:13–18, and Philippians 1:9–11, have all clearly influenced Bucer in the construction of his prayer. Bucer, who had a good knowledge of patristic literature, knew well that the church of an earlier age had included such concerns in prayers. Bucer's reform was based on Scripture, to be sure, but it was also informed by his knowledge of the practice of the ancient church.

These two core prayers, the General Confession and the Prayer of Intercession, were translated into French and through Calvin's (1509–1564) influence were made part of the liturgy of the Church of Geneva as we discover in the *Genevan Psalter* of 1542. From that point on these two core prayers became a regular feature of Reformed worship. John Knox (1513–1572) used these two prayers as patterns and so we find an elaboration of these two prayers in the *Book of Common Order* of the Church of Scotland.

From the earliest *Strasbourg Psalters* there is evidence that the Evangelical pastors wanted to allow for the developing of the gift of some sort of free or extemporaneous prayer. At the same time they recognized that prayer forms were needed as well. What developed was that the two core prayers were used pretty much as they appeared in the printed text of the psalter, but then there were other prayers in the service which were supposed to be formulated by the minister. In a way quite similar to their other liturgical activities the Reformers were trying to get away from a mere *opus operandi* saying of prayers. It was not a matter of wanting to be original or creative in their prayer. They saw it to be important to pray as Christ had taught them to pray. From the eighth chapter of Romans they learned that prayer was a sanctifying work of the Holy Spirit in their hearts. Learning to pray and growing in holiness went together.

Calvin was quite clear that not every minister could be expected to have the gift of leading in public prayer. Evidently Calvin normally led the Prayer of Confession and the Prayer of Intercession pretty much out of the book. It was the same thing with the accustomed prayers at matins and vespers on weekdays. On the other hand, after preaching the Reformer was accustomed to extemporize. Hundreds of the extemporized prayers of Calvin have come down to us. These prayers were offered after the sermon at morning or evening prayer and were carefully taken down by the stenographer who was responsible for recording the sermon. For Calvin, hearing the Word of God naturally leads to prayer. In searching the Scriptures it becomes clear that there are things in our lives which need to be set in order; there are things in the church or in the community which need to be corrected. For example, when Calvin was preaching through the book of Amos, he dealt in one sermon on the stubbornness of Israel in refusing to follow God's commandments. In the prayer which followed the sermon Calvin prayed ''that we might turn our hearts to thy service and submit ourselves to the yoke of thy word.'' As one studies these extemporaneous prayers of Calvin one sees that it is through prayer that one moves from the Word to the world.

There is a certain symmetry in the discipline of public prayer as it is found in the worship of the *Genevan Psalter*. Not only do we find a balance between prayer forms and free prayer, we also find a balance between the General Prayer of Confession and the Prayer of Intercession. Each represents a distinct aspect of Christian prayer. The prayer of confession and supplication is by nature more subjective and introspective. It is turned inward while the intercessions are turned outward, directed toward the building up of the church and the redemption of the world. The Prayer of Confession is baptismal prayer while the intercessions are communion prayers. In baptisms we are baptized unto the forgiveness of sins. Baptism is the sign under which we pray that we might die unto sin and live unto righteousness. Baptism calls us to prayers of repentance and supplications for growth in grace. On the other hand the intercessions are more closely related to communion.

The intercessions look forward to and pray for the consummation of the kingdom, to the wedding feast of the Lamb. The intercessions pray for the building up of the church, the conversion of the nations, and the perseverance of the saints. There is yet another dimension to this symmetry. Balancing these liturgical prayers of the church are the metrical psalms, particularly the psalms of praise and thanksgiving. The *Genevan Psalter* shows an awareness of the great variety of Christian prayer.

With the seventeenth-century Puritans the order of prayers at the ordinary Sunday service was changed considerably. The *Westminster Directory of Worship* outlines the content of the prayers for the Sunday morning service. It provided for a short Invocation at the beginning of the service and a short prayer after the sermon. The main prayer of the ordinary Sunday service however was to be a full, comprehensive prayer including the elements of praise, confession, petition, intercession, and thanksgiving. The desire of the Puritans for this kind of prayer arose from the Congregational wing of the Puritan movement rather than the Presbyterian wing. In fact the position found in the *Westminster Directory* represents a compromise made by the Assembly which decided in favor of the Congregationalists with the compensating concession to the Presbyterians that there might be an Invocation at the beginning of the service and a prayer after the sermon. The Congregationalists would have been happy to have had quite simply one long comprehensive prayer. Nevertheless, the full, comprehensive prayer became the regular prayer of churches which followed the *Westminster Directory* from that point on. Even in Presbyterian Scotland the new arrangement of prayers supplanted the old Genevan arrangement. This comprehensive prayer, or Pastoral Prayer as it was called, was to be said between the Scripture reading and the sermon.

There were some real weaknesses to the arrangement of prayers provided by the *Westminster Directory*. In the first place, it made for an unbearably long prayer which only the most mature Christians could follow with profit. In the second place, it disturbed the very ancient order of the dominical service by putting the prayer between the Scripture lesson and the sermon rather than its more accustomed place between the sermon and the communion service. It tended to have the effect of diminishing the intercessory character of the prayer. It was no longer so much a prayer for the peace of the world, the progress of the gospel and the salvation of all people, but rather a general all-purpose prayer. Finally, because the prayer was supposed to be "framed" by the minister in his own words it was very much dependent upon the gifts of the minister leading the prayer. Unfortunately too many ministers neglected developing this gift and in the popular imagination the minister's long prayer was apt to be a rather tedious part of the service.

There were masters of the pastoral prayer and when it was done well, it was done very well! Developing the gift of leading in public prayer needed preparation just as developing the gift of preaching needed long study and practice. There were a number of manuals for this purpose. Isaac Watts (1694–1748) and John Wilkins (1614–1672), the bishop of Chester, produced such works but by far the most influential was Matthew Henry's *A Method of Prayer*. Over thirty editions of this work appeared between 1712 and 1865. The work takes up in turn the different aspects of prayer, praise and adoration, confession, thanksgiving, petition and supplication, and finally intercession. Henry (1662–1714) had gone through the whole of Scripture studying all the prayers, teachings about prayer, and examples of prayer in order to make clear the nature of each of the various prayer genre. Henry's knowledge of Scripture was prodigious. Today, more than 250 years later, his commentary on the complete Bible is as popular as ever. What Henry attempted to do was to learn the biblical language of prayer. He well understood that one learns a language by imitation and so he gathered together the biblical language of praise, the biblical language of supplication, and the biblical language of intercession. Henry's work is a seminal work. He suggests to us how we can deepen our experience of prayer by turning to the Scriptures and saturating ourselves with the biblical language of prayer. Still today such an approach will help us to develop disciplines of prayer which are Reformed according to the Word of God.

VII
The Lord's Supper

The roots of the sacrament of the Lord's Supper go back to the very dawn of the biblical tradition. We find them as far back as the covenant meals of the patriarchs. One thinks of the story of Melchizedek bringing out bread and wine to share a meal with Abraham after his victory in the battle of the kings. Then there was Abraham's meal with the three heavenly visitors and the meal Jacob prepared for his father Isaac when he sought from him the covenant blessing. These meals were covenant meals which established a profound relationship between those who shared them.

Even more significant, however, is the Passover meal which the children of Israel ate before leaving Egypt. In chapters 12 and 13 of Exodus, we have a detailed description of how the Passover feast was to be celebrated. The narrative makes clear that it was not a feast eaten once at a time way back in history, but rather that it was to be a perpetual memorial.

> "This day shall be for you a memorial day, and you shall keep it as a feast to the LORD; throughout your generations you shall observe it as an ordinance for ever."
>
> (Exodus 12:14)

It was the eating of the feast itself that was the service of worship. Each of the foods eaten had its particular meaning. Much of the meaning of the feast had to do with understanding the meaning of the foods that were eaten.

The two most important foods in the Passover service were the roasted lamb and the unleavened bread. As we shall see, other foods will appear in the paschal rite as time goes on; the wine, bitter herbs, the fruit puree, and so forth. Each of these foods was invested with a particular meaning much as an American Thanksgiving feast is made up of foods which have particular significance. The turkey is a bird unique to North America, the pumpkins used for pumpkin pie were unknown in Europe, the same was true with the corn for the corn bread. When we eat the turkey, we can think of the Pilgrims going out into the woods with a blunderbuss in hand to hunt that extraordinary bird. When we eat the corn bread and the pumpkin pie, we remember how the Indians taught the settlers to plant that strange new cereal; how in the same field at the same time one could grow both corn and pumpkins, foods that could be stored all winter long. Without that essential instruction in the local agriculture, the Puritans would never have survived. Each food we eat at Thanksgiving reminds us of the Pilgrims and the hardships they went through to found our land. It was the same way with the lamb and the unleavened bread for the Passover.

Scholars will tell us that behind the celebration of Passover there must have originally been two separate feasts and that what we find in Exodus 12 and 13 is the splicing together of a primitive nomadic lambing feast and an agricultural first fruits feast. The joining together of these feasts must have happened a long time ago, and it is almost impossible from the texts which have come down to us to reconstruct the two separate feasts. Let us look at the meaning given to these two central foods.

In Exodus 13:1-2 and 11-16 we read of the consecration of the first born. Presumably behind this is the idea of the sacrifice of the first fruits or the firstborn of the flocks. It was a lamb which had been born that same season the year before which was to be prepared for the feast. Whatever undertones of sacrifice there may have been in this story, the eating, not the sacrificing, of the lamb was central. The blood of the lamb was to be put on the lintels of the house in which the lamb was eaten. When this was done as God had directed, the angel of the Lord would spare all those in the house. The angel seeing the blood would pass over the homes of the Hebrews while going through the land of Egypt executing judgment on the Egyptians. The blood on the doorposts was a sign of the Covenant which those who were within had with God. They were to be spared because God had graciously put a covenantal mark upon them. In later generations, however, the lamb was to remind those who ate of the whole story of the Passover and Exodus. It was to remind generations of Jews how God strengthened his people for their journey and protected them from his judgment on Egypt and led them out of the land of bondage. Whatever traces there may be of a primitive nomadic lambing festival, the text in Exodus makes the memorial of the history of God's saving acts central.

The unleavened bread likewise had memorial significance as well as covenant significance. It was to be eaten "because on this day I brought you out of the land of Egypt." It was to remind Israel of the haste with which the Jews had left Egypt. Somewhere in the background there must have been the thought of offering the first fruits of the year, but in our text the nature rites have been succeeded completely by the memorial of God's act of redemption from Egypt. Furthermore, we find very clear evidence that the eating of the unleavened bread had covenant significance, "for if any one eats what is leavened, that person shall be cut off from the congregation of Israel." (Exod. 12:19).

In Exodus 12:43 we read that no foreigner is to eat of the Passover meal. A slave or a sojourner or a hired servant may eat of the Passover only if he has first been circumcised. Having gone through these rites he is a member of the community and therefore he may participate in the Passover. All this makes very clear that the Passover is a covenant meal and that to participate in the meal is constitutive of the community.

An important part of the rite of Passover was recounting the saving acts of God which the meal celebrated.

> "And you shall tell your son on that day, 'It is because of what the LORD did for me when I came out of Egypt.' "
>
> (Exodus 13:8)

The account in Exodus carefully provides the retelling of the story of God's redemption of Israel from servitude in Egypt. Three times the account directs that the father on the day of the feast is to tell his children the story of the deliverance from Egypt (Exod. 12:26; 13:8; 13:14). It should be carefully noted, however, that the father is to *tell* his son. Nothing is said about dramatizing the event. Nothing is said about redoing the Exodus in our day. There is nothing here resembling the Mesopotamian Creation Myth which was re-enacted each year to make the power of creation relevant to a new year. There is no cyclical interpretation of history! The events of the Exodus remain firmly attached to the past. What God did then was done once for all. The Exodus did not need to be repeated. Quite to the contrary each generation needed to be made a part of that unique saving event. "It is because of what the LORD did for me when I came out of Egypt." By participating in the meal, each new generation was added to that people who had been saved from the armies of Pharaoh and the slave-masters of Egypt.

To understand what the Passover was really about, it is essential to see its relation to time. The rites of Passover did not involve any magic tampering with time. It is not as though the rites of Passover were some sort of time machine which made an event in the past leap the intervening centuries. Nor is it a retrogressive time machine which magically takes us back to the days of old. It was rather the forming of a covenant with an eternal God who revealed himself in the past as the Savior of his people and seeks with us that same redemptive relationship in our own time and our own age.

The Synoptic Gospels tell us of how Jesus celebrated the Passover with his disciples at Jerusalem just before his Passion. The Jewish Passover as it was celebrated at the time, while it retained much that was prescribed in the account of Exodus, had been modified in certain respects. From rabbinical sources we are able to reconstruct much of the Passover liturgy of the time with fair probability and the account we find in the Synoptic Gospels becomes increasingly clear when set beside a reconstruction of the Passover Seder.

Let us look at the account in the Gospel of Mark. While Jesus customarily stayed in the suburban village of Bethany when visiting Jerusalem, he moved into the city itself for the celebration of the Passover (Mark 14:3, 12–16). The Passover meal needed to be eaten in the precincts of the holy city. The Synoptic Gospels make a great point of the providential nature of the choice of the room in which the meal was to be eaten. The room, the text tells us, would be "furnished and ready." In this sacred hour, there is nothing casual or happenstance. It has all been arranged by the plan and foreknowledge of God.

Mark recounts that in the course of the meal Jesus took the bread and blessed it and broke it and gave it to the disciples. It is the unleavened bread that is taken. The short benediction over the bread which Jesus, following the Passover Seder, must surely have said was

> Blessed art thou, O Lord God, King of the Universe, who hast brought bread from the earth.

It is a prayer of thanksgiving for creation. To this was added a blessing of the feast day, that is, a blessing of the feast of Passover. Whether the blessing of the feast day is really that old is not altogether clear, but if both were in use at that time, then we have a short prayer of thanksgiving both for the works of creation and redemption.

Jesus then takes the bread and says, "This is my body broken for you." At this point the Passover Haggadah explained that the bread was unleavened because of the haste with which they had left Egypt. Jesus however, gave yet a new meaning to the bread. He broke the bread as a prophetic sign of the giving of his life for his disciples on the day that was to follow, much as Jeremiah had broken the potter's vessel as a prophetic sign of the fall of Jerusalem. Jesus, by means of the covenant meal, joined his disciples to himself before he offered himself up as a sacrifice for their sin and the sin of the world. He joined them to himself because what he was about to do he was doing for them. He shared that meal with them that they might be joined to him in his death.

One notices that nothing is said here about the eating of the Passover lamb. It is mentioned a few verses earlier that it was "the first day of Unleavened Bread, when they sacrificed the passover lamb" (Mark 14:12), but nothing is said of the Passover lamb in the actual meal. The Passover liturgy did not have a special blessing for the lamb. Undoubtedly roast lamb was part of the meal. It should be carefully noticed that the sacrifice of the lamb had taken place well before the meal began.

The account of the Passover in Exodus had said nothing about wine, but the Passover Seder in the first Christian century gave great attention to the drinking of the wine. There were four different cups in the course of the meal. The major blessing was said over the third cup, the cup of blessing. The prayer started out

> Blessed art thou, O Lord God, King of the Universe, who bringeth forth fruit from the vine.

The blessing goes on to mention the covenant with Abraham and the gift of the promised land. It gives thanks for the kingdom of David and God's covenant with David to preserve his son upon the throne and to establish his holy city Jerusalem.

This prayer of thanksgiving first for creation and then for these major acts of the history of redemption has profound significance. By giving thanks for God's gifts, one appropriated them to one's own use (cf. 1 Tim. 4:3–4). This is an old principle of biblical prayer. Giving thanks blesses or consecrates the gifts one has received so that one may use those gifts for one's own enjoyment and profit. In the Passover benedictions the devout Jew gave thanks for the history of salvation and thereby made it the history of his salvation. By giving thanks for the release from bondage in Egypt, he claimed his own freedom, by giving thanks for the gift of the land, he made it his land, by giving thanks for the kingdom of David, he was assured of his place in it.

Here again Jesus invests the sacramental food with a new meaning. "This is my blood of the covenant, which is poured out for many" (Matt. 26:28). The covenant aspect of the meal is here underlined by Jesus just as clearly as it had been indicated by the account in Exodus. Just as each Israelite family had been sealed in a covenant relationship by the blood on the doorposts of their homes in Egypt before the night of judgment, now Jesus bound his disciples to himself in this covenant meal before he went to the cross and passed from death to life.

"And when they had sung a hymn, they went out to the Mount of Olives" (Mark 14:26). This undoubtedly refers to the singing of the Hallel, Psalms 113—118, which was already, in the days of Jesus, part of the Jewish Passover Seder. This series of psalms is a remarkable prayer starting out with an invocation of the name of the Lord (Ps. 113). It moves to a hymnic recounting of the Exodus (Ps. 114—115). Then in a full votive thanksgiving psalm the prayer recognizes the obligation which receiving God's mighty acts of salvation had put upon Israel. "What shall I render to the LORD for all his bounty to me?" (Ps. 116). In Psalm 117, all nations are called to worship the Lord and then is unfolded in Psalm 118 the messianic hope. The stone rejected by men has been chosen by God and is become the foundation stone of a new kingdom. With confidence in the covenant faithfulness of God, Israel cries out "Hosanna! Save now we beseech thee, oh Lord. Blessed is he who comes in the name of the Lord.'' This is how Jesus and his disciples prayed, as Joachim Jeremias so aptly puts it, when Jesus went to the cross.

In the Gospel of Luke we find among the stories of the appearances of the risen Jesus the story of two disciples who met Jesus on the road to Emmaus (Luke 24:13–35). The story takes place on the afternoon of the first Easter Day. It is in many ways a story about the Lord's Supper and what it meant to the first Christians. As they go along Jesus joins them and opens to them the Scriptures. And beginning with Moses, the psalms and all the prophets he explains to them how it was necessary for the Messiah to suffer and to rise again. So having studied the Scriptures they finish the day by sharing a meal together. They did not yet know that it was Jesus who was explaining the Scriptures to them, but when they sat at the table together and when Jesus blessed the bread, then their eyes were opened and they recognized that it was Jesus with whom they were eating. One wonders if there was something unique in the way Jesus broke the bread or in the prayer of thanksgiving that he used to bless the bread. Perhaps already Jesus had transformed the prayers said over the bread and wine so that they were not only prayers of thanksgiving for creation, but also prayers of thanksgiving for God's acts of redemption in his own death and resurrection. There is something even more significant about the story of this supper with the Lord and that is the time when it took place. It took place on the first day of the week, on the first Lord's Day. It was just before Jesus went to the cross that he joined himself to his disciples by means of the supper that they might participate in his suffering and its redemptive power. Now the risen Jesus once more shares a meal with his disciples that they might participate in his victory over death and his resurrection unto eternal life (compare John 21:9–14).

Now let us turn to the Apostle Paul. That the communion is a covenantal meal is particularly evident in the tenth chapter of 1 Corinthians. In an argument to show the Corinthians that they should not participate in pagan cultic meals, he gives the following reason: ''The cup of blessing which we bless, is it not a participation in the blood of Christ? The bread which we break, is it not a participation in the body of Christ? Because there is one bread, we who are many are one body, for we all partake of the one bread.'' Paul goes on to say, ''You cannot drink the cup of the Lord and the cup of demons" (1 Cor. 10:16–21). The reason is simple; partaking of the meal was the act of entering into a covenant with the Lord. If the Christian had entered into a covenant with Christ, how could he enter into a covenant with the pagan gods?

There is another interesting point here. The Christians evidently shared one loaf of bread and drank from a common cup, "because there is one bread, we who are many are one body, for we all partake of the one bread" (1 Cor. 10:17). This is an integral part of the sign of the Supper and it should not be tampered with by the introduction of those little individual glass cups which at the turn of the century American Protestants invented. In the same way the little celluloid disks used in high church circles or the sugar cubed bits of bread used by others should never take the place of the one loaf of bread. The breaking of the one loaf, just as the pouring out and sharing of the one cup, is part of the sign.

In the following chapter, Paul again returns to the subject of the celebration of the Lord's Supper. He introduces his remarks by saying, "When you assemble as a church, I hear that there are divisions among you" (1 Cor. 11:18). The Greek here is very interesting. It might be translated, "when you come together to make the church." The text seems to imply that it is in the meeting together for the purpose of sharing the meal that these individuals become the church, the body of Christ. It is this supper which constitutes the church. Once again it is clear that the Lord's Supper is a covenant meal. Those who participate in it become members of the covenant community.

Here let us think for a moment about the fact that the service is called "the Lord's supper" (1 Cor. 11:20). Very few things in the New Testament are called the Lord's. We hear of the Lord's Supper, the Lord's Table, the Lord's Cup, and the Lord's Day. That is about it. These things all belong together. The Lord's Day is distinguished by the fact that it is the day for the celebration of the Lord's Supper at the Lord's Table, sharing all together the Lord's Cup. Why are all these things called the Lord's? It is because it is here above all that we celebrate the memorial of our Lord, the memorial which he instructed his disciples to observe. It was the Lord's Table, the Lord's Cup, and the Lord's Supper because he was the host. It was by means of these that through his Holy Spirit he was present among them. It was the Lord's

Day because this was the day on which he chose to meet them again and again.

Going on Paul recites the oral tradition which he had received using the formula which a rabbi normally used when reciting oral tradition. "For I received from the Lord what I also delivered to you" (1 Cor. 11:23). Was this oral tradition always recited at the Lord's Supper like the Passover Haggadah was recited in the Jewish Seder? It would seem to have been, but, yet, it is not completely clear that it was. "The Lord Jesus on the night when he was betrayed took bread, and when he had given thanks, he broke it, and said, 'This is my body which is for you. Do this in remembrance of me'" (1 Cor. 11:23–24). The Jewish Passover Haggadah had explained the meaning of the meal by recounting the story of the Exodus from Egypt. The Passover had been a memorial of the redemption of God in freeing the children of Israel from Egypt but now the eating of the sacred meal is to celebrate not only that act of redemption but even more God's act of redemption in Christ.

"Do this in remembrance of me" (1 Cor. 11:24). Quite important to a true understanding of the sacrament of communion is an understanding of what is meant by celebrating "in remembrance of me." "Do this in remembrance of me" is in effect Jesus' interpretation of the fourth commandment, "Remember the sabbath day, to keep it holy" (Exod. 20:8). We have already spoken about this at some length. Something else needs to be said here. Neither Jesus nor Paul had in mind a simple mental recollection. They had in mind far more. The text says "*Do this* in remembrance of me." They had in mind holding a religious service. In a true celebration of a covenant meal the remembering of God's saving acts had an essential function. It was through God's gracious acts of redemption that he laid claim to his people; by remembering those saving acts one confessed and acknowledged that claim. In holding the memorial one acknowledges God's Lordship and the service which one therefore owes to God. In the hymnic remembering and confession of the history of redemption one pledges allegiance to God and one claims the benefits of those redemptive acts. In so doing one lays hold of the Covenant and assumes both the obligations and the prerogatives of the covenant people.

Paul goes on to explain, "For as often as you eat this bread and drink the cup, you proclaim the Lord's death until he comes" (1 Cor.

11:26). How was it precisely that this proclamation was made? Was the proclamation done in the context of the elaborate prayer over the cup in which the main events of salvation history were recounted? That might have been in Paul's mind. We have already spoken of how the thanksgiving prayer by which Jesus blessed the bread and wine mentioned the cardinal events in the history of salvation. Certainly the first Christian eucharistic prayers contained a hymnic recounting of acts of creation and redemption. There was undoubtedly more than this, however. Surely Paul had in mind as well the preaching which normally preceded the celebration of the Lord's Supper. We remember how Jesus met the two disciples on the road to Emmaus and how he explained the Scriptures at length before coming to the inn and sitting down to supper with them. It would seem more than likely that the central proclamation of the Lord's Day worship was in preaching!

Finally, it must be said that for Paul the dimension of the fellowship of the Christian community was extremely important. This is after all the main point of this passage in chapter 11. The celebration should express the mutual concern of the members of the church one for another. It was important to discern the Lord's body and to wait for one another. It was not like eating in a cafeteria where each one eats the food one has chosen, or where each one has as much as one can pay for. Those who had plenty were to share with those who did not have enough. It was a covenant meal wherein the individual entered into a covenant not only with God but with the total Christian community. Paul's concern for the poor of the community was completely in keeping with the nature of the covenant meal.

Having very briefly gone over these passages of the Apostle Paul, let us take a look at the Gospel of John to see what it tells us about the Lord's Supper. In the Gospel of John we do not have an account of the celebration of the Last Supper but there are a number of passages which show us how John understood the celebration of the sacrament.

The story of the wedding feast of Cana has important sacramental implications. Jesus uses the simple village wedding as a sign of the coming of the kingdom, showing himself to be the true bridegroom by providing the wine, a wine delicious beyond the expectations of the guests. In that feast, the new Solomon played on the themes of the Song of Solomon. The Messianic son of David provided a foretaste of the wine of heaven and the wedding feast of the Lamb (2 Sam. 7:1–17; Prov. 9:1–6; Matt. 22:1–14; Rev. 19:9). Here the Fourth Gospel emphasizes the eschatological dimensions of the eucharist. From the story of the wedding at Cana we understand that the sacrament is a celebration of the joyful life of the coming kingdom.

The Gospel of John specifically calls the changing of the water into wine at Cana a sign. As C. H. Dodd has so beautifully shown, John's use of the word *sign* draws on the rich meaning of the word *sign* which we find all the way through Scripture. Again and again God reveals his will through signs. The rainbow which God set in the heavens after the flood, the burning bush from which he spoke to Moses, the opening up of the sea, the pillar of cloud and fire which led Israel through the wilderness, the manna which nourished the children of Israel, the sweetening of the waters of Marah, and the water from the rock were all signs of God's redemptive presence among his people. It is clear that for John the sign at Cana as well as the sign of the feeding of the multitude are signs of a very similar sort. When we speak of the sacraments being signs, we should have in mind the profound force of the word *sign* found in the Gospel of John.

In discussing Johannine eucharistic teaching the story of the feeding of the multitude (John 6:1–14) with the five loaves and two fish and the bread of life discourse (John 6:35–65) which follows it are of central importance. Here we must pay careful attention to two elements of Old Testament tradition. The first of these is the wisdom tradition. Sapiental themes abound in the Gospel of John. The prologue to the Gospel presents Jesus as the Word of God, that is, the divine wisdom from on high. We have already suggested that the first sign of Jesus recounted by John, the sign of turning water into wine, is to be understood from the standpoint of the wisdom tradition. When we get to the story of the multiplication of the loaves and the feeding of the multitude we find the wisdom theme recurring. The scene John recounts evokes the memory of Moses delivering the law to Israel. Then, in the bread of life discourse, Jesus interprets the text from Exodus 16:4–15 "He gave them bread from heaven to eat." The text comes from the story of God feeding the children of Israel with manna in the wilderness. Following the Alexandrian exegesis, the manna is presented as a sign or sacrament of the divine wisdom revealed in the law of Moses. Jesus tells his listeners that in his feeding of the multitude there was a sign to be seen just as there was in the manna. The sign which Jesus gave, however, points to a teaching which leads to eternal life (John 6:26–27). The prophets had spoken of the day when God himself would teach his people (Isaiah 54:13) and that day has now come. The Word of God, who was God from the beginning, is now revealed as the bread of life. This teaching of the Word of God is of far greater value than the teaching of Moses. "Your fathers ate the manna in the wilderness, and they died." The teaching of the gospel of Christ unlike the teaching of the law of Moses gives eternal life. Jesus tells them, "I am the bread of life" (John 6:47–48). By this he means that those who receive his teaching will receive eternal life. Repeatedly Jesus urges his hearers to believe. Justification by faith is one of John's recurring themes. Just as they ate the loaves which were a sign of the divine wisdom or a sacrament of the Word so now they should believe the gospel. Eating and believing go together. In fact eating the bread and drinking the wine of the eucharist is an act of believing.

The bread of life discourse has far more in mind than telling us that the teachings of Jesus on the good moral life will nourish us unto eternal life. "I am the living bread which came down from heaven; if anyone eats of this bread, he will live forever; and the bread which I shall give for the life of the world is my flesh" (John 6:51). It is to be sure the gospel of his saving death and resurrection which is meant. When Jesus tells us that it is his flesh which is the bread which he gives for the life of the world it is his sacrificial death to which he refers. He gives himself up for the life of the world (John 3:16). At the very beginning of the Gospel of John, Jesus is identified as the sacrificial Lamb of God who takes away the sin of the world. To those who first read the Gospel of John there was nothing obscure or novel about the idea that the eating of a sacrificial meal was a sign of receiving the divine wisdom. It was along this line that the Alexandrian exegesis had interpreted the sacrifices of the law long before the Gospel of John appeared on the scene. Even before that, as Father Raymond Brown has pointed out, we find in the book of Proverbs that wisdom invites her children to the sacrificial feast, "Wisdom has built her house, she has set up her seven pillars, she has slaughtered her beasts, she has mixed her wine . . . . 'Come, eat of my bread and drink of the wine I have mixed. Leave simpleness, and live, and walk in the way of insight'" (Prov. 9:1–6). Essential for understanding the bread of life discourse is the recognition that it is the Lamb of God who is the Word of God. It is the crucified and risen Christ who is the divine wisdom. We are not to be offended by the death of Christ. We are to accept his death as God's act for our salvation. In it the wisdom of God is revealed. When this wisdom is received it nourishes us to eternal life. For John to eat the bread and drink the wine, the signs of Christ's sacrifice, is to receive the wisdom which nourishes unto eternal life.

The second thing we need to consider in our attempt to understand the sixth chapter of the Gospel of John is Passover. Allusions to the Passover and the events which Passover celebrated recur constantly in the chapter. We are specifically told that the feeding of the multitude took place at the Passover season. Then Jesus in the bread of life discourse interprets the feeding of the multitude in terms of Israel receiving manna in the wilderness. The theme of Passover involves of course the Passover meal itself (Exod. 12—13). It also involves quite naturally the meal of manna (Exod. 16:1–36). There is a third meal involved in the Passover traditions and that is the covenant meal on the top of Mt. Sinai (Exod. 24:3–11). That this third meal is alluded to is very clear from the fact that the Gospel tells us that Jesus "went up on the mountain" and there fed the multitude (John 6:3). Let us look at this story. After the law had been given, Moses proclaimed the law to Israel and the people vowed, "All the words which the LORD has spoken we will do." Sacrifices were made, half the blood was sprinkled on the altar, and half the blood was sprinkled on the people, and Moses said, "Behold the blood of the covenant which the LORD has made with you in accordance with all these words." Then Moses and the seventy elders of Israel went up on the mountain and there, "they beheld God, and ate and drank." By sharing that meal with God on the top of Mt. Sinai the Covenant was sealed. God became their God and they became his people. It is on these themes that John 6:52–59 plays.

Here then is John's understanding of the Lord's Supper. It is through the Lord's Supper, the covenant meal of the New Covenant that the Christian is joined to the crucified and risen Christ and therefore has eternal life. What John says here is very similar to what the Apostle Paul said in the tenth and eleventh chapters of 1 Corinthians. When we ask how Jesus can give us his flesh to eat, the answer is that he gives us his flesh by becoming our Passover Lamb, the Lamb of God, and offering himself up for us. His death and his resurrection are for us because we have been joined to him in a covenant relationship; what is his is ours and what is ours is his. Through eating the bread we share in his broken body, through drinking the cup we become partners in the New Covenant. We have been consecrated for the new life of the kingdom of God.

One should point out that this whole discourse underlines the importance of understanding that Christ is present at the eucharistic meal. With a covenant meal everything turns on with whom the meal is shared. When Jesus fed the multitude "on the mountain" it is essential to observe that they ate with Jesus. At the heart of the sign was that the meal they shared, they shared with God himself. It should be equally clear that the discourse on the bread of life puts in high relief the close relation of word and sacrament. It makes clear that when we participate in the covenant meal we engage ourselves to live by the Word of God.

Before leaving our consideration of the celebration of communion in the New Testament one very important question must be asked. Did the church of New Testament times understand the celebration of communion to be a sacrifice?

Undoubtedly the earliest Christians understood that participation in the communion united them to Christ in his sacrificial death. Paul put it this way, "The cup of blessing which we bless, is it not a participation in the blood of Christ?" (1 Cor. 10:16). This does not mean that the bread and wine that have been blessed are then offered to God as a sacrifice. It means that the covenant meal of bread and wine unites us to the one who gave himself as a sacrifice. At the Passover in the time of Jesus the lambs were sacrificed at the Temple but the lambs were eaten in the home. The Passover meal itself was not a sacrifice. To be sure, without a sacrifice there could have been no covenant meal, but in those days the sacrifice took place before the Passover Seder began. "Christ, our paschal lamb, has been sacrificed. Let us, therefore, celebrate the festival" (1 Cor. 5:7–8). Christ was sacrificed at one particular time and place in history, yet the feast is celebrated in many times and places.

Undoubtedly the earliest Christians understood that praise and thanksgiving had taken the place of the Temple sacrifices (Romans 12:1–2). Their prayers were the spiritual sacrifices of the royal priesthood which they offered daily (1 Peter 2:1–10). One could therefore logically move from this general understanding of prayer and thanksgiving as a spiritual sacrifice to understanding the prayer of thanksgiving over the bread and wine as a sacrifice, although the New Testament does not specifically indicate that the earliest Christians had come to such conclusions. Nowhere does the New Testament speak of the Supper as a sacrifice of praise and thanksgiving.

The Scriptures provide us with a very full theology of thanksgiving. It is found particularly in the thanksgiving psalms which accompanied the thank offerings of the Temple. A thank offering was not propitiatory. Such a sacrifice did not atone for sins; it was far more an appropriation of God's grace and favor which one had already received. Having received the blessing of God one was obligated to witness to God's blessing in a public act of thanksgiving. This was done by presenting at the Temple a thanksgiving sacrifice, an important part of which was the recitation of a psalm of thanksgiving. For the Jews of the first century it was the "spiritual sacrifice," that is, the psalm or prayer of thanksgiving, and the public witness of recounting God's favor was regarded as being more important than the actual animal sacrifice. The thanksgiving consecrated the gracious acts of God to one's own use (1 Tim. 4:4–5). The earliest Christians, however, seem to have understood the thanksgiving over the bread and wine not so much in terms of the thanksgiving sacrifices of the Temple as they understood it in terms of the thanksgiving prayers of the Passover Seder (1 Cor. 10:16). It is quite different to regard the prayer of thanksgiving at communion as an appropriation of Christ's atoning sacrifice on the cross for our salvation and to regard that thanksgiving as a sacrifice for the forgiveness of sin. Surely, there is no evidence that the early church confounded the two in such a way that they regarded the communion as a repetition of Christ's sacrifice. On the other hand the New Testament, in the clearest possible terms speaks of Christ's death on the cross as the unique sacrifice, which never needed to be repeated, which once and for all put away sin (Heb. 10:12–14).

We summarize this cursory investigation of the celebration of the Lord's Supper in the New Testament with the following observations.

The celebration by the earliest Christians was in terms of liturgical form very much like the Passover Seder. It was, like the Passover meal, a covenant meal but it was shared with the risen Christ as a celebration of his passage from death to life and as a prophetic sign of the heavenly banquet in the last day. By the end of the New Testament period the Christian celebration of this meal had undergone a number of modifications. First, it had become a weekly celebration held every Lord's Day morning in celebration of Christ's resurrection. Second, it was no longer a rite observed by a small group of ten people, but a celebration of the whole Christian community in a given area. It was by means of this service that Christians came together as the church. Third, the celebration was closely connected with the proclamation of the gospel. It is not clear whether the service of the Word and the service of the Supper had been joined into a single liturgy by this time, but surely this was beginning to happen in New Testament times. Fourth, the sacrament already had diaconal significance. The meal was to be shared with the poor, the widowed, and the hungry. It was a sign of concern for those who were in need. Fifth, the content of the prayers had been changed so that they were a thanksgiving for God's mighty acts of redemption in Christ. Finally, the whole service was a memorial of God's mighty acts which the church proclaimed to the world "until he come."

One hesitates to embark on a brief and simple account of the historical development of the eucharistic liturgy. To do this requires going over much detailed work in a most summary way. Every author whom we must treat is capable of a wide variety of very subtle interpretations. The subject of sacramental theology has been treated by some of the greatest minds of Christendom and as yet there is far from being any unanimity. We must approach the subject with a sense of humility. It is with only the greatest apologies that one ventures to write on the subject in such a summary fashion.

The most important document we have concerning the celebration of communion in the earliest days of church history is a small collection of directions for ordering the affairs of the church called the *Didache*. From this document we discover that the Christians of the late first century or the early second century celebrated a communion service which, liturgically considered, was very close to the Passover Seder. The liturgical form of the service seems to have remained the same with separate prayers over the bread and the wine at the beginning of the meal and a longer prayer over the cup of blessing at the end of the meal. The theological content of the prayers is different. The prayers of the *Didache* are a thanksgiving for creation and for our redemption in Christ as well as the celebration of the Christian hope for the consummation of the kingdom. Although the full text of the prayers is given, there is no mention of the words of Jesus being repeated as part of the prayers. For this reason scholars abound who insist that what the *Didache* reports is not to be regarded as a celebration of the sacrament. Surely this opinion is in error even if it means we are faced with the fact that in the oldest eucharistic liturgy we have had no words of consecration. The dominical words may have been repeated elsewhere in the liturgy but they were obviously not part of either of the two eucharistic prayers.

It is here in the *Didache*, rather than in the New Testament, that we find the first hint of the doctrine of the eucharistic sacrifice which begins to develop in the following centuries. We read toward the end of the document that before partaking of the communion, Christians were to confess their sins in order that "their offering be pure." What seems to have been meant, however, is not much more than the idea which we have already mentioned, that prayer is the Christian sacrifice of praise and thanksgiving. The passage goes on to allude to the prophecy of Malachi 1:11, "in every place and time offer me a pure sacrifice" (*Didache* XIV, 3). Christians often understand this as a prophecy of the worship of the church, the spiritual sacrifice of the royal priesthood (1 Peter 2:1–10). In other words what is being said is not as much that the communion is a sacrifice but that it is analogous to the Jewish sacrifices. The sacrifices of the law were the types or foreshadows of the Christian forms of worship. The Christian eucharist may have succeeded the Jewish offerings but that did not mean they really were sacrifices.

Shortly after the middle of the second century Justin Martyr gives us a picture of the way the communion was celebrated. From this picture we gather that the several blessings of the Passover Seder have been consolidated into a single prayer of praise to the Father and thanksgiving for his works of creation, providence, and redemption. This prayer has not yet been codified into a formulated canon. The one presiding followed certain customs as to what was to be included in the prayer, but he prayed in an extemporary fashion and we are told that he prayed at length. When he was finished the whole congregation said the Amen. This prayer of thanksgiving forms the heart of the liturgy Justin describes. When the prayer has been said over the bread and wine this food has thereby been blessed or in some sense consecrated. It is the "eucharist," that is, "thanked-over" bread and wine. One would like to say more about how Justin understood this consecration but he seems to be purposely vague and ambiguous. Justin seems to indicate that the words of institution were recited as part of the liturgy but it is not clear at what point in the service. For Justin they are words of institution in that they communicate that what is done is at the bidding of the Savior and thereby receive his promised blessing. They are not a formula of consecration. Justin does not suggest that he considers the sacrament a sacrifice, although he does understand it to fulfill the prophecy of Malachi that the Gentiles will offer up pure sacrifices to God's name (Malachi 1:11). The covenant aspect of the celebration is evident. Those who participate are baptized and are those who keep or intend to keep God's commandments. Special significance is given to the fact that the whole Christian community gathers together in one place for the celebration and that the eucharist is celebrated on the Lord's Day.

By the beginning of the third century we notice further developments. Hippolytus gives us considerably more detail as he writes down what he understands to be the apostolic tradition for the celebration of communion. First we notice that the bread and wine which are brought to the bishop are called an offering or oblation. The presenting of the bread and wine at the table has come to have special significance; it is an offertory. The prayer over the bread and wine gives thanks for the sending of a Savior who was "born of Holy Spirit and a Virgin," a Savior who suffered that he might abolish death and demonstrate the resurrection. Here we recognize the logos theology of Hippolytus. This portion of the prayer was no doubt marked by the author's particular understanding of the person and work of Christ. Yet, the text of the prayer was supposed to be flexible enough to allow for such individual expressions. There was as yet no formulated canon. Particularly to be noticed is the fact that the words of Jesus concerning the bread and cup are recited in the midst of the prayer. This is done in such a way that they function as words of consecration. Then the bread and wine are offered to God, "because thou hast bidden us to stand before thee and minister as priests to thee." The communion has clearly become a sacrifice. It is not completely clear in what sense it was considered a sacrifice. Much has been written on the subject but exactly how Hippolytus understood the sacrament remains uncertain. Furthermore Hippolytus seems to have some idea that the saying of the eucharistic prayer did something to the bread and wine, but again it is not too clear whether it was through the recitation of the words of Jesus, "This is my body . . . this is my blood" or because of the invocation of the Holy Spirit. From this point on the communion service begins to become more and more an act of consecration and sacrifice. The eucharistic prayer begins to occupy greater and greater importance as the act of consecrating or transforming the bread and wine and as presenting them as an oblation or sacrifice to God.

At the end of the fourth century, some time between A.D. 380 and 390, we have a series of sermons on the sacraments preached at Milan by its great bishop Ambrose (339–97). This series, entitled *De sacramentis,* was a sort of communicants class preached just before Easter and intended to prepare those who were to be baptized for their baptism and first celebration of communion. From this document we learn much about how communion was celebrated at the time and how it was understood. One of the most beautiful things about these two works is the poetic use they make of the Old Testament types of the sacraments. Explaining the sacraments by means of the Old Testament types goes back to the New Testament itself and ever since has been one of the most important means of trying to perceive the meaning of the signs. Particularly important is that in the *De sacramentis* we find for the first time a number of the prayers which eventually found their way into the canon of the Roman mass. Ambrose makes the point that before the words of Jesus, "This is my body . . . this is my blood," what we have is bread and wine but after those words of Jesus, we have the body and blood of Christ. Very clearly, then, Ambrose understands that when the words of Jesus are quoted in the eucharistic prayer they are words of consecration by which bread and wine are transformed into the body of Christ. The eucharistic prayer goes on, "Therefore remembering his most glorious Passion and his Resurrection from Hell, and his Ascension into Heaven, we offer to thee this immaculate host, reasonable host, unbloody host, this holy bread and cup of eternal life, and we desire to pray that this oblation be accepted by thy sublime altar . . . " (Ambrose, *De sacramentis* IV, 21–23 [author's translation]). It is equally clear that for Ambrose the consecrated bread and wine are offered as a sacrifice to God in the course of the eucharistic prayer. One notices however that with his increased emphasis on consecration and oblation, the aspects of thanksgiving and covenant have receded into the background.

Toward the end of the fourth century, another important series of developments begins to appear. Christians begin to come to church to see the communion service performed but without participating in it by receiving the bread and wine. Both John Chrysostom in the East and a bit later Augustine in the West began to admonish their congregations against the growing practice of watching the liturgy but not taking part in the holy meal. In vain they exhorted. Their preaching inhibited the growing practice in no way. This reticence to participate was partly due to the fact that Christian preachers and teachers were putting such a strong emphasis on worthy participation that weaker Christians were discouraged from receiving communion for fear that it would be to their judgment. On the other hand, it was partly due to the fact that the liturgy was beginning to take on elements of the drama. This is particularly noticed in the explanations of the liturgy given by Cyril of Jerusalem (315–86) in the second half of the fourth century. One also finds this tendency in the pilgrimage journal of a Spanish nun, Aetheria, who told of the services of worship in the city of Jerusalem toward the end of the same century. It was natural perhaps that the worship of the city of Jerusalem should begin to develop in this direction. Pilgrims from all over the Christian world flocked to the Holy Land and they made up a large portion of the worshiping congregation in the Church of the Holy Sepulchre. Particularly during the Easter season the pilgrims came to see the room where Jesus had eaten the Last Supper, the garden where he had prayed before his Passion, the place where he had been crucified and the sepulchre from which he rose again. It was only natural that on Good Friday the pilgrims would retrace the footsteps of Jesus, stand beneath the cross and wait before the tomb. The idea of re-enacting the Passion of Christ came easily, particularly to a Greek-speaking culture which had so much love for the theater.

In Cyril of Jerusalem's *Mystagogical Catechism* we begin to get a clear picture of an increasingly important conception of the liturgy. The very title of the work makes clear what is beginning to happen. A mystagogical catechism was the explanation of the sacred rites of one or another of the Greek mystery religions. The Hellenistic world was filled with these mystery religions. The Mithras cult, the Eleusinian mysteries, the Orphic rites and the mysteries of Isis were among the most popular. One obtained salvation in these mystery religions by going through a sacred initiation in which one was illuminated in the teachings of the cult by experiencing them in a sacred drama or ceremony. These initiation services still survive in a rather pale form in the initiations of college fraternities and sororities or various lodges. A mystagogical catechism was an explanation of the sacred mystical rites. The Greeks loved these dramatic rites and it could have been expected that Christians would begin to understand their sacraments as though they were Greek mysteries. The idea behind these mysteries was that the dramatic representation of the redemptive event made that past event contemporary so that its redemptive power was available to those who were being initiated. The great paschal baptisms of the fourth century were indeed dramatic with their preparatory rites during the weeks leading up to Easter, their dramatic immersions in the dark of night, their anointing with perfumed oil, their robing in pure white gowns, and their solemn procession into the church to receive first communion at dawn. One can see real similarities to the cult mysteries of the day. It was an easy way for a Christian preacher to explain things to a popular audience. The question is whether Cyril was leading the church into a profoundly Christian understanding of sacraments or whether he was confusing the Christian sacraments with the pagan mysteries.

About the same time another attitude toward the liturgy began to develop which also had great consequences for the development of worship. It was the introduction of a devotional attitude of sacred fear. One of the first places we begin to mark this is in the works of Theodore of Mopsuestia (350–428). It was an attitude which became very popular with the Christians of Syria and the churches of the East. The celebration of the eucharist was an awe-filled mystery. "Let all mortal flesh keep silence and with fear and trembling stand" is a hymn we sing today which was translated from one of the oriental liturgies which comes to us from this period, the *Liturgy of St. James*. It expressed this devotional posture quite well. In the course of time the most sacred part of the service tended to be hidden from human eyes and spoken in a reverent hush. In the East the most holy moment of the consecration of the host was moved behind the iconostasis, a screen constructed of sacred pictures or icons. In the West the prayer of consecration came to be spoken with such profound reverence that it was inaudible to the congregation. The moment when the consecration had been performed was marked by the ringing of bells and the prostration of the celebrants. When the host was offered up, the people could not hear the prayer in which the offering was made; they could only see the elevation of the host from afar as they bowed deeply to the ground.

Augustine, one of the most fertile thinkers of Christian antiquity, had a tremendous effect on the sacramental theology of the Western church. His thought developed in a very different direction from Cyril's. He re-emphasized a number of the fundamental biblical teachings regarding the Lord's Supper. While the trend at the beginning of the fifth century was to forget the covenantal aspects of the sacrament, Augustine re-emphasized it. The Latin word *sacramentum*, which originally signified a sacred oath of allegiance, naturally lent itself to the re-emphasizing of the covenantal aspects of the Supper. Augustine also re-emphasized the initiative of God in the sacrament. The sacrament was a God-given sign. Against the Donatists he stressed that it was the work of God in the sacrament which made it effective, not the worthiness of the minister of the sacrament. Against the Pelagians he stressed that the sacrament was a sign of God's grace. It was Augustine who gave the classic definition of a sacrament as an outward and physical sign of an inward and spiritual grace. The most interesting aspect of Augustine's sacramental teaching is the way he returned to the themes of the Gospel of John and came up with an explanation of the sacrament as the Word of God made visible. As we shall see, the Reformers found Augustine's insights at this point very helpful. Unfortunately these insights of Augustine were to fall on hard days. Even as Augustine was preaching his last sermon the Vandals were destroying classical civilization in North Africa. Learning was in retreat before the barbarians. In the centuries which followed much that was said by Augustine and other Church Fathers would be either misunderstood or understood in a magical and superstitious way.

By the time of Charlemagne (742–814), the power of Christendom had moved North across the Alps. Islam had begun to eclipse the influence of the Christian East but the barbarian tribes of France and Germany were infusing fresh vigor into the Christian faith. Although for these Northerners Latin was a foreign language, they wanted their religion to be Roman just as they wanted to make their barbarian empire Roman, and so they maintained Latin, the Roman language, in their worship. It gave their worship a mystique of learning and culture. Not understanding the liturgical language, the use of ceremonies, symbols, vestments, pictures, and images began to be more and more important. About the year 800, Alamar of Metz, one of Charlemagne's bishops, wrote a commentary on the liturgy which gave an allegorical meaning to every gesture, every movement, every act of the liturgy. More and more the faithful understood the liturgy as a sacred drama to be watched with awe. The allegorical explanations which began to multiply from this time on had the effect of inspiring even more ceremonials which could be interpreted and read by the spectators. Even though the worshipers might not understand the liturgical language, they could understand the visual ceremonies.

By the end of the Middle Ages, the Lord's Supper had already a long time before become the sacrifice of the mass. It was a sacred drama which re-enacted the sacrifice of Christ on the cross, a most solemn mystery celebrated in a language unknown by the common people. It was, in the eyes of many, a magical ceremony which transformed bread and wine into the body and blood of Christ and made God present on the altar there to be worshiped and adored in sumptuous religious rites. The idea of eating Christ's flesh and drinking his blood had developed in such a way that the awesomeness of communion led to the practice of receiving it but once a year and even then only the bread was eaten; the cup was withheld from the people. Many churches were filled with dozens of altars and every day flocks of priests would offer the sacrifice of the mass for the salvation of the living and the dead. The private mass had become an institution. The splendid celebration of the Roman mass in a Rhineland cathedral in the year 1500 had developed into something quite different from the celebration of the Passover Seder which Jesus observed with his disciples in the Upper Room.

Toward the end of the Middle Ages, the need to reform the worship of the church was generally felt and widely expressed, but with the beginning of the Protestant Reformation the cry for specific liturgical reforms became increasingly urgent. For the Reformers of classical Protestantism, that is Luther, Melanchthon, Zwingli, Bucer, and Calvin, there was agreement about the most pressing liturgical reforms needed in the celebration of the communion service. The first thing was to translate the communion prayers into the language of the people and for the celebrant to speak them in a loud and distinct voice. The second was to remove from the liturgy the sacrificial elements both in regard to the offertory prayers which were said when the bread and the wine were brought to the table and those prayers in the canon of the mass in which the consecrated bread and wine were offered to God as a sacrifice. Third, the Reformers were agreed that when communion was celebrated, an indispensable part of the celebration was the participation of the faithful in both the eating of the bread and the drinking of the cup. It was not sufficient for the priest alone to commune, nor was it enough for the congregation to receive only the bread. No more was the communion to be a show for those who simply watched but did not participate. The first stage of the liturgical reform, then, was to translate the text, remove the prayers of sacrifice and to emphasize the actual communion of the faithful.

Late in 1523 Luther published his *Formula Missae,* which was a proposal for the reform of the celebration of the communion service. In some ways it was a rather moderate proposal. It advocated a gradual introduction of German into the liturgy and provided that there would always be occasions for the use of Latin in worship. The first part of the service up to the offertory was to remain unchanged, but from that point on, as Luther put it, the whole thing "reeked with sacrifice." For the Reformers generally, the removal of the elements of sacrifice from the mass was one of the most pressing of reforms. The offertory, that is the ceremony by which the bread and wine were brought to the altar and offered to God, Luther felt should be completely discontinued. The canon of the mass, that is the prayer of consecration said over the bread and wine, Luther wanted to rearrange completely so that any prayers which implied the presenting of the consecrated bread and wine as a sacrifice to God should be omitted. For Luther the sacrament of communion was not to be understood as a sacrifice to God but as a gracious gift from God.

What was it that Luther and the other classical Protestant Reformers objected to so much in the doctrine of the eucharistic sacrifice? At the very core of Protestant theology is the affirmation that the sacrifice of Christ on the cross was full, sufficient and perfect. Christ offered himself up once for all. His sacrifice never has to be repeated. His sacrifice is more than sufficient to redeem the whole of the human race from all its sin. Once a doctrine of a eucharistic sacrifice has developed, then the doctrine of the sufficiency of Christ's sacrifice has been compromised. Equally important to classical Protestantism is the doctrine of the substitutionary atonement. Christ died for us and in our place. He made the sacrifice which we could not make. Christ's sacrifice was unique because he was the Lamb without blemish. Once the mass is regarded as a sacrifice the uniqueness of Christ's sacrifice disappears. In this question what is really at play is the Reformers' Augustinian theology of grace.

In Wittenberg there seemed to be no hurry to implement the suggestions made in Luther's *Formula missae,* but in Strasbourg it was another matter. A few months later, in February 1524, Diebold Schwarz, Matthew Zell's assistant at the Cathedral of St. Lawrence, celebrated a German mass much like the service Luther proposed. The entire service was conducted in German, the offertory was removed, all prayers from the canon implying any doctrine of eucharistic sacrifice were struck out, and communion in both kinds was offered to the congregation. The *Strasbourg German Mass* of Diebold Schwarz was not a Reformed communion liturgy, it was an expurgated mass, but it was an important step toward a truly Reformed celebration of the sacrament.

The first important attempt to celebrate a Reformed communion service took place almost a year later. At the end of the year 1524 Bucer published a work, *Grund und Ursach,* in which he explained the liturgical reforms which he and his colleagues were trying to achieve. Then in the succeeding months several editions of the *Strasbourg Psalter* appeared. These writings witness to the liturgical changes which were gradually taking place.

The first thing we notice in these documents is that the communion itself is emphasized. The sharing of the bread and the cup by the whole people of God becomes the heart of the service. The Reformers place the emphasis here rather than in the consecrating, the sacrificing, or the adoring of the bread and wine. The altar is replaced by a table. Here we see the Reformers' concern for the recovery of a basic biblical sign. The communion is to look like a meal.

The second thing we notice is that the Strasbourg Reformers strove to restore the basic unity between word and sacrament. The words of Jesus are to be proclaimed as the promises of the gospel rather than recited as a formula of consecration. When the sacrament is celebrated it is essential to preach the gospel. Sermon and supper go together.

Already we notice that the Reformers are beginning to turn to the Old Testament concept of covenant to understand the Lord's Supper. The covenantal nature of the holy meal is underlined by an attempt to get the whole church to participate in one celebration of communion each Lord's Day. The Communion Invocation which follows the Prayer of Intercession draws on and develops the themes of the Covenant. In the earliest Strasbourg psalters the Communion Invocation asks the Holy Spirit to write the law upon our hearts, that Christ live in us and we in him, that we be members of Christ's body and serve him in the building up of his church. In later editions of the psalter it is put even more expressly. In communion we are to become partakers of the eternal testament, the covenant of grace.

If the Word of God is to be visible as Augustine had taught, then it is to be visible in terms of the bread and wine of communion not in terms of liturgical art. All statues of the saints, pictures of Christ, and liturgical images or icons have been removed from the churches of Strasbourg. We see from this document that from the very beginning the use of images in worship is completely antithetical to a Reformed concept of worship. In the first place it is clearly forbidden by Scripture. Reformed theology, just as both Old Testament and New Testament, understands that we are to serve God not by our creating images of God but by our being the image of God. The glory of God is not reflected in our works of sacred art but in holiness of life, sharing with those in need and in the witness to a life of peace and justice. Clearing the churches of those images and icons which God had forbidden put the emphasis on the visible signs which God had commanded.

Finally the connection between eucharist and Lord's Day is underlined. The celebrations of the sacrament are reserved to the Lord's Day. Here again we find the same concern at work—the concern to recover

the basic biblical signs of the liturgy. The Lord's Supper is to be celebrated on the day of resurrection that both Christ's death and resurrection be observed and that the sacrament be received as a sign of the last
day, the day of consummation. The reform which these documents of
the Church of Strasbourg envision has much that is truly consequential.

Ulrich Zwingli (1484–1531) drew up another attempt at a Reformed
eucharistic liturgy. It was celebrated in the Church of Zurich at Easter in
1525. The service is very short. We note the following things. The
"dominical action," that is, the sharing of the bread and the cup occu-
pies the central position in the service. The doxological and eucharistic
aspects of the service are likewise put in high relief through the reciting
of the Gloria, the Apostles' Creed, and Psalm 113. Zwingli is quite
aware that this is the first of the Hallel psalms traditionally used in the
Passover Seder. Finally, the ecclesial or covenantal aspect of the service
is emphasized in the Communion Invocation. The communion is seen
as a sign of the uniting of the whole church in the body of Christ.
Zwingli's communion rite has often been misunderstood by an attempt
to understand it from his "sacramentarian" theology. Theologians have
often tried to show that this service demonstrates Zwingli's teaching
that the sacrament is "only a subjective memorial." A more helpful key
to understanding Zwingli's liturgical reform is the title which he gave to
the service, *The Act or Way of Observing the Memorial or Thanksgiving
of Christ.* Obviously even for Zwingli the celebration of communion
was not just a subjective remembering, it was a quite objective act of
thanksgiving. It was the observing of the memorial Christ had appointed.

In the city of Basel, a bit later that same year, John Oecolampadius
attempted to develop a celebration of communion following much the
same principles adhered to by his colleagues in Strasbourg and Zurich.
Oecolampadius (1482–1531), as we have already had several occasions
to remark, was not only an outstanding biblical scholar but an outstanding patristic scholar as well. Oecolampadius realized that one of the
great problems in the history of the liturgy was the concept of mystery.
The Reformer of Basel realized that the word mystery (*mysterion*) was
the word the Greek church used for sacrament. He knew well what
pagan Greek meant by the word. He studied the usage of the word in the
New Testament and showed that what Scripture meant by mystery was

very different from what the mystery religions meant. As Oecolampadius understood it, the Christian mysteries are God's sending of his Son to establish a kingdom in which all things will be united under his sovereign will. The Christian mysteries are the mysteries of Christ—the gospel, our faith and God's faithfulness, the church, and the coming of the kingdom. Oecolampadius realized quite well that Cyril of Jerusalem had something quite different in mind by the word mystery than the Apostle Paul. It is not surprising, therefore, that the communion service developed by the Church of Basel is marked by great simplicity.

For almost twenty years the Reformers of the Upper Rhineland had been working on the reform of the communion liturgy. When John Calvin published the *Genevan Psalter* of 1542, he drew on the experience of his predecessors. Let us look briefly at this service. Psalms are sung as the congregation gathers. The minister begins the service with the Invocation. Then, he leads the congregation in a general prayer of confession and supplication. This is followed by the singing of a metrical psalm. The reading of the Scriptures is prefaced by the Prayer for Illumination, asking God "the grace of His Holy Spirit to the end that His Word be faithfully preached to the honor of His name and the building up of the Church." A sermon is then preached on the lesson. After the sermon and the usual prayers of intercession, the actual celebration of communion begins with the singing of the Creed. The Creed is a hymnic recital of God's mighty acts of creation and redemption as well as a celebration of the Christian hope of the resurrection of the body and the life everlasting. The Creed is said to testify that the people "wish to live and die in the Christian faith."

Calvin's Communion Invocation appears at different points in the various editions of the liturgy. He seems to have preferred it after the Creed. The prayer consists of three elements: first, it is a prayer of invocation, or an epiclesis, asking that we might receive the grace promised in the sacrament; second, it is a prayer of thanksgiving rendering praise and thanks to God and celebrating his redemptive work in Christ; third, it is a prayer in which the covenant vows are renewed. The prayer is concluded by the Lord's Prayer.

After this the Words of Institution are recited from 1 Corinthians. The Exhortation follows from the Words of Institution. In it the unrepentant are warned not to participate and the faithful encouraged and invited to receive the communion. This "fencing of the table" was an attempt to take seriously the warning of the Apostle Paul (1 Cor. 11:27–32). It was largely shaped by the dismissals of the catechumens and penitents as the Reformers learned about this practice from the works of John Chrysostom. This Exhortation is in effect a short sermon setting forth the benefits of the sacrament and an invitation to come to the table to renew the covenant vows. It ends with these words, "Lift up your hearts and minds on high where Christ is seated in the glory of his Father, whence we expect his coming at our redemption." The whole service is thereby given an eschatological dimension. It is an invitation to enter into an invisible and heavenly reality. This done, the bread and wine are distributed to the people, the ministers serving the bread and the deacons the cup.

During the distribution, a psalm of thanksgiving, Psalm 138, is sung by the congregation. It should be underlined at this point how central the psalmody is to the liturgical structure of the celebration. It is in the psalmody, sung by the whole congregation, that the central act of praise and thanksgiving is to be found. When all have received, there is a prayer of thanksgiving for the sacrament in which the people dedicate themselves to live out the rest of their lives to the glory of God and the well-being of their neighbors. Then the congregation sings a final hymn of praise and thanksgiving such as Psalm 103 or 113. The use of Psalm 113 is obviously appropriate because it was one of the Hallel psalms which even in the time of Jesus belonged to the Passover Seder. For the same reason Psalms 116, 117, or 118 were considered equally appropriate. The Reformers were well aware that it was to the Hallel psalms that the Gospels referred when they tell us that Jesus and the disciples sang a hymn before leaving the Upper Room. The communion liturgy of the *Genevan Psalter* concluded when the minister lifted up his hands and dismissed the congregation with the Aaronic Benediction (Num. 6:23–26).

Let us look for a moment at the theology behind this service. While a covenantal understanding of the sacrament was clearly to be seen in the earlier communion liturgies of Strasbourg and Zurich, it comes to full bloom in the Genevan order. Earlier, in our chapter on baptism, we spoke of the reasons for the development of Covenant theology among the High Rhenish Reformers of the early sixteenth century. It was among these theologians that biblical Hebrew was recovered by the Western church. It was quite natural that the full semitic color of Scripture should become evident to them in a way it had not been evident to Christian theologians for over a thousand years. Moreover the Hebrew concept of covenant gave the early Reformed theologians an alternative to Scholastic theology and its attempt to explain the sacraments in terms of Aristotelian philosophy. Just as the recovery of the Hebrew concept of covenant had opened up to the Reformers a more profound understanding of baptism, so it opened up a much deeper understanding of communion as well.

One of the first places one notices this is in the relationship between word and sacrament. Calvin's writings on eucharistic theology always gave ample attention to this subject. Calvin understood quite well how often in the Scriptures the sharing of a meal was the way an agreement was sealed. As Calvin understood it, the proclamation of the covenant promises at the celebration of communion was an essential element of the service. Calvin reminds us of the teaching of Augustine that the sacraments are the visible words of God. The celebration should always include teaching that what is seen might be understood. It was important that the covenant promises be understood, because in sharing the bread and the cup the covenant promises were sealed. Calvin tells us that our Lord clearly had this in mind when he said, "This cup is the new covenant in my blood." It is clear from this, Calvin tells us, that the signs of bread and wine are the signs of the Covenant which he has made with us (Calvin, *Opera selecta* II, 14). For Calvin, sharing in the communion seals to us the promises proclaimed in the preaching of the word.

If Calvin wanted to follow Augustine's maxim that the sacraments are the visible words of God, he wanted on the other hand to guard against dissolving the sacraments into words. God gave us the sacraments because our minds are not able to grasp the fullness of God's redemptive work. Again and again Calvin speaks of the mystery of the Lord's Supper being far greater than any of our explanations or attempts to explain it. The communion itself, that is partaking of the bread and wine, should be the heart of the service. As Calvin sees it, it is important during the celebration of the Lord's Supper to meditate on the sacramental signs of bread and wine and contemplate the deeper meaning. "As bread nourishes, sustains, and keeps the life of the body, so Christ's body is the only food to invigorate and enliven our soul. When we see wine set forth . . . we must reflect on the benefits which wine imparts to the body and so realize that the same are spiritually imparted to us by Christ's blood" (Calvin, *Institutes* IV: xvii, 3). For Calvin the sacrament is above all a sign of our being fed by the body of Christ, and therefore, the liturgical celebration preserved the outward sign of the meal. The celebration of the sacrament at Geneva did precisely that. The service was celebrated around a table rather than before an altar. The receiving of the bread and wine itself was the high point of the service.

For Calvin the discourse on the bread of life in the sixth chapter of the Gospel of John is of the greatest possible importance in understanding the sacrament. Putting the discourse in the context of the whole of the Johannine literature, Calvin reminds us that the Gospel of John begins by telling us that in Christ is life, "In him was life and the life was the light of men." Then calling on the first epistle of John, the Reformer tells us that this life "was manifested only when, having taken our flesh, the Son of God gave himself for our eyes to see and our hands to touch" (Calvin *Institutes* IV: xvii, 8). Having set this context he returns to the words of the bread of life discourse, "I am the bread of life . . . which came down from heaven . . . the bread which I shall give for the life of the world is my flesh" (John 6:48–51). Calvin tells us that Christ is life, life in itself, the life which God intended. Being then that life which God intended, he entered into this world that we might be alive as he is alive. The inward grace of communion is then the gift of life, the life of the Son of God.

Calvin is not talking about divinization or *theosis* in the sense of Neo-Platonic philosophy. Reformed theology has never been much attracted by Neo-Platonism and has never shown much interest in those Church Fathers such as Origen (185–254), Gregory of Nyssa (330–395), Dionysius the Areopagite (c. 500), or John of Damascus (675–749) who were so obviously influenced by it. What Calvin is concerned about is the restoration of true human life, not the divinization of humanity.

One more thing needs to be said about the relation between word and sacrament. If for Calvin the sacraments are the visible words of

God, it must be underlined that they are effectual. The sacraments are not only signs of the word but seals of the word as well. The outward sign of the meal speaks of nourishment for eternal life. The worshiper taking part in the service can be sure that what the outward and visible sign promises will indeed take place inwardly and invisibly. This inward and invisible fulfillment of the signs of promise is the work of the Holy Spirit.

It is likewise from the standpoint of covenant that we can best understand Calvin's doctrine of Christ's presence at the Supper. In a covenant meal it is of the greatest significance with whom one eats. So many of the stories of covenant meals make the point in one way or another that it is with God that the meal is shared. The fact that the Lord's Supper is a meal shared with the Lord escaped in no way Calvin's notice. Calvin, indeed, understood Christ to be present at the Supper. What needs to be understood is the nature of that presence. According to Calvin we must respect Christ's ascension. Our Lord, ever since the ascension, has been at the right hand of the Father. Nevertheless, through his Spirit he is still present with us. We read for example in the Gospel of John, "I go to prepare a place for you." As we read further in the Gospel of John we discover that Jesus promises the disciples the Holy Spirit which the disciples could not receive unless Jesus left them. Nevertheless, leaving the disciples Jesus sent his Holy Spirit that he might dwell within them. As Calvin understood it, although Christ is clearly in heaven, at the right hand of the Father, he is nevertheless present among us through the Holy Spirit. As Calvin understood it, Christ's presence at the Lord's Table is not so much a local presence as it is a personal presence. Again, it is not so much that Christ is present on the table as that he is present at the table. It is by sharing a meal with him that the Covenant is sealed.

It is here that Calvin's doctrine of the Holy Spirit once more comes into play. Obviously for Calvin our union with Christ is of the greatest possible significance. This union is brought about by the Holy Spirit. It is through the inner working of the Holy Spirit that Christ abides in our hearts. One should not overlook, however, that for Christ to abide in our hearts implies that he rule in our hearts. Calvin makes a point of our being nourished by our union with Christ who is both crucified and risen. It is not that the Holy Spirit pours into our hearts some sort of spiritual fluid. It is rather that the Holy Spirit makes Christ present by sanctifying us. The Holy Spirit nourishes us by uniting us to the death of Christ so that we too die to sin. The Holy Spirit nourishes us by the resurrection of Christ so that we too live in newness of life.

Another important element of Calvin's eucharistic theology is his working out of the Pauline concept of the body of Christ. Here again the influence of the biblical concept of covenant is in evidence. Calvin begins with the first chapter of Ephesians where we read that the mystery of God's will is to unite all things in Christ (Eph. 1:9–10). Our participation, our communion, our sharing in Christ's body is indeed a great mystery. Paul is talking about the kingdom of God and the reign of Christ which God in his sovereign will ordained before creation. The creation of Adam and Eve, the giving of the Covenant to Abraham, the revealing of the law to Moses, the establishment of the throne of David all built toward that plan, that in the fullness of time all things might be united in Christ. Now how is this unity of the body of Christ to be understood? Is it to be understood in terms of the mystery religions or is it to be understood in terms of the Old Testament concept of the Covenant? Admittedly Paul is using a Greek vocabulary which can very easily be understood in terms of the Hellenistic mystery religions. He even uses the word mystery! But Calvin understands Paul quite correctly. He sees Paul against the background of the Old Testament rather than of Greek philosophy. Calvin's commentary on the first chapter of Ephesians makes it clear that what makes for the unity of the body of Christ is Christ's reign over that body. Of the very essence of our union with Christ is covenant faithfulness. It is "to do justice, to love kindness, and to walk humbly with your God" (Micah 6:8). Ever since the days of Amos the Hebrew prophets had insisted on the integrity of worship and conduct. If true humanity is to be restored then the human community must be healed. Human life as God intended it is life in community.

For Calvin the Lord's Supper had profound ethical and moral implications. The communion is not only with God in heaven; it is participation in the Christian community as well. The Lord's Supper was both an invitation to the rich banquet of the grace of God and a call to the righteousness and justice of Christ's kingdom. Just as the sharing of the Passover meal in Egypt was to strengthen the children of Israel for their passage to the Promised Land so, for Calvin, the Supper nourishes us in our pilgrimage to the heavenly Jerusalem. The hungering and thirsting after righteousness we have cried out for the grace of God and we have been granted that grace. We have been granted through the death and resurrection of Christ new and eternal life. We have been joined to Christ in his death to the old life and in his resurrection to new life. Now, using covenant terms once again, we are obligated to give thanks to our Savior and to confess the obligation this lays upon us. This confession is a witness, recounting the story of God's mighty acts of redemption and at the same time a vow dedicating one's life to the service of the everfaithful God who has heard our cry. It is in this way that the prayer of dedication at the end of the service is to be understood.

> Now grant us this other benefit: that thou wilt never allow us to forget these things; but having them imprinted on our hearts, we may grow and increase daily in the faith which is at work in every good deed. Thus may we order and pursue all our life to the exaltation of thy glory and the edification of our neighbor.
>
> (Bard Thompson, *Liturgies of the Western Church,* 208)

Having received communion we are obligated to live in holiness, justice, and peace.

It would be a mistake to regard the service used by Calvin in Geneva as the ideal Reformed communion liturgy. The *Genevan Psalter* offered many significant liturgical reforms, but there were still others which needed to be made.

The Italian Reformed theologian, Peter Martyr Vermigli (1500–62), had a profound effect on the Reformed doctrine of the Lord's Supper and on the way the sacrament has ever since been celebrated in Reformed churches. His writings are perhaps the most thorough treatment of eucharistic theology by any Reformed theologian. Vermigli was born in Florence to a family which had been greatly influenced by the famous reformer of that city, Savonarola (1452–98). Joining the Augustinian order Vermigli became prior of an Augustinian community at Naples in the early fifteen thirties. While in Naples he came to know Juan de Valdes (1500–41), who was already recognized as the most eminent of the Spanish Reformers. De Valdes introduced Vermigli to a circle of prominent Spaniards and Italians who aspired to the reform of the church. This group included Princess Vittoria Colonna, Cardinal Gonzaga, Benedetto Ochino, and even the great painter and sculptor, Michelangelo. After some time Vermigli became prior of the important Augustinian community at Lucca and while there tried to institute reforms. Official opposition to these reforms made it necessary for Vermigli to leave Italy. In 1547 Archbishop Thomas Cranmer (1489–1556) invited him to England and had him appointed as Regius Professor of Divinity at Oxford. In 1549 he took part in the great eucharistic disputation held at Oxford and from that time on had a tremendous influence on Anglo-Saxon eucharistic theology.

Vermigli gave a lot of attention to studying the biblical concept of sign. As Vermigli saw it the giving of signs is part of the divine condescension involved in God's self-revelation. God graciously accommodates himself to human weakness. Humans can not understand divine things as they are; therefore God reveals himself in signs, shadows, and types in order that by analogy we might rise to some intimation of divine truth. Following the line of thought made so popular by the fourth-century Church Father, Hilary of Poitiers, Vermigli gave much attention to the Old Testament types as sacraments of Christ. Joseph McLelland even goes so far as to say that Vermigli's typology is his real sacramental theology (Joseph McLelland, *The Visible Words of God*, 94). In this appreciation for typology, Vermigli is typical of sixteenth- and seventeenth-century Reformed theologians. The great depth of thought involved here is only beginning to be fathomed by contemporary theologians.

Vermigli's doctrine of the Lord's Supper is particularly significant for his profound sense of the analogy between the Lord's Supper and the doctrine of the incarnation. For Vermigli it is Christ himself who is the ultimate sacrament, the sign and promise of our redemption. As the Italian Reformer so often put it, it is important that in our doctrine of the Supper we respect both the divinity and the humanity of Christ. Appealing to Chalcedonian Christology, Vermigli reminds us that we should not confuse, mix, or separate the true humanity and the true divinity of Christ. Christ's humanity remains even after the resurrection and ascension. His humanity is not turned into divinity. His divinity does not destroy or efface his humanity. Rather, it redeems it, sanctifies it, and glorifies it. In the same way, at the Lord's Supper bread is not changed into God. Bread remains bread but it becomes a sign of the body of Christ. It is at the Lord's Table, by means of the signs of bread and wine, that we encounter the body of Christ. In the incarnation, the humanity of Christ is not turned into divinity but rather sanctified. Likewise, when we come to communion it is not for divinization but rather that through this communion with Christ we might become holy as he is holy. Our human flesh and blood remain human flesh and blood but being sanctified we become the humanity God always intended us to be. We become true children of God, heirs and joint heirs with Christ, the firstborn among many brethren (Rom. 8:17). As true children of God we inherit eternal life.

Another feature of Vermigli's sacramental theology is his profound appreciation of the biblical theology of thanksgiving. Vermigli liked to use the word eucharist in referring to the sacrament, because that word emphasized that the Lord's Supper is a feast of praise and thanksgiving. As Vermigli understood it, one of the cardinal actions of the liturgy is the eucharistic prayer in which the church gives thanks in joyful profusion for God's mighty acts of creation and redemption. Vermigli, as the other Reformers, very much opposed making the sacrament into a sacrifice. To be sure, the sacrament is a memorial and a thanksgiving for Christ's sacrifice. To be sure, Christians having received the benefits of Christ's sacrifice owe to God the sacrifice of thanksgiving and the offering of their lives to his service, but it is by Christ's sacrifice alone that our salvation has been won. Vermigli distinguished carefully between a propitiatory sacrifice which saves us from our sins and a eucharistic sacrifice which gives thanks to God for the salvation which God has already granted us. Our giving of ourselves to his service, our giving of alms, our self-dedication is entailed by Christ's obedient sacrifice of himself, but it must not be confused with his sacrifice.

This concern to respect the uniqueness of Christ's sacrifice explains a number of the features of the Reformed communion service. It explains the absence of what in the mass is called the offertory. The early Reformed liturgies studiously avoided anything which looked like or even sounded like the offering of bread and wine to God. If bread and wine were brought to the Holy Table during the service it was done so in a manner which could not possibly be considered an offering. In order to avoid confusion, alms were collected at the end of the service. The same concern explains the fact that during the Eucharistic Prayer itself there is no kind of oblation nor any offering of "ourselves, our souls and our bodies." We do find quite typically, a post-communion prayer of thanksgiving and dedication in which the worshipers give themselves to God's service. This comes quite intentionally after the congregation has received the bread and wine. Thus it is made clear that we give ourselves to God because he first gave himself to us. "We love him because he first loved us" (1 John 4:19).

What one normally finds particularly in the early Anglo-Saxon Reformed liturgies, where Vermigli's influence was especially strong, is two distinct prayers. The Eucharistic Prayer is a hymnic setting forth of God's mighty acts of creation and redemption. With this central prayer of the liturgy devoted to extolling Christ's death and resurrection, his humiliation and exaltation for our salvation, there is no question as to the eucharistic and doxological emphasis of the service. These early Reformed liturgies do indeed "proclaim the Lord's death until he comes." After all have participated in the meal, there is a prayer which thanks God for the benefits received from the sacraments and dedicates the congregation to a faithful confession before the world, the doing of good works, and the advancement of God's glory.

With the Reformation of the Church of Scotland in 1560 John Knox was given the responsibility of drawing up a Reformed liturgy. While the intention of John Knox was to follow the Genevan liturgy he improved it considerably, particularly in regard to the Eucharistic Prayer. The prayer is a thanksgiving for the works of creation and redemption and a celebration both of the grace and mercies which we have received in life and those to which we look forward in the kingdom of heaven.

> O Father of Mercy, and God of all consolation! Seeing all creatures do acknowledge and confess thee as Governor and Lord: It becometh us, the workmanship of thine own hands, at all times to reverence and magnify thy godly Majesty. First, for that thou hast created us in thine own image and similitude: But chiefly in that thou hast delivered us from that everlasting death and damnation, into the which Satan drew mankind by the means of sin, from the bondage whereof neither man nor angel was able to make us free.
>
> We praise thee, O Lord! that thou, rich in mercy, and infinite in goodness, hast provided our redemption to stand in thine only and well-beloved Son, whom of very love thou didst give to be made man like unto us in all things, sin excepted, in his body to receive the punishment of our transgression, by his death to make satisfaction to thy justice, and through his resurrection to destroy him that was the author of death; and so to bring again life to the world, from which the whole offspring of Adam most justly was exiled.

O Lord! we acknowledge that no creature is able to comprehend the length and breadth, the depth and height of that thy most excellent love, which moved thee to show mercy where none was deserved, to promise and give life where death had gotten the victory, to receive us in thy grace when we could do nothing but rebel against thy justice.

O Lord! the blind dullness of our corrupt nature will not suffer us sufficiently to weigh these thy most ample benefits; yet, nevertheless, at the commandment of Jesus Christ our Lord, we present ourselves at this His table, which he hath left to be used in remembrance of his death, until his coming again: to declare and witness before the world, that by him alone we have received liberty and life; that by him alone thou dost acknowledge us thy children and heirs; that by him alone we have entrance to the throne of thy grace; that by him alone we are possessed in our spiritual kingdom to eat and drink at his table, with whom we have our conversation presently in heaven, and by whom our bodies shall be raised up again from the dust, and shall be placed with him in that endless joy, which thou, O Father of Mercy! hast prepared for thine elect before the foundation of the world was laid.

And these most inestimable benefits we acknowledge and confess to have received of thy free mercy and grace, by thine only beloved Son Jesus Christ: for the which, therefore, we thy congregation, moved by thine Holy Spirit, render all thanks, praise, and glory, for ever and ever. Amen.

(*The Presbyterian Liturgies*, 124–126)

This Eucharistic Prayer has been composed with a very clear understanding of the biblical theology of thanksgiving. It celebrates in hymnic terms God's mighty acts for our redemption in the incarnation, redemptive sacrifice, and life-giving resurrection of Christ. It declares and witnesses before the world what God has done of his own mercy and grace. For Knox, as for the English Puritans, an important part of the sign was the actual breaking of the bread, the pouring out of the wine, and actually sitting about the table. In fact Scottish churches were often built in such a way that the congregation sat around three sides of the table. When the congregation had received the bread and wine there was a prayer of thanksgiving for the sacrament in which the worshipers dedicated themselves to live in praise to God and love toward their neighbors. This was followed by singing a psalm of thanksgiving. Psalm 103 is specifically indicated. In the course of Scottish liturgical history the use of this psalm became almost invariable. The great emphasis which Knox put on the eucharistic aspects of the service is clear.

Knox was very conscious that the Gospels tell us that when Jesus took the bread and wine, he gave thanks.

The English Puritans developed a number of the insights of the sixteenth-century Reformers in a most positive manner. During the Puritan period, not only in England but in Scotland and New England as well, a distinctive eucharistic piety began to develop. In the middle of the seventeenth century we find the following instructions in the *Westminster Directory*. First, either on the Sunday before the Lord's Supper or during the week immediately beforehand, there is to be a preparatory service that "all may come better prepared to that heavenly Feast." Then, when the day comes for the administration, the sermon being completed, the minister is to give a brief exhortation on the proper use of the sacrament. The people are to sit about or at the table, then the minister is to set apart the bread and wine "by the Word of Institution and Prayer." The words of institution are to be read out of the Gospels or from 1 Corinthians. Then follows the eucharistic prayer. The prayer is to give thanks for all God's benefits, "and especially for that great benefit of our redemption, the love of God the Father, the suffering of the Lord Jesus Christ the Son of God, by which we are delivered; and for all the means of Grace." This prayer included a very clear invocation of the Holy Spirit "to sanctify these Elements both of Bread and Wine, and to bless his own Ordinance, that we may receive by Faith the Body and Blood of Jesus Christ crucified for us, and so to feed upon him that he may be one with us, and we with him."

What is most notable here is the elaboration of the invocation or epiclesis. Richard Baxter (1615–91), one of the most influential of the Puritans further elaborated the epiclesis in his *Reformed Liturgy* of 1662.

> Most Holy Spirit, proceeding from the Father and the Son: by whom Christ was conceived; by whom the prophets and apostles were inspired, and the ministers of Christ are qualified and called: that dwellest and workest in all the members of Christ, whom thou sanctifiest to the image and for the service of their Head, and comfortest them that they may shew forth his praise: illuminate us, that by faith we may see him that is here represented to us. Soften our hearts, and humble us for our sins. Sanctify and quicken us, that we may relish the spiritual food, and feed on it to our nourishment and growth in grace. Shed abroad the love of God upon our hearts, and draw them out in love to him. Fill us with

thankfulness and holy joy, and with love to one another. Comfort us by witnessing that we are the children of God. Confirm us for new obedience. Be the earnest of our inheritance, and seal us up to everlasting life. Amen.

The invocation of the Holy Spirit was a characteristic liturgical concern of the Puritans. Indeed, the element of invocation is to be found in the prayers of Strasbourg, Zurich, and Geneva, but in nothing like the fullness we find here.

Returning to the *Westminster Directory* we find that the bread and wine are distributed much as in other Reformed liturgies. The sharing of the bread and wine complete, there follows a post-communion prayer. One assumes that the *Westminster Directory* has in mind the usual communion psalmody but it is not specifically mentioned. By this time there were well established traditions in regard to which psalms were appropriate for communion. Among the favorites were Psalms 23, 24, 34, 103, 113, 116, 118, and 133. Something is mentioned, however, which is of great importance, and that is the collection of alms for the poor. This had been an important aspect of the eucharistic piety of continental Reformed churches although it is not often specifically mentioned in the liturgical documents. It is a long-honored practice of Reformed piety that on communion Sundays there is a special collection of alms which is turned over to the deacons for distribution to the poor.

From this presentation it should be clear that the classic Reformed communion service should include a number of different facets: the covenantal, the eucharistic, the epicletic, the eschatological, the kerygmatic, and the diaconal. Each of these the Reformers discovered in Scripture and each of these was emphasized at one point or another in the development of the tradition.

VIII
Daily Prayer

The worship of the Temple was daily worship. It had been so since earliest times. To be sure, the worship of the weekly Sabbath was specially important. The annual feasts of Passover, Pentecost, and Tabernacles were great occasions at the Temple too. But the worship of the Temple was also an every day affair. Every morning and every evening there were sacrifices at the Temple. These daily sacrifices were called the *tamid*, the continual sacrifice. They were accompanied by prayers and particularly the singing of the psalms. It is from these continual sacrifices of the Temple that the Christian discipline of daily prayer is ultimately derived.

In the book of Daniel we read of how faithful Jews maintained the continual sacrifices of the Temple even when they were far away from Jerusalem. We are told that three times a day at the regular hours of the Temple sacrifices Daniel went to his room, opened his window toward Jerusalem and said his prayers. (When the third daily sacrifice was added is not known.)

There is another very ancient root of Christian daily worship. In the book of Deuteronomy we find an old version of the Ten Commandments followed by a summary of the law which for centuries Jews have called the *Shema*.

> "Hear, O Israel: The LORD our God is one LORD; and you shall love the LORD your God with all your heart, and with all your soul, and with all your might. And these words which I command you this day shall be

upon your heart; and you shall teach them diligently to your children,
and shall talk of them when you sit in your house, and when you walk by
the way, and when you lie down, and when you rise."

(Deuteronomy 6:4–7)

From very early times faithful Jews took quite literally the admonition to recite the *Shema* "When you lie down and when you rise."
Every morning and every evening the devout Jew would repeat the
summary of the law. Rabbinical scholars of our day tell us that in the
days of Jesus the reciting of the *Shema* included the reciting of
the whole of the Ten Commandments in addition to what is regarded as
the *Shema*. In doing this they kept the law constantly in their hearts and
minds; they meditated on the law day and night (Ps. 1:2). Perhaps, if in
those days people had had inexpensively printed Bibles as we do today,
they might have read a chapter of their Bibles each morning and evening. Copies of the Torah were very expensive in the days before printing and only very rarely would an individual have a personal copy. It
was therefore important to have a summary of the law, such as the
Shema, which every man, woman, and child could memorize. Each
morning and evening this core of the law was recited as a religious duty
or devotional practice. From earliest times daily prayer included a portion of Scripture.

By New Testament times the Jews had well established customs for
daily worship. In fact from the time of the council of Jamnia (A.D. 110)
the maintaining of the discipline of daily prayer was considered obliga-
tory. The service of daily prayer consisted of three parts. First there was
the repetition of a number of psalms, then the saying of the *Shema* with
its introductory and concluding prayers, and finally the Prayer of the
Eighteen Benedictions. It is quite certain that Jesus and the Apostles
maintained this prayer discipline and that in the earliest Christian church
daily prayer was maintained much as it was in the synagogue. In fact
when the Apostle Paul tells us to pray continually or to pray without
ceasing, what he surely has in mind is that we are to maintain the daily
discipline of morning and evening prayer (Rom. 12:12, 1 Thess. 5:17, 1
Tim. 5:5).

One of the places we most clearly see the first Christians maintaining the discipline of daily prayer is in the Acts of the Apostles (Acts
4:23–31). After Peter and John were released from prison they went to

find their friends and they knew just where to find them. They were gathered together for daily prayer as they did each morning and evening. The contents of that prayer meeting follow amazingly closely the pattern of daily prayer as it was practiced by the synagogue. The congregation, we are told, lifted up their voices together in prayer. A line from Psalm 146 is quoted. We can take this to mean that the service began with the congregation chanting several psalms. The synagogue normally began morning prayer with the chanting of Psalms 145 through 150. A passage of Scripture is quoted at length and the meaning of that passage of Scripture to the situation of the church at that time is discussed. This is followed by a prayer of intercession for the needs of the church. This prayer service held by the Apostles, like the prayer service of the synagogue, was made up of three elements, the chanting of psalms, a passage of Scripture, and prayers of supplication and intercession.

A good number of early Christian documents witness to the practice of holding daily prayers at the church as well as to the fact that Christian families maintained daily prayers at home. The *Didache*, for example, tells us that Christians were expected to pray the Lord's Prayer three times a day. We learn from Hippolytus that about the year 200 daily morning and evening prayer was regularly held at the church. From the *Apostolic Constitutions* we get a rather full report of the daily prayer services in Antioch at the end of the fourth century.

With the development of monasticism the service of daily prayer began to be cultivated with great care. Even from the very beginning the monks of the Egyptian desert began to give great attention to the memorizing and praying of the psalter. St. Anthony (251–356), one of the founders of Egyptian monasticism, knew the whole psalter by heart and in this respect he was typical of the desert saints. The monks often understood one of their main reasons for existence to be the service of daily prayer. They understood the saying of daily prayer to be their "office," that is, the work which God had called them to perform. Monks still refer to their services of daily prayer as the saying of the "daily office."

At the beginning of the sixth century, Benedict of Nursia (480–550) led a reform of monasticism which aimed at organizing the monks into Christian communities. St. Benedict had a keen perception into one of the fundamental truths of the Christian faith. Christian life is life in community and Christian prayer is essentially common prayer. Christian prayer is more truly Christian when it is shared with others. At the heart of Benedict's monastic reform was the organization of the daily prayer services and his division of the psalter so that in the course of time the whole psalter would be said. The cultivation of daily prayer reached such a high point in the Middle Ages that the monks held a series of seven services of prayer each day. This "liturgy of the hours," as it was called, developed elaborate musical settings. The artistic perfection which was frequently achieved in the saying of the liturgy of the hours must have been remarkable. It was in the Eastern church, however, that the saying of daily prayer reached its most sublime. The story goes that in the Church of Hagia Sophia in Constantinople the service of daily prayer became so rich in its musical setting that it required three choirs of monks working in relays to provide the music.

Unfortunately, with this elaborate development the saying of daily prayer became almost a monastic prerogative. Those not engaged in "religious vocations" hardly had either the training or the leisure to maintain such a complicated discipline of daily prayer.

With the Reformation it was necessary to restore the service of daily prayer to the regular members of the church. This entailed simplifying the service so that it could be maintained by those who were engaged in secular work and family responsibilities. Again it was Strasbourg which led the way in the reorganizing of the daily prayer services. In the first place the series of seven services which began at earliest morning and ran through the whole course of the day was reduced to a very simple program of morning prayer and evening prayer. That it was reduced to two services rather than a single service or to three services, morning, noon, and night is not explained. Be that as it may, the custom of holding daily prayers at morning and evening became characteristic of the Protestant reform of the daily office. Each service began with the singing of one or more psalms. Great attention was given to the production of a collection of metrical psalms and canticles which could be sung to simple tunes and in the German language. The daily prayer services in Strasbourg included a program of daily preaching. There were two main prayers. At the beginning of the service was a prayer of confession and supplication. After the sermon there was a comprehensive prayer of intercession for the needs of the church, for the Christian magistracy, for the perseverance of the saints, and for those suffering from any adversity. The service was concluded with another psalm and the giving of a benediction by the minister.

Very similar daily prayer services were held in the Reformed Church of Augsburg. Augsburg developed its own psalter, although in other ways the worship of the Church of Augsburg was greatly influenced by Strasbourg. In time Geneva too developed a daily morning and evening prayer service.

In the seventeenth century it became more and more the practice to emphasize the discipline of daily family prayer. Particularly in England and Scotland the maintaining of the discipline of daily prayer was understood as a family responsibility. Richard Baxter (1615–1691) in his *Christian Directory* wrote at considerable length on how daily morning and evening prayer was to be conducted by the father of each family. Baxter insists that daily family prayer is one of the divinely ordained functions of the family. A family, Baxter tells us, is a little church. Family prayer should include the following things. First there was to be the singing of one or more psalms, then the reading of a chapter of Scripture, and finally the head of the house was to offer a full and comprehensive prayer.

The General Assembly of the Church of Scotland drew up a special chapter on secret and family prayer which it added to the *Westminster Directory* shortly after its adoption in 1647. The fact that the Scottish General Assembly found it necessary to add such a chapter to the *Westminster Directory of Worship* is interesting itself. Originally the chapter was much longer than what we now have. According to the *Directory*, family prayer should be held morning and evening each day. It should include prayer, reading the Scriptures, and singing praises.

Matthew Henry (1662–1714), pastor of a Presbyterian church in Chester, England, had a pastoral concern for cultivating family prayer. He produced a number of aids for those who bore the responsibility of leading family prayers. First there was his classic *A Method of Prayer*. Then there was a collection of psalms and canticles, *Family Hymns*. This was an anthology of the best metrical psalms which Henry was able to gather from a number of collections which were then available in the English language. In addition to these, Henry wrote several popular essays on the subject of daily prayers which give us an insight into how the English Puritans understood this important devotional discipline. For Matthew Henry the discipline of daily morning and evening prayer was the fulfillment of the continual sacrifices of the Temple. These daily services were the spiritual sacrifices of praise and thanksgiving offered by the royal priesthood. He saw a very definite devotional rhythm in morning and evening prayer. In the morning we go to God in praise and adoration. We ask his guidance through the course of the day. Such an approach was natural for a Reformed theologian for whom the doctrine of providence was so important. Then having finished the day one comes to God again in thanksgiving for his guidance, mercies, and blessings.

For classical Reformed spirituality, morning and evening family prayer was one of the foundations of piety. It was at the heart of the day to day exercising of Christian faith. This made sense to those for whom Covenant theology was so formative. The unity of the family was a significant feature of Covenant theology. With the coming of pietism, daily family prayer was unfortunately replaced with private devotions.

Pietism was very individualistic and many of this persuasion had a hard time understanding why children should be baptized. There was no sacred unity in the family. Each single human being stood before God alone. With the demise of pietism, private devotions began to develop atrophy. They finally became not much more than "five minutes a day." Today as we seek to recover a Reformed spirituality, we need to reach behind pietism and recover the older classical Protestant discipline of daily morning and evening prayer.

IX

Alms

When Martin Bucer (1491–1551) in his *Grund und Ursach* of 1524 tried to summarize what should be included in the service of worship, he appealed to the text of Acts 2:42, "And they continued in the teaching and fellowship of the Apostles, in the breaking of bread and the prayers." As Bucer understood this, the service of worship which aspired to follow the apostolic example should include preaching and teaching, the giving of alms, the celebration of communion and the service of prayer. Perhaps most of this would seem self-evident except for the second of the four parts, the giving of alms. Bucer's approach to the Greek text of the book of Acts, if a bit original, was certainly sound enough. The Greek word in question is *koinonia* which can mean communion or fellowship or very practically the sharing of material goods with those who are in need. We can leave aside the question of whether Bucer's translation was completely appropriate. His sense of liturgical balance was impeccable. The giving of alms should always be regarded as one of the constituent elements of Christian worship.

In the days of Jesus the giving of alms to the poor was considered as one of the standard good works which the faithful Jew was supposed to practice. As pious Jews understood it, the giving of alms was something quite different from the paying of tithes. Tithes were a sort of tax which was paid for the support of the Temple and other religious institutions. Alms were gifts to the poor. The word alm comes from the Greek word for mercy. To give alms is therefore to make a gift as an act of mercy, to relieve those who are in need. Normally when one entered or left the synagogue, there were beggars asking alms. That Peter and John should meet with a beggar on entering the gates of the Temple is not at all remarkable; there were always beggars there (Acts 3:1ff.). To be sure, this was not the only way of giving one's alms. We read in the Gospel of Mark, for example, the story of the widow's mite (Mark 12:41–44). Jesus while teaching in the Temple saw an obviously poor woman putting a gift into the alms chest and commended the fact that even in her poverty she gave alms. The story is witness to the fact that the Temple maintained an alms chest that the faithful might give anonymously. No doubt similar chests were to be found in each synagogue. The giving of alms was well organized among first-century Jews. The synagogue regularly appointed some of its most respected members to be almoners. These almoners were charged with reminding people of their responsibility toward those in need, collecting alms, and distributing food and other necessities of life to the poor, the sick, the widowed, and the orphaned.

In the Sermon on the Mount Jesus turned his attention to the subject of almsgiving. He was concerned in his teaching with correcting certain abuses which accompanied the giving of alms in his day:

> Thus, when you give alms, sound no trumpet before you, as the hypocrites do in the synagogues and in the streets, that they may be praised by men. Truly, I say to you, they have received their reward. But when you give alms, do not let your left hand know what your right hand is doing, so that your alms may be in secret; and your Father who sees in secret will reward you.
>
> (Matthew 6:2–4)

What is striking, however, is that this instruction on the proper way to give alms is found in a series of teachings about prayer. Almsgiving, as Jesus evidently understood it, is an auxiliary discipline to the discipline of prayer. It was for this reason that pious Jews gave alms when they went to the synagogue or to the Temple to pray.

Very early in the life of the church it was necessary for Christians to establish something like the almoners of the synagogue. In reading the sixth chapter of Acts we find the church doing just that. As the church had grown, the care of the poor had become an increasingly time-consuming task. The primitive church realized that the care of widows and orphans, the crippled, the blind, and the disturbed was an essential part of the ministry of Jesus and so specific members of the church were charged with maintaining this ministry. It is most interesting that the text of Acts 6 makes such a point of the division of labor between the Apostles who were to devote themselves to prayer and the ministry of the word and the deacons who were to devote themselves to the ministry of tables. Deacon really means one who serves at the table; a deacon is a waiter. This kind of service or ministry is essential to the church. The ministry of the Christian deacon is grounded in the ministry of Jesus himself. It was Jesus himself who came "not to be served but to serve." Here Jesus was making a play on the Greek word from which the word deacon comes. Jesus often claimed for himself the role of the deacon, that is, the role of the servant. One place where this became particularly clear was in the Upper Room where Jesus washed the disciples' feet and told them, "If I then, your Lord and Teacher, have washed your feet, you also ought to wash one another's feet" (John 13:14). So important is the diaconal ministry of the church!

Another place where we get an intimation of the place of almsgiving in the worship of the church is the Apostle Paul's instructions to the Corinthians regarding the collection for Jerusalem (1 Cor. 16:1–4). The Apostle directs that on the first day of the week, that is, on the Lord's Day, the day when communion was celebrated, each one is to put aside some money for the saints of Jerusalem. One gathers that a collection was made at the worship assembly, but perhaps after the actual service of worship was over. The money was then to be kept, no doubt by the deacons, until the Apostle's arrival. In this the Apostle Paul was only following the teaching and example of Jesus regarding the true nature of the true Sabbath. It was to be a day of release, a day of healing, and a day of charitable works. What could be more appropriate to the Lord's Day than to collect funds for the relief of the poor? How could the church more appropriately remember Jesus? In works of mercy the death and resurrection of Jesus were eloquently remembered.

During the first centuries of church history, generosity in the giving of alms was characteristic of Christians. That the church maintained funds for the care of the poor we learn from many early sources. Of particular interest is a passage in the *Apology* of Tertullian, written at the end of the second century, which makes clear the diaconal aspect of the celebration of communion. True *koinonia* was at the same time communion with God and sharing with the poor. That marvelous Greek word meant both at the same time.

Rarely has the Christian church lost sight of the importance of almsgiving. The charitable works of the deacons of the early church often left a profound impression. Lawrence, a deacon of the city of Rome in the middle of the third century, is a particularly well-remembered example. Even the briefest remarks on the subject should mention John Chrysostom (347–407) who may be reckoned as the greatest alms preacher in the history of the church. Frequently his sermons end up with an appeal to the congregation to remember the poor as they leave the church. The monastic orders of the Middle Ages often provided Christendom with extensive diaconal services. Francis of Assisi (1181–1226) was perhaps the most famous of all deacons. His whole ministry emphasized the importance of the care of the poor.

The Reformation brought a radical reshaping of the church's ministry to the poor. It is to the Free Imperial City of Nuremberg that the credit should go for taking the lead in the reform of charitable institutions during the early sixteenth century. Nuremberg was among the most cosmopolitan centers of Germany and from the very beginning of the Reformation Nuremberg took a strong stand for Protestantism. Hand in hand with a new baptismal rite and a translation of the liturgy into German, the city published a new order for the care of the poor. Those who were in genuine need were to be taken care of at public expense. There was to be no more begging in the streets. Homes for the care of the elderly, the widowed, and the orphaned were established and maintained by the deacons with the help of the city treasury as well as the giving of alms.

Strasbourg followed the lead of Nuremberg very quickly. The eleemosynary institutions, that is institutions supported by alms, were completely reorganized so that the city supported a comprehensive program for the care of the sick, the blind, and any others in need. The new approach to the care of the poor won widespread approval for the city of Strasbourg. Gerard Roussel, the chaplain to the Queen of Navarre, reported after his visit to Strasbourg in 1526 that the care of the poor was one of the most impressive aspects of the Reformation. Much of the reorganization of the charitable institutions of Strasbourg goes far beyond the scope of this book but there are a number of these reforms which were clearly liturgical.

Early in the Reformation the liturgy of Strasbourg eliminated the offertory. No collection was taken in the service of worship itself. Nevertheless a chest was put in each of the churches so that on leaving the church worshipers could deposit their alms. The collection of alms as people left worship became characteristic of Reformed churches. We hear of this being the practice of the Reformed Church of Augsburg. In Basel, after the minister had given the Benediction, he was to remind the congregation to contribute to the care of the poor, and as the people left the service they put their alms in one of the alms chests which stood near the door.

In Strasbourg we begin to find a reform of the ministry of the deacon. In about the fifth century, after the introduction of the hierarchical principle into the organization of the Christian ministry, the office of deacon tended to become the first rung up the hierarchical ladder. One had to become a deacon before one could become a priest and so gradually the church lost sight of the uniqueness of the diaconal ministry as a ministry of mercy to those in need. The Reformers of Strasbourg did much to recover the charitable orientation of the diaconate. This was picked up by Calvin who likewise interpreted the office of deacon in the light of the sixth chapter of Acts. For Calvin the deacon performed one of the distinct ministries of the church and that distinct ministry was the care of the poor. This understanding of the office of deacon soon became characteristic of the Reformed doctrine of the ministry. In England, for example, when Thomas Cartwright (1535–1603) and the Cambridge Presbyterians drew up their admonitions to Parliament, one of the specific reforms which they advocated regarded the recovery of the diaconal ministry. They wanted deacons whose primary concern was the care of the poor.

Let us look very briefly at the diaconal ministry of the Church of Geneva. As in most of the Protestant cities of the Rhineland, public begging, even at the doors of the churches, was discontinued soon after the city accepted the Reformation. The care of the poor was to be taken care of in other ways. One of the most important of these was the establishment of a hospice or hospital. Robert Kingdon has given us a vivid picture of the work of this institution. In those days a hospital was a much more comprehensive institution than what we usually understand today. In Geneva it was housed in a large building in the center of the city, surrounded with stables, barns, courtyards, and gardens. Several dozen people were cared for in that building. They ranged from orphaned children to elderly widows too feeble to care for themselves. This hospital was presided over by a hospitaller and his wife. Several servants cared for the extensive gardens and the large kitchen. This was important because the garden and the kitchen provided a considerable amount of food for needy families who did not live in the hospital. There was even a resident tutor, who was usually a theology student. The tutor's job was to help care for the children in the hospital. The hospital was under the care of the deacons. It was their job to see to it that the hospital was well funded and well administered.

Another diaconal work of the Genevan Church was the French Refugees Fund. This was presided over by Jean Budé, the son of the great Renaissance Greek scholar, Guillaume Budé. This fund was to care for those who had had to flee from France because of religious persecution. The fund was generously supported by a number of very wealthy French refugees living in Geneva including Jean Budé himself. Robert Estienne, the famous printer, and Laurent de Normandie were generous supporters, and Calvin himself made regular contributions from his own salary. He too was a French refugee. According to Professor Kingdon, the French Refugee Fund spent its money for a great variety of projects. The fund was used to help obtain housing for recently arrived refugees, to provide furniture for families, and tools to help artisans set themselves up in business. It provided fees for young men who needed to enter apprenticeship and dowries for women wanting to get married. Food and medical care was supplied by the fund for those in need and it even supported the widows and orphans of Reformed pastors who had lost their lives in the service of the gospel. The fund's distributors were concerned with evangelism too. They sent missionary pastors back into France and saw to the printing and distribution of Protestant literature in the French homeland. The French Refugee Fund was precisely the sort of social service which was needed in Geneva at the time. Refugees poured into Geneva at such a rate that while Geneva had a population of perhaps ten thousand at the beginning of the Reformation, twenty years later the population had doubled, largely because of the refugees. Ge-

neva was kind to its refugees. It is interesting to note that more than four
hundred years later Geneva is still maintaining this tradition as a haven
for refugees.

Finally, the *Westminster Directory* provided for the giving of alms
in three ways. In its chapter on the sanctification of the Lord's Day we
are told that among the duties of the day are to be reckoned the
". . . visiting of the sick, relieving the poor, and such duties of piety,
charity, and mercy." Nothing is said about a collection during the ordinary service of worship; nevertheless there might have been one. This
would especially be the case when some special cause needed to be
supported. On the other hand, when communion was celebrated there
was quite definitely to be a collection for the poor. The ancient connection between the Lord's Supper and the giving of alms is patently recognized. The third place the *Westminster Directory* provides for the giving
of alms is found in the chapter on the observing of days of public
thanksgiving. There we are told, "At one or both of the publick meet-
ings that day, a collection is to be made for the poor, . . . that their
loins may bless us, and rejoice the more with us. And the people are to
be exhorted at the end of the latter meeting, to spend the residue of the
day in holy duties, and testifications of Christian love and charity one
towards another, and of rejoicing more and more in the Lord as be-
cometh those who make the joy of the Lord their strength." It is significant that for the Puritans almsgiving belongs to thanksgiving. It is a way
of expressing holy joy. It is a way of rejoicing in all the riches of grace
and all the benefits of salvation which we have received from God.

X

Tradition and Practice

Having covered all these pages on the subject of what the Reformed tradition in worship is, let us take a few more pages and speak of how this tradition should shape our current practice. Let us think for a few moments about what the Reformed liturgical heritage has to offer American Protestants of today.

In our considering this there are two extremes to be avoided. The first is a sort of archaeological reconstruction in the English language of the *Genevan Psalter* or a meticulous following of the *Westminster Directory*. Simply *going back* to either of these classics would not really constitute a reform of worship. One problem with doing this is that our tradition at its most simple and at its most classical revolves around these two foci, the Continental Reformers of the sixteenth century and the English Puritans of the seventeenth century. There will always be those who will tend more toward Geneva, others who will tend more toward Westminster. Luther, Zwingli, Bucer, and Calvin did not always agree, nor did the Scottish Presbyterians and the English Puritans. There is quite a spread between Richard Baxter and Matthew Henry. Some are going to be more attentive to Manton, some to Bucer. The Reformed tradition has been collegial from its very beginning. This was made abundantly clear as early as the Synod of Berne in 1528. We are not the devotees of some single, star Reformer. Reformed is not the same thing as Lutheran, Zwinglian, or Calvinist.

Then there is the obvious fact that there is a gap between the classical age of Reformed theology and our age. Reformed theology suffered its baroque period and its mannerist period. With the coming of pietism and rationalism Reformed churches began to worship in ways that were very different from the Reformers. That is, their worship was motivated by other considerations. The Great Awakening and the revivals which followed it had their influence on worship. The romanticism of the High Church movement began to have its effect about the middle of the last century. One could have traced this story, going into considerable detail. It would have been interesting to have spoken of Jean-Frederick Osterwald and his influence on the French Huguenot liturgy, or to have become quite engrossed in the work of the German Reformed hymnodist Joachim Neander or the Czech educator Jan Komensky. The Dutch Reformed pastor and statesman Abraham Kuyper wrote much interesting material for the liturgist. The Scottish hymnodist Horatius Bonar deserves considerable attention. In America, Charles W. Baird, Henry van Dyke, and Louis F. Benson led a significant liturgical revival. John W. Nevin and the Mercersberg school make a most important chapter in the history of Reformed liturgics. Philipp Doddridge, Jonathan Edwards, and Samuel Miller all had their influence on the worship of Reformed churches. One should certainly mention the influence of the Wesleys on Reformed worship as well as the influence of Alexander Campbell and the English Calvinistic Baptist Charles Haddon Spurgeon. They often did in one respect or another a masterful job of representing the Reformed tradition.

An archaeological reconstruction rarely meets the needs of the time. Too many things have happened in the meantime. No longer can one expect a whole town or city to share a common faith, when the church can exercise any kind of discipline. Today the church cannot expect civil law to support the church's calendar. Today we have much more friendly feelings toward Roman Catholics and we are not apt to avoid a religious practice simply because it appears papist. We are beginning to discover much in the monastic tradition which is admirable and much in Scholastic theology which we rather like. In fact, the first draft of this work included quite a bit on the worship of the Middle Ages. It had to be left out. Things have indeed changed since the sixteenth and seventeenth centuries. There was a time when for most people the church was the only place where one could experience music or one could hear an interesting speaker. Now the church is in constant competition with the entertainment industry for the attention of its members. This cannot help but affect the worship of today's church. One could go on and on in this vein, but the point has so often been made we hardly need to repeat the obvious.

Just because one seeks to recover a tradition, one is not necessarily committed to what we have called an archaeological reconstruction of the tradition. For a Reformed theologian any tradition, the Reformed tradition as well, needs to be measured against Scripture to determine whether it is of value. It is Scripture which has authority and the tradition only has authority when it is based on Scripture. The tradition needs to be evaluated and re-evaluated and those elements in it which are most solid emphasized. In any tradition there are elements which have played a significant role because of the needs of the day, but which in a few generations no longer seemed meaningful. In every tradition, there are the marks of compromises with the culture. There are things the religious leaders would have liked to have done but which the state would not permit or the people would not support.

A particularly good example of this was the way the Reformers wanted to restore to the church the weekly communion of the faithful. In Strasbourg Bucer and his colleagues tried to get the whole population of the city to come to one celebration of the Lord's Supper at the cathedral each Lord's Day. Unfortunately the Reformed pastors of Strasbourg were never able to bring about that reform. A similar thing happened in Geneva. Calvin wanted a weekly celebration of communion in Geneva. Evidently the faithful who had been accustomed under the old order to receive communion but once a year just could not make that kind of transition, and so, quarterly observance became the rule. In Geneva communion was celebrated only four times a year, Christmas, Easter, Pentecost, and the first Sunday in October. That was an advance over the Medieval custom, but before too long Reformed churches were stuck with a tradition which was not "according to Scripture." Alexander Campbell tried to set that matter in order at the beginning of the last century. We need to get back to that reform again.

There are certain recurring aspects of our tradition which we really do not need to continue. The Reformed liturgical tradition has usually been read as being rather ascetic in its attitude toward music. Occasionally it has gone in the direction of exclusive psalmody. This attitude still has supporters among the Reformed Presbyterians here in America and in certain Reformed churches in the Netherlands. It is a most venerable sort of hyper-conservatism. It certainly has patristic support. There have been long periods when the church or large portions of the church refused to sing anything but the psalms. On the other hand Reformed churches of today can appeal to the example of Constance and Strasbourg to support the use of hymnody in addition to psalmody. It is much the same way with the use of instrumental music. Zwingli had the organ closed up in the Zurich minster but he never claimed scriptural support for doing so. One can only speculate what his reasons might have been. Calvin did his best to get talented musicians for the Church of Geneva but the city council constantly frustrated his desires. The city fathers were not willing to pay the salary of good musicians. What finally was taken for the tradition was a compromise with the bland musical taste of the burghers of Geneva. Luther did not have to fight that kind of opposition. Consequently German Lutherans had much better church music than the Zwinglians and the Calvinists of Switzerland.

In sixteenth-century Reformed communion liturgies there was always a long Communion Exhortation in which unrepentant sinners were warned not to approach the table and the faithful encouraged to receive the sacrament. These exhortations normally went into considerable detail as to who was allowed to receive communion and who was not. They usually elaborated the proper doctrine of the Lord's Supper at great length. Reading these exhortations must have taken ten to twenty minutes. They were quite necessary in those days when the Reformers needed to explain again and again the reasoning behind their reforms. The Reformers strove valiantly to establish true church discipline. Besides, for the members of the congregation the exact formulation of eucharistic doctrine was of great interest. It was a matter of public discussion and the more alert members of the congregation could be counted on to follow these exhortations with the closest attention. It would be foolish to revive these long Communion Exhortations. Today most of us would find them tedious. This is not necessarily to our credit. It is much more because we have lost our church discipline and we are apathetic in matters of theology. One might say that the temperature of devotion in American Protestantism is not sufficiently high to support such a conscientious approach to public worship. But on the other hand we might be able to find more effective ways of fulfilling the scriptural admonition to examine ourselves before coming to the table and being sure we discern the Lord's body. At the heart of the Reformed tradition is this witness to the moral implications of the sacrament. The Reformed tradition recognizes this to be a fundamental aspect of what Scripture teaches us about the proper celebration of the Lord's Supper. One can guard the Reformed tradition without having to copy everything that was done in Geneva in the mid-sixteenth century. On the other hand a celebration of communion which ignores its moral implications has lost contact with the Reformed tradition.

The Puritans in both England and America as well as the Dutch Calvinists often developed the observance of the Lord's Day to unfortunate extremes. Surely we do not want to resuscitate all this. Nevertheless an important aspect of the Reformed liturgical heritage was the recovery of a biblical theology of the Lord's Day. The more left wing Puritans totally rejected the liturgical year and celebrated the Lord's Day alone. Reformed churches today would probably be better advised to follow the practice of the Continental Reformed churches which reemphasized the weekly celebration of the Lord's Day but also allowed for the celebration of what they called the five evangelical feast days, Christmas, Good Friday, Easter, Ascension, and Pentecost. The recent efforts to bring back the celebration of the old liturgical calendar has suspicious similarities to a revival of the nature religions, natural theology, a cyclical interpretation of life, and the resurgence of the religions of fortune and fertility. One does penance in Advent when winter sets in and then one rejoices at Easter when the flowers reappear in the spring. It is all quite natural, but this fascination with liturgical seasons sometimes seems not much more than a revival of Canaanitism. One thing should be clear, the primary emphasis of any Reformed liturgical calendar should be the weekly observance of the Lord's Day. Very significantly, the seven day cycle of the biblical week is not related to any of the nature cycles! The celebration of the resurrection is primarily the weekly celebration of the Lord's Day, not the yearly celebration, which in certain parts of the world is connected with spring. To drape the worship of any Sunday in penitential purple is contrary to the best our tradition teaches us.

There is another extreme. Archaeological reconstruction we have identified as the one extreme. Liturgical romanticism we would identify as the other. On the one hand we do not want mechanically to reproduce the tradition but on the other hand we do not want to give ourselves up to perpetual liturgical revision. One often explains the name Reformed by the motto "reformed and always reforming." That motto can be understood in more than one way. It can point to the fact that "Reformed" must always mean reformed according to Scripture. At best this motto points to the fact that our obedience cannot become a static matter which was once worked out in the sixteenth century and seventeenth century and never needs to be reconsidered. It can mean that our church doctrine and practice must always repeatedly be set against the measure of Scripture. "Reformed and always reforming" can be understood in another way. It can be understood as a sort of theological Trotskyism. It can mean submitting the worship of the church to perpetual revolution. Romanticism, we remember, had a tendency to glorify revolution. To call for perpetual revolution in liturgical matters, however, is to lose sight of the value of having a liturgy.

There are good reasons for having an established liturgy and these reasons have often been recounted. In the first place liturgical forms are a good means of teaching the essentials of the Christian faith. When familiar liturgical forms and texts are used again and again it gives us the opportunity to meditate on them and to penetrate their meaning more deeply. When there are well established procedures with which everyone is familiar it makes it easier to concentrate on the content rather than the outward form. Any athlete understands the importance of mastering form. Such simple things as breathing must be done correctly. It takes a long time to get some of these simple techniques down correctly, but this is essential so that eventually they can be done spontaneously, without effort, without thinking about them. The concentration must be on other things. Forms are a means to an end and if they are constantly changing they obscure the end rather than leading to it.

A tradition which gets radically changed every generation is not really a tradition. For tradition to be tradition it must have a considerable amount of permanence and changelessness. Tradition can only become tradition when it is passed from one generation to another. That is what the Latin root *tradere* means, to hand over, from one hand to another, from one generation to another. Tradition can not be invented. It can be discovered or recovered, but it must be received from someone else. A liturgical tradition cannot be concocted by a General Assembly task force. Such a task force can recognize that over the generations such and such a liturgical tradition has been passed on to us. It can evaluate these traditions asking whether they are adequate or inadequate for our day or whether they are true to Scripture. Tradition can be received or rejected but it cannot be invented.

The story is told of a well known Presbyterian liturgist who held a workshop in liturgy at some ecumenical study conference center. The liturgist having all sorts of credentials in music and the arts was instructing the workshop in the creation of liturgies. When the course drew to a close the liturgist gave an assignment to his class. Each participant was to create his or her own liturgy. It happened that among those in the class was a woman from the Orthodox Church of Ethiopia. To her the assignment was the cause of great confusion. At last she approached the liturgist and explained her confusion. How could she write a liturgy? A liturgy was something which had developed over the centuries. How could she just sit down and make one up in the course of a few hours? The liturgist, realizing he was dealing with someone from a very primitive culture, patiently sat her down and explained that it was really all very easy. For an hour or so he worked at putting together a liturgy for matins. Since he was responsible for leading matins the next morning he had the service mimeographed and then performed the next morning. When the performance was over the liturgist asked the woman what she thought of it. She shook her head and said, "The liturgy can only come from many tears." She understood what liturgy really is. It is participation in a fellowship of suffering and joy which has gone on for centuries.

On the other hand tradition must always be reinterpreted. That is of the very nature of tradition. This is true for liturgical tradition just as it is for music. Today when a Mozart trio sonata is played in a concert before a modern audience an important part of the artists' work is the interpretation of Mozart's composition. There is a certain amount of adaptation which must be made. Today two hundred years after Mozart the musical instruments used will be different from those used in Mozart's day. The musical instruments of Mozart's day were much more delicate. Performances took place in drawing rooms or salons rather than concert halls. Then there is the matter of the phrasing and the tempo. A good interpreter recognizes subtle harmonies, contrasts and balances. The interpreter underlines them and brings them out so that the listener hears them too. Artists who are sensitive to the composer can make these compositions fascinating, but on the other hand a poor interpretation can make them dry and boring. There is something quite analogous to this in the celebration of the liturgy. One cannot celebrate the liturgy without interpreting it. The pastor of an American Protestant church today must evaluate the liturgical heritage of his or her church and decide what things are important to include in the amount of time set aside for worship. The pastor must decide how to divide up that time between preaching, prayer, praise, and sacraments. He or she must decide how much to be guided by the contemporary liturgical books offered by the denomination, how much to be guided by the great classics of the tradition and certainly the pastor will have an ear tuned to the capacity of the congregation. A celebration of vespers on Easter Sunday in a large city church where there is a well trained choir and a professional organist will obviously be quite different from the holding of vespers on a camping trip with a group of a dozen teenagers. There is a real art to adapting the liturgical forms of vespers to two such very different situations. One could of course just ignore these forms, but on the other hand a far greater depth can be gained in the worship if these forms are used as a guide to the shaping of the prayers of the group.

There is great value in maintaining the tradition. More and more this is becoming recognized today. Let us look at some reasons for maintaining the tradition.

The first reason we would like to suggest is quite simply that we human beings feel a need to keep in contact with our roots. Often in history there has been a violent reaction against the tradition. Nevertheless one eventually gets around to going back and trying to recover the tradition. Something in us reaches out for the tradition just as something in us pushes us to pass on the tradition. This concern for the tradition corresponds to a basic human need. For the Christian this is not at all surprising. God made us to live in community and so we find it natural that we should reach out to our neighbors. As Christians we recognize a need to maintain fellowship with Christians in other parts of the world.

For the same reason we recognize a need to maintain fellowship with Christians who have gone before us. The universality of the community has temporal dimensions.

The importance of having roots has recently been illustrated by Alex Haley in his book which simply bears the title *Roots*. As an American of African ancestry he went searching for his roots in Africa. The fact that he found them gave millions of black Americans a new appreciation for the value of their own life today. Even more it gave millions of American whites a new appreciation for Blacks.

We reach out for the tradition because we want to see who we are and where we came from and where we are going. We want to see our own lives in a larger perspective of history. We want to know who we are as American Protestant Christians at the end of the twentieth century.

A second reason for maintaining the tradition is that the tradition contains material of lasting value. The church has maintained great respect for the Fathers of the earliest Christian centuries, particularly those Christians of the second and third centuries such as Irenaeus, Cyprian, Origen, Clement of Alexandria, Lactantius, Hippolytus, and Tertullian who did their work amidst the persecutions and harassment of a hostile civil authority. One is amazed that the church produced any literature at all during this period. Nevertheless, they preserved for us a vivid picture of the nature of the Christian life. They reveal a vitality and purity which we cannot do other than emulate. With the establishment of the church in the fourth century the number of great Christian thinkers, preachers and writers increased enormously. Athanasius, Hilary of Poitiers, Ambrose of Milan, John Chrysostom, Basil of Caesarea, Gregory of Nazianzus and Gregory of Nyssa, Cyril of Jerusalem and Cyril of Alexandria, Augustine, and Jerome were all men of intellectual prowess who provided extraordinary leadership for the church. Whenever Christians talk about tradition, the Fathers figure prominently in the discussion. The reason is not hard to discover. We respect them because of their brilliance.

It is a strange thing about the Fathers, for very few of us are they really fathers. Only a very few American Protestants have Italian or Greek ancestors. We have neither racial nor ethnic relation to the Fathers of the ancient church. Most of us can claim no saints in the branches of the family tree, not even in the most remote twigs. There are some American Protestants who can after the flesh, claim Abraham and Sarah as ancestors, but most of us claim them as ancestors according to the lineage of faith. In fact, when we think about it, do we not think of Abraham and Sarah as being our ancestors far more than any proto-Germanic or Celtic tribesmen who might have been tramping around northern Europe in that age when Abraham was called out of Ur of Chaldees? It is an old custom to call John Chrysostom "our Father among the saints." John Chrysostom, however, was a celibate. Not one of us can claim him as our ancestor. What makes him then our Father? Augustine had one son who died at the age of twelve. Besides that Augustine was an African of racially mixed parentage. He seems to have had some Roman ancestry but for the most part he was a descendant of Punic stock. Racially he is quite distant from most of us. How is it that we call such men Fathers?

The answer is this: Chrysostom, Augustine, and Jerome have again and again engendered spiritual children. It has happened in one generation after another. It has happened in one culture after another. The Schoolmen of the High Middle Ages quoted Augustine more than anyone else. The Reformers feasted on him. In our own country the Mercersburg school paid him the highest deference. Augustine's commentaries on Scripture, his theological essays and his introspective thoughts get great minds thinking. They have the power to inspire thought. He, as the other Church Fathers, was a seminal thinker. Their thinking inspires others to think. The Fathers were the seminal thinkers of Christian theology. If it were not for this ability of theirs to speak to the most devout and fertile of minds of every age and nation they would have been forgotten long ago.

For the American Protestant of today the Fathers and the Reformers occupy much the same position. As Karl Barth puts it, the Reformers recognized much the same sort of authority in the Fathers of the ancient church as the modern Protestant recognizes in the Reformers of the sixteenth century. It was inevitable that the Reformers should respect Basil of Caesarea. He was a great ethical thinker and a man of such moral integrity. He wrote about the Christian life so clearly. Ambrose of Milan could not help but capture the imagination of the Reformers. He was a man of such courage and political ability. Cyril of

Alexandria's commentary on the Gospel of John is such a brilliant exposition of orthodox Christology that when the first generation of Reformers read it, they were thoroughly convinced. Cyril was a great theologian regardless of where and when he lived.

It is now approaching five hundred years since the Reformers did their work and it is becoming very clear that they were great thinkers far beyond the accidents of time and culture which produced them. Luther is far more than a German folk hero. He is far more than a reaction against certain religious abuses of a certain age in the history of the church. Luther is not really explained or explained away by the economics and politics of his day. He gained a very fresh and clear insight into some lasting realities. He perceived the radical nature of God's grace revealed in the death and resurrection of Christ. He perceived the transcendent authority of the Word of God. He clearly perceived the priority of faith in the Christian life. It was because he saw this so clearly and because he wrote about it so clearly that we recognize his leadership in the church. Luther was not alone. In Oecolampadius we recognize a great biblical philologist who had a profound sense of how one interprets Scripture. Oecolampadius helped bring into focus many biblical concepts which had become blurred over the centuries. He was an outstanding patristic scholar who translated for the first time into a Western language a sizable portion of the treasures of Greek Christian literature. In Calvin we recognize a great interpreter of Scripture. It is amazing the way Calvin's biblical commentaries still speak to us today even though biblical research has gone far beyond him. Thomas Manton's sermons on the epistle of James are to this day the most practical sort of instruction on the Christian life. Matthew Henry's commentaries are as popular today as they were when they were first written. In fact few people realize they are getting close to three hundred years old. This is the nature of the classics! They transcend the merely ethnic, the merely national, the merely cultural.

The classics whether in theology or any other field are classics because they are so good. It is a matter of quality. The tradition becomes important when we recognize that what the tradition preserves is important. The way we evaluate the tradition has certain points in common with the way we evaluate great music. Generation after generation listens to Bach simply because his music is so good. We do not listen to his music because it is German or because it is an expression of Baroque culture. The more one studies music the more the genius of Bach becomes clear. The sophisticated craftsmanship of Bach is simply unsurpassed. That Bach is among the greatest of composers is not simply a matter of subjective opinion or mystical experience. He was able to solve problems of harmony and counterpoint with a classic simplicity that amazes the musician of today. The breadth of Bach's genius is illustrated by the great variety in his work. There are the great choral works, the chamber music, the delicate works for harpsichord and the mighty organ works. Another amazing thing about him is the volume of his work. This is typical of a real genius. Bach's genius was not a trickle or an occasional spurt. It was a mighty river constantly flowing in full force. The classics themselves set the standard of quality. We do not really measure the classics; they measure us. It is somewhat the same way with theology.

But to return to the Reformers. Were they really any better than the theologians of any other age? Should we really place them in some sort of Golden Age of theology? By what standard do we give them any more respect than theologians of any other age? These questions are often asked but in fact it is hard not to recognize the genius of the sixteenth-century Reformers. We do not recognize them as great because they lived in a Golden Age and therefore have to be recognized as great. We recognize them as great because they were great! One place we recognize the genius of Luther for example is that he sufficiently mastered both Greek and Hebrew that he was able to do an original translation of both the Old and New Testament which has never been surpassed. That feat alone should win for Luther our abiding respect. Calvin's brilliance is recognized in the many facets of his theological endeavor. He was a most able commentator on Scripture. He was a master of the original languages and an excellent biblical philologist. He was a systematic theologian too. Few theologians have achieved distinction in both fields. In the *Institutes* he treated the whole range of Christian thought. His letters reveal him to have been an excellent pastor. He was a capable preacher as well. It is the quality of Calvin's work which has won him the respect he has enjoyed among theologians ever since the sixteenth century. Again, Luther and Calvin were not alone. Bullinger was a man of enormous ability. Educated at the University of

Cologne in pure *via antiqua* Scholasticism he knew Thomas Aquinas, Bonaventure, and Duns Scotus well. His knowledge of patristic, exegetical, and historical literature was encyclopaedic. He had read everything in his long life. He started out as a child prodigy succeeding Zwingli while he was still twenty-seven years old and for more than forty years he capably directed the Reformation of Zurich securing for it an international influence. It was not simply because the politics of Europe were favorable to the Reformation that it succeeded. The Reformation had very capable leadership. The Reformers were great scholars and men who exercised spiritual leadership of the highest quality. At the center of their reform was a concern for the reform of worship, and they had a profound insight into the nature of worship. That is why we are interested in what they had to say.

The third point we want to make is that we should maintain the tradition because it witnesses to the authority of Scripture. Above all the leadership of both the Fathers and the Reformers is to be found in the fact that they understood Scripture so well. They were *testes veritatis*, that is, witnesses to the truth. It is because the Fathers and the Reformers point us to the Scriptures so unequivocally and open up Scripture so widely that we listen to them.

Just before the beginning of the Reformation when Erasmus published his first edition of the complete works of St. Jerome, he was sure it was going to clear up the theological atmosphere. Jerome was the greatest biblical scholar of the ancient Latin Church. It was he who produced the standard Latin translation of the Bible. He made his translation from the Hebrew Old Testament and the Greek New Testament and he devoted a lifetime to the work. The Christian Humanists of the early sixteenth century who recognized Erasmus as their leader read the enormous nine volume folio edition of the complete works of Jerome with high expectations. Here they had before them the fulfillment of the Christian Humanist ideal. Erasmus in his edition of Jerome was indeed bringing his generation *ad fontes,* he was bringing them to the purest sources of the tradition. The sharpest students of Erasmus, men like Zwingli, Oecolampadius, and Bucer read Jerome, and Jerome pointed them to Scripture. They went further than Erasmus. Zwingli tells us that the ink was hardly dry before he had the first volume under his nose. He read the whole thing with the most careful attention. Jerome opened to him the study of Scripture. When he finished Jerome he realized it was Scripture he had to study.

Erasmus gave Oecolampadius the job of preparing the index volume for his edition of Jerome. Erasmus was a great Latinist and he had also mastered Greek, but he did not know Hebrew; Oecolampadius on the other hand, like Jerome, was a master of all three ancient languages. Erasmus set Oecolampadius at the job of preparing an index of all the Hebrew words discussed by Jerome and then an index of all the Greek words discussed by that master biblical philologist. This work of Oecolampadius opened up modern biblical philology. It became a Rosetta Stone for theologians. The work of Oecolampadius made it possible to see how Jerome, the master of Latin, Greek, and Hebrew, had translated the original biblical words into Latin. It made it possible to discover what those original biblical words really meant. Jerome had a passion for discovering the "Hebrew verity," and from Jerome the Reformers learned the importance of searching out the original Hebrew concepts. No wonder Oecolampadius, Zwingli, and Bullinger rediscovered the meaning of covenant! They had carefully studied Jerome, and Jerome taught them the importance of studying the Hebrew text. Jerome, as Cyril of Alexandria, as John Chrysostom, and as one Father after another, pointed the Reformers to Scripture.

For us as twentieth-century Christians the Reformers are tradition just as the Fathers were tradition for the Reformers. To be sure the Fathers are tradition for us too. If we accept the Fathers and the Reformers as important constituents of our tradition then we need to be interested in them not in themselves but interested in them because of what they point out to us about Scripture. We are interested in what they have to say about how Scripture teaches us to worship.

Reformed theology has always made a very clear distinction between Scripture and tradition. Scripture has authority and tradition has the value of witnessing to that authority. In the *Church Dogmatics* of Karl Barth is a chapter entitled "Authority under the Word." In this chapter he shows how and in what sense tradition witnesses to Scripture. The authority of tradition is secondary, derived from and dependent upon the authority of Scripture. In the last analysis we are not as much concerned with what tradition tells us about worship as we are concerned with what tradition tells us about what Scripture has to say about worship. We are concerned to hear what those great biblical scholars have had to say about worship. Few matters of concern in Reformed worship are merely matters of tradition. Most things we do in worship we do because God has commanded us to do them. It is because of this that we preach the gospel, we praise God in psalms and hymns, we serve God in prayer, we baptize in the name of Christ. Some things we do in worship not so much because they are specifically taught in Scripture but because they are in accordance with Scripture. What is meant by that is that some of the things we do in worship we do because they are demanded by scriptural principles. For example we baptize in the name of the Father, the Son, and the Holy Spirit because this is specifically directed by Scripture. It is on the basis of scriptural principles that before the baptism we offer the Baptismal Invocation asking the Holy Spirit to fulfill inwardly what is promised in the outward sign. The basic acts of worship we perform because they are clearly commanded in Scripture. The ways and means of doing them we try to order according to scriptural principles. When something is not specifically commanded, prescribed, or directed or when there is no scriptural example to guide us in how we are to perform some particular aspect of worship we should try nevertheless to be guided by scriptural principles. As we discover in the first chapter of the *Westminster Confession* such is often the case with the public ordering of worship. In fact one might say that it is the essence of the Reformed tradition that worship should be far more than merely tradition. The *adiaphora*, the indifferent things, are quite appropriately matters of merely human tradition, but the essential elements of worship are those which we do in obedience to the Word of God.

Let us look for a moment at some of the most valuable worship traditions which are at the heart of the heritage of Reformed Protestantism; liturgical traditions which commend themselves to us because they are above all according to Scripture.

1. At the head of the list should certainly be expository preaching. This has always been the glory of Protestant worship. At the present it seems to have fallen on hard days, but it needs to be revived. The fifteen and twenty minute homilies which have become the regular practice in most American Protestant churches today amount to not much more than a surrender of the tradition. Unfortunately, far too few ministers

are equipped to do expository preaching. Even worse, few congregations are willing to give their ministers the time to do expository preaching. To be sure, there should be other kinds of preaching as well. On Sunday evenings it might be well to preach a major series of catechetical sermons each year, but the preaching of the Lord's Day morning should be devoted to expository preaching. Preaching should not be neglected at weddings and funerals. Needless to say, the quality of preaching will have to be improved considerably before we can expect the faithful to support a genuine preaching ministry.

2. Very closely related to expository preaching is the use of *lectio continua*. This was one of the most significant reforms of the sixteenth century resting solidly on the practice of both the synagogue and the ancient church. Nothing could have a more salutary effect on preaching than the regular systematic preaching through of one book of the Bible after another. It gives a great opportunity for both the preacher and the congregation to study the Scriptures. In time many in the congregation will develop the habit of reading along with the preacher and will arrive for worship having studied the passage on which the sermon is to be preached. This kind of preaching needs to be done in a sensitive way, with a recognition of the capacity of the congregation. It also needs to be supported by good Bible study in Sunday school for both children and adults. After several years of using the *lectio continua* the congregation will discover itself to have learned an amazing amount of Scripture.

3. Another excellent Reformed liturgical tradition which needs to be cultivated is the praying of the psalms. The singing of metrical psalms and the responsive reading of the psalms should both be cultivated. There are plenty of excellent versions of metrical psalms which are available. Another way of using the psalms in worship is to have a lector read the text and the congregation sing a three fold Hallelujah or some other antiphon after each stanza.Certainly we should not overlook the use of choral settings of psalms. Here we find a great wealth of material. Psalm settings are available in every conceivable style of music. New arrangements of psalms should always be encouraged. So much has been learned about the psalms in the last few decades that many of us regard psalm study as one of the most fascinating branches of biblical research. Enriched by modern psalm study we need to ap-

proach the praying of the psalms once more. Surely this will do much to deepen the prayer life of the church today.

4. We have spoken several times of the way the Reformed tradition in worship has emphasized a full diet of prayer. This sense for the full range of prayer found implicitly in the Strasbourg and Genevan psalters is elaborated explicitly in the *Westminster Directory*. Here we are specifically told that prayer should include praise, confession, thanksgiving, supplication, and intercession. Today, this appreciation of the varieties of prayer has taken on new interest because of what has been learned about the various genre of the psalms and the different theologies of prayer behind each genre. There are different prayer types in another level. We have pointed out that the *Genevan Psalter* provides for the singing of psalms as prayer, the reading of set prayers, and the use of extemporaneous prayer. Surely the ability to frame prayers appropriate to the occasion has a venerable heritage and it is important to maintain this heritage. The Puritans learned much of great value in regard to the prophetic nature of prayer and in regard to prayer being the work of the Holy Spirit. The literature on prayer, which is quite extensive, needs to be carefully restudied. Extempore prayer, as the Westminster Fathers expressly remind us, takes a great deal of preparation and a deep understanding of the nature of prayer.

5. The first generation of Reformers recovered a number of different aspects of the celebration of the Lord's Supper. In the first place they rediscovered the Supper as a meal. For so long the emphasis had been on the consecrating and sacrificing of the bread and wine. The Reformers put new emphasis on the communion itself, that is on the sharing of the bread and wine by the whole church. They tried to make their celebration look like a real meal. They replaced altars with tables and they used bread which looked like real bread. In many places they actually sat at the table. The Reformers as we have shown recovered a covenantal understanding of the Lord's Supper and here is one of their most valuable contributions. Again, we should point out, advances in biblical theology today enormously enhance the work of the Reformers. Thanks to modern biblical research we can appreciate the work of the Reformers in this field much better than before. The Reformers were going in the right direction when they tried to understand the Lord's Supper as a covenant meal.

6. The appreciation of the Lord's Supper as eucharist which we find particularly in Vermigli and in John Knox also needs to be maintained. John Knox's eucharistic prayer could well serve as a model for a Reformed eucharistic prayer. It is truly a hymnic recounting of the works of creation and redemption. So many eucharistic prayers have been obsessed with walking the tightrope of theological formulation that they have lost the doxological spirit. They have become formulas of doctrine rather than hymns of praise.

7. The epicletic nature of the Lord's Supper needs to be maintained as well. There is real genius in the tradition developed in Strasbourg and Geneva in which the Prayer of Intercession is expanded by a Communion Invocation when the sacrament is celebrated. It is as though the Prayer of Intercession gathers all Christians together about the Lord's Table in much the same way as the High Priestly Prayer of Jesus in the seventeenth chapter of the Gospel of John. In that prayer Jesus prays for the unity of the church, the sanctity of the church and the continuity of the church. Here is where the real epiclesis of the Reformed eucharistic liturgy is to be found. It is in the Prayer of Intercession. A Reformed epiclesis is a prayer for the church. It is a prayer for the consecration of the body of Christ through the work of the Holy Spirit. It is a prayer for the gathering, the uniting, the illumination, and, above all, the sanctifying of the church.

8. The diaconal aspect of the Lord's Supper is an important aspect of the tradition which needs to be clearly expressed in the contemporary Reformed liturgy. The keynote of this part of the service is the post-communion prayer of thanksgiving and dedication. The essence of this part of the service is magnificently expressed by the hymn of Isaac Watts which so often we sing after communion.

> When I survey the wondrous cross
>   On which the Prince of Glory died,
> My richest gain I count but loss,
>   And pour contempt on all my pride.
> . . . .
>
> Were the whole realm of nature mine,
>   That were a present far too small;
> Love so amazing, so divine,
>   Demands my soul, my life, my all.

Likewise the singing of Psalm 116 is appropriate because it makes clear that our giving is thanksgiving. Such texts remind us that our giving of tithes and alms is an act of thanksgiving for our redemption. Surely the fact that this giving of ourselves and our substance comes at the end of the service demonstrates that our charitable works are enabled and empowered by our communion with God. Collecting tithes and alms at the end of the service is a liturgical practice consistent with a theology which emphasizes grace. It is much more in accordance with Scripture than the practice of having an offertory before the communion. This transition from the service of God to the service of the neighbor should be a clear and distinct part of every Reformed communion service.

9. In regard to baptism several features might be singled out. Covenant theology needs to be re-emphasized. (By Covenant theology we do not of course mean any one of the very elaborate systems of theology developed by various seventeenth-century theologians. By Covenant theology we have something much more simple in mind. We are thinking primarily of a recovery of the biblical concept of covenant and a theology of the sacraments which has that in mind.) It is important to understand baptism as a sign of the Covenant. This should be the theology on which we build our baptismal practice. In fact, one can go so far as to say that Covenant theology is Reformed sacramental theology. To understand baptism in terms of the Hellenistic mystery religions may develop dramatic liturgical rites, but these rites will neither be according to Scripture nor Reformed. When baptism is understood in terms of covenant then it is clear that the children of the covenant community should be baptized.

10. Any Reformed celebration of baptism should be very clear in maintaining the unity of the sacrament. There is one baptism for the forgiveness of sins and the gift of the Holy Spirit. No secondary rite, such as anointing, should be introduced which might suggest that those who had been merely baptized with water now needed to receive the gift of the Holy Spirit. The washing of water should be presented as an outward sign of an inward gift of the Holy Spirit.

11. Baptism should be explained as a sign given at the beginning of the Christian life of what happens to us through the whole of the Christian life. As long as we live here on earth we are living out our baptism as we more and more die unto sin and live unto God.

12. Baptism should always entail the teaching of ''all things which I

have commanded you.'' The Reformers were eager to revive the catechetical discipline of the ancient church. They had to adjust this discipline to a church which existed in a society which in name at least was
Christian. They did this well by providing thorough catechetical instruction for children baptized in infancy once those children had achieved
sufficient age to understand basic Christian teaching. Upon completing
this course of instruction the children were admitted to the Lord's Table
on the basis of a profession of faith. This historic Protestant catechetical
discipline does justice to two great biblical truths. It recognizes that
baptism is a sign of entrance into the covenant community and therefore
should be given at the beginning of the Christian life, and it recognizes
that baptism should be accompanied by teaching and a profession of
faith.

13. One aspect of our tradition which particularly needs our attention is the daily service of morning and evening prayer. This needs to be
cultivated both in relation to the service of daily prayer maintained by
Christian families in their homes and in relation to the service of daily
prayer maintained at the church. Today a revival of daily prayer at the
church has become increasingly important because of the great number
of Christians who live alone. Christian prayer is the prayer of the body
of Christ. It is prayer in fellowship with other Christians. For many of
us, single or married, if we are going to pray in the fellowship of other
Christians then the church is the place we are most likely to find that
kind of prayer fellowship. Most singles need more than coffee klatch
fellowship. There are plenty of people who live in families who need
stronger prayer support than they can find at home. It should be in the
context of the daily prayer services that pastoral care should take place.
Let us leave counseling couches to the psychologists and make the
service of daily prayer the heart of our ministry of pastoral care.

14. The Puritans developed the discipline of daily family prayer
with particular insight. They understood the family to be a little church.
The family is a divinely created organism; a reality established by God.
As such it owes worship to God. The maintaining of family prayer
demonstrates the family to have a sacred reality.

15. The greatest single contribution which the Reformed liturgical
heritage can make to contemporary American Protestantism is its sense
of the majesty and sovereignty of God, its sense of reverence, of simple

dignity, its conviction that worship must above all serve the praise of God.

This program for the renewal of worship in American Protestant churches of today may not be just exactly what everyone is looking for. In our evangelistic zeal we are looking for programs that will attract people. We think we have to put honey on the lip of the bitter cup of salvation. It is the story of the wedding of Cana all over again but with this difference. At the crucial moment when the wine failed, we took matters into our own hands and used those five stone jars to mix up a batch of Kool-Aid instead. It seemed like a good solution in terms of our American culture. Unfortunately, all too soon the guests discovered the fraud. Alas! What are we to do now? How can we possibly minister to those who thirst for the real thing? There is but one thing to do, as Mary the mother of Jesus, understood so very well. You remember how the story goes. After presenting the problem to Jesus, Mary turned to the servants and said to them, "Do whatever he tells you." The servants did just that and the water was turned to wine, wine rich and mellow beyond anything they had ever tasted before.

Bibliography of Works on Worship

THE BIBLICAL AND PATRISTIC PERIODS

Achtemeier, Elizabeth. "Overcoming the World: An Exposition of Psalm 6." *Interpretation* XXVIII (1974): 75–88. (This issue of *Interpretation* has a number of excellent articles on the worship of ancient Israel as it is reflected in the psalms.)

Agaesse, Paul. *Saint Augustine, Commentaire de la première épître de S. Jean.* Paris: Editions du Cerf, 1961.

Aland, Kurt. *Did the Early Church Baptize Infants?* Translated by G. R. Beasley-Murray. Philadelphia: Westminster Press, 1963.

Ambrose of Milan. *Des sacrements, Des mystères, Explication du symbole.* Paris: Editions du Cerf, 1961.

Arens, Anton. "Die Psalmen im Gottesdienst des altern Bundes." Trier Theologische Studien, Band 11. Trier: Paulinus Verlag, 1968.

Audet, J. P. *La Didaché: Instructions des Apôtres.* Paris: J. Gabalda, 1958.

Augustine of Hippo. *Sermons pour la Pâque.* Edited by Suzanne Poque. Paris: Editions du Cerf, 1966.

Bauer, Walter. *Der Wortgottesdienst der ältesten Christen.* Tübingen: Mohr, 1930.

Baumgarten, Joseph M. "Sacrifice and Worship Among the Jewish Sectarians of the Dead Sea (Qumran Scrolls)." *Harvard Theological Review* 46 (1953): 141–59.

Baumstark, Anton. *Liturgie comparée: principes et méthodes pour l'étude historique des liturgies chrétiennes.* Third edition, Chevetogne, Belgium: Editions de Chevetogne, 1953.

Baumstark, Anton. *Nichtevangelische syrische Perikopenordnungen des ersten Jahrtausends.* Münster in Westphalia: Aschendorff, 1921.

Baumstark, Anton. *Nocturna laus, Typen früchristlicher Vigilienfeir und ihr Fortleben vor allem im römischen und monastischen ritus.* Münster in Westphalia: Aschendorff, 1967.

Baur, Chrysostomus. *John Chrysostom and His Time*. 2 vols. Translated by M. Gonzaga. Westminster, Maryland: The Newman Press, 1959. (Particularly interesting in regard to the preaching of John Chrysostom.)

Benoit, André. *Le baptême chrétien au second siècle, la théologie des pères*. Paris: Presses Universitaries de France, 1953.

Betz, Johannes. *Die Eucharistie in der Zeit der griechischen Väter*. Freiburg: Herder, 1955.

Beyer, Hermann Wolfgang. *"εὐλογέω." Theologisches Wörterbuch zum neuen Testament* 2, pp. 751–62. Edited by Gerhard Kittle. 8 vols. Stuttgart: W. Kohlhammer, 1933–73.

Beyerlin, Walter. *Die Rettung der Bedrängten in den Feindpsalmen der Einselnen auf institutionelle Zusammenhaug untersucht*. Göttingen: Vandenhoeck und Ruprecht, 1970.

Billerbeck, Paul and Hermann L. Strack. *Kommentar zum neuen Testament aus Talmud und Midrasch*. Third edition. 8 vols. Munich: C. H. Beck, 1961. (See the articles on the celebration of the Passover, on the preaching of the synagogue, and on prayer in volume 4.)

Boobyer, George Henry. "'Thanksgiving' and the 'Glory of God' in Paul." Dissertation, University of Heidelberg, 1929.

Bornkamm, Günther. "Zum Verstandnis des Gottesdienstes bei Paulus in: 'Das Ende des Gesetzes.'" *Beiträge zur evangelischen Theologie* 16 (Munich 1952): 113–32.

Botte, Bernhard. "L'ange du sacrifice et l'épiclèse de la messe romaine au moyenâge." *Recherches de theologié ancienne et médiéval* I (1929).

Botte, Bernhard. *La tradition apostolique de saint Hippolyte*. Münster in Westphalia: Aschendorff, 1963.

Botte, Bernhard, "L'épiclèse de l'anaphore d'Hippolyte." *Recherches de théologie ancienne et médiévale* XIV (1947).

Botte, Bernhard. "L'épiclèse dans les liturgies syriennes orientales." *Sacris erudiri* VI (1954).

Botte, Bernhard. "Les dénomination du dimanche dans la tradition chrétienne." *Le dimanche*. Lex orandi, vol. 39, pp. 7–18. Paris: Editions du Cerf, 1965.

Botte, Bernhard. "Problème de l'anamnèse." *Journal of Ecclesiastical History* V (1954).

Bright, John. "A Prophet's Lament and Its Answer: Jeremiah 15:10–21." *Interpretation* XXVIII (1974): 77–88.

Brown, Raymond E. *The Gospel According to John*. Garden City: Doubleday & Company, Inc., 1970.

Brueggemann, W. "From Hurt to Joy, From Death to Life." *Interpretation* XXVIII (1974): 3–19.

Childs, Brevard S. *The Book of Exodus*. Philadelphia: Westminster Press, 1974.

Childs, Brevard S. *Introduction to the Old Testament as Scripture*. Philadelphia: Fortress Press, 1979.

Childs, Brevard S. *Memory and Tradition in Israel*. London: SCM Press, 1962.

Chirat, H. "Le dimanche dans l'antiquité chrétienne." *Etudes de pastorale liturgique*. Lex orandi, vol. 1. Paris: Editions du Cerf, 1944.

Clerici, Luigi. *Einsammlung der Zerstreuten: liturgiegeschichtliche Untersuchung zur Vor-und Nachgeschichte der Fübitte für die Kirche in Didache 9,4 und 10,3*. Münster in Westphalia: Aschendorff, 1965.

Congar, Yves. "La théologie du dimanche." *Le jour du seigneur*. Liturgical Congress in Lyons, Sept. 1947, pp. 131–80. Paris, 1948.

Congar, Yves. *Le Mystère du Temple*. Paris: Editions du Cerf, 1963.

Connolly, Richard Hugh. *The So-called Egyptian Church Order*. Cambridge: The University Press, 1916.

Conzelmann, H. and W. Zimmerli. "εὐχαριστία." *Theologisches Wörterbuch zum neuen Testament* 9, pp. 349–405. Edited by Gerhard Kittle. 8 vols. Stuttgart: W. Kohlhammer, 1933–73.

Cross, F. L. *St. Cyril of Jerusalem's Lectures on the Christian Sacraments: The Procatechesis and the Five Mystagogical Catecheses*. London: S.P.C.K., 1951.

Cullman, Oscar. *Die ersten christlichen Glaubensbekenntnisse*. Zürich: Evangelischer Verlag, 1943.

Cullmann, Oscar. *Die Tauflehre des neuen Testaments*. Zürich: Zwingli-Verlag, 1948.

Cullmann, Oscar. *Early Christian Worship*. Translated by A. Stewart Todd and James B. Torrance. London: SCM Press, 1953.

Cullman, Oscar. *Sabbat und Sonntag nach dem Johannesevangelium: In memoriam of E. Lohmeyer*. Stuttgart, 1951.

Cullmann, Oscar and F. J. Leenhardt. *Essays on the Lord's Supper*. Richmond: John Knox Press, 1958.

Cyril of Jerusalem. *Catéchèses mystagogues*. Edited by Auguste Piédagnel. Paris: Editions du Cerf, 1966.

Daniélou, Jean. "Le dimanche comme huitieme jour." *Lex orandi*, vol. 39. Paris: Editions du Cerf, 1965.

Daniélou, Jean. "La doctrine patristique du dimanche." *Le jour de seigneur*. Liturgical Congress in Lyons, Sept. 1947, pp. 105–30. Paris, 1948.

Daniélou, Jean. *Etudes d'exégèse judeo-chrétienne*. Paris: Beauchesne et ses fils, 1966.

Daniélou, Jean. *Les figures du Christ dans l'ancien testament "sacramentum futuri."* Paris: Beauchesne et ses fils, 1950.

DeClerck, Paul. *La "prière universalle" dans les liturgies latines anciennes: Temoignages patristiques et textes liturgiques.* Münster in Westphalia: Aschendorff, 1977.

Delling, Gerhard. *"ὕμνοσ-ψαλμος."* *Theologisches Wörterbuch zum neuen Testament* 8, pp. 492–506. Edited by Gerhard Kittle. 8 vols. Stuttgart: W. Kohlhammer, 1933–73.

Delling, Gerhard. *Worship in the New Testament.* Philadelphia: Westminster Press, 1962.

Dix, Gregory. *The Shape of the Liturgy.* London: Dacre Press, 1943.

Dix, Gregory, ed. *The Treatise on the Apostolic Tradition of St. Hippolytus of Rome.* Published for the Church Historical Society. London: S.P.C.K. New York: The Macmillan Company, 1937.

Dodd, Charles Harold. *The Apostolic Preaching and Its Developments.* London: Hodder & Stoughton, 1936.

Dölger, Franz Joseph. "Die Planetenwoche der griechisch-romischen Antike und der christliche Sonntag." *Antike und Christantum* 6, 1941.

Dölger, Franz Joseph. "Sol salutis, Gebet und Gesang im christlichen altertum." *Liturgiegeschichtliche Forschungen,* 4/5. 2 aufl. Münster in Westphalia: Aschendorff, 1952.

Dumaine, H. "Dimanche." *Dictionnaire d'archéologie chrétienne et liturgie* IV (1921): col. 970–94. Paris: Letouzey et Ané.

Elbogen Ismar. *Der jüdische Gottesdienst in seiner geschichtichen Entwicklung.* Hildesheim: Georg Olms, 1962.

Elfers, Heinrich. *Die Kirchenordnung Hippolyts von Rom.* Paderborn: Bonifacius-druckerei, 1938.

Fischer, Balthazar. "Die Psalmen frömigkeit der Regula S. Benedictli." *Liturgie und Mönchtum: Laacher Hefter,* vol. 4, 1949.

Fischer, Balthazar. *Die Psalmen-Frömmigkeit der Martyrerkirche.* Freiburg: Herder, 1949.

Funk, F. X., ed. *Didascalia et Constitutiones apostolorum.* 2 vols. Paderborn: Ferdinand Schoening Library, 1905.

Gavin, Frank Stanton. *The Jewish Antecedents of the Christian Sacraments.* London: S.P.C.K. 1933.

Greeven, Heinrich. *Gebet und Eschatologie im neuen Testament.* Gütersloh: Bertelsman, 1931.

Greeven, Heinrich and Johannes Herrman. "εὔχομαι." *Theologisches Wörter-buch zum neuen Testament* 2, pp. 774–808. Edited by Gerhard Kittle. 8 vols. Stuttgart: W. Kohlhammer, 1933–73.

Hanssens, Jean Michel. *Nature et genèse de l'office de matines*. Rome: Gregorian University Press, 1962.

Harkins, P. W. *St. John Chrysostom: Baptismal Instruction*. Westminster, Maryland: The Newman Press, 1963.

Hauck, Friedrich. "κοινωνία." *Theologisches Wörterbuch zum neuen Testament* 3, pp. 789–810. Edited by Gerhard Kittle. 8 vols. Stuttgart: W. Kohlhammer, 1933–73.

Hedegord, David. *Seder R. Amram Gaon*. Lund: Ph. Lindstedts, 1951.

Heiler, Friedrich. *Das Gebet, eine religionsgeschichtliche und religionspsychologische Untersuchung*. 4th ed. Munich: Verlag von Ernst Reinhardt, 1921.

Idelsohn, Abraham Zebi. *Jewish Liturgy and Its Development*. New York: Schocken Books, 1960.

Idelsohn, Abraham Zebi. *Jewish Music in Its Historical Development*. New York: Tudor Publishing Company, 1944.

Jeremias, Joachim. "Das tägliche Gebet im Leben Jesu und in der ältesten Kirche." *Abba: Studien zur neutestamentlichen Theologie und Zeit-geschichte*. Göttingen: Vandenhoeck und Ruprecht, 1966.

Jeremias, Joachim. *The Eucharistic Words of Jesus*. Translated by Norman Perrin. Philadelphia: Fortress Press, 1977.

Jeremias, Joachim. *Infant Baptism in the First Four Centuries*. Translated by David Cairns. Philadelphia: Westminster Press, 1960.

Jungmann, Joseph A. "Beginnt die Christliche Woche mit Sonntag?" *Zeit-schrift zur Kirche und Theologie* 55 (1931).

Jungmann, Joseph A. *Die Stellung Christi im liturgischen Gebet*. 2nd edition. Münster in Westphalia: Aschendorff, 1962.

Jungmann, Joseph A. *The Early Liturgy to Gregory the Great*. Translated by Francis A. Brunner. Notre Dame: The University of Notre Dame Press, 1959.

Jungmann, Joseph A. *The Mass of the Roman Rite*. Translated by Francis A. Brunner. 2 vols. New York: Berziger, 1951–55.

Keet, C. C. *A Liturgical Study of the Psalter*. New York: The Macmillan Company, 1928.

Kelly, J. N. D. *Early Christian Doctrines*. Revised edition. San Francisco: Harper & Row, 1978.

Kraus, Hans-Joachim. *Gottesdienst in Israel*. 2nd edition. Munich: Chr. Kaiser, 1962.

Kraus, Hans-Joachim. *Psalmen*. 2nd edition. 2 vols. Neukirchen: Neukirchener Verlag, 1961.

Kretschmar, Georg. "Die Geschichte des Taufgottesdienstes in der alten Kirche." *Leiturgia: Handbuch des evangelisches Gottesdienstes,* vol. 5. Edited by Karl Ferdinand Müller and Walter Blankenburg. Kassel: Johannes Stauda-Verlag, 1954.

Kucharek, Casimir. *The Sacramental Mysteries: A Byzantine Approach*. Allendale, N. J.: Alleluia Press, 1976.

Kunze, G. "Die gottesdienstliche Zeit." *Leiturgia: Handbuch des evangelischen Gottesdienstes,* vol. I. Edited by Karl Ferdinand Müller and Walter Blankenburg. Kassel: Johannes Stauda-Verlag, 1954.

Lampe, G. W. H. *The Seal of the Spirit*. 2nd edition. London: S.P.C.K., 1967.

Leipoldt, Johannes. *Der Gottesdienst der ältesten Kirche jüdisch? griechisch? christlich?* Leipzig: Dörffling & Franke, 1937.

Leo the Great. *Sermons*. Edited by Jean Leclerq and René Dolle. 3 vols. Paris: Editions du Cerf, 1957–64.

Lietzmann, Hans. *Messe und Herrenmahl*. Bonn: A. Marcus und E. Weber's Verlag, 1926.

Lohmeyer, Ernst. *Das Vater Unser*. Göttingen: Vandenhoeck und Ruprecht, 1946.

Lohmeyer, Ernst. *Kultus und Evangelium*. Göttingen: Vandenhoeck und Ruprecht, 1942.

Lohse, E. "Jesu Worte über den Sabbat." Judentum-Urchristentum-Kirche: Festschrift für J. Jeremias zum 60 Geburtstag. *Beihefte zur Zeitschrift für die neutestamentliche Wissenschaft* 26 (1960).

Lohse, E. "σάββατον." *Theologisches Wörterbuch des neuen Testament* 7, pp. 1–30. Edited by Gerhard Kittle. 8 vols. Stuttgart: W. Kohlhammer, 1933–73.

Macdonald, Alexander B. *Christian Worship in the Primitive Church*. Edinburgh: T. & T. Clark, 1934.

Mann, Jacob. *The Bible as Read and Preached in the Old Synagogue*. 2 vols. New York: KTAV Publishing House, Inc., 1971.

Martimort, A. G., ed. *L'église en prières: Introduction à la liturgie*. Paris: Tournai, 1961.

Mateos, Juan. *De officio matutino et vespertino in ritibus orientalibus*. Rome: Athenaeum Sancti Anselmi, 1969.

Menoud, Philippe. "Les Actes des Apôtres et l'Eucharistie." *Revue d'histoire et de philosophie religieuses* 33 (1953): 21–36.

Mingana, A. *Commentary of Theodore of Mopsuestia on the Lord's Prayer and on the Sacraments of Baptism and the Eucharist.* Cambridge: The University Press, 1933.

Moeller, Bernd. *Johannes Zwick und die Reformation in Konstanz.* Quellen und Forschungen zur Reformationsgeschichte, vol. 28. Gütersloh: Gerd Mohn, 1961.

Moore, George Foot. *Judaism in the First Centuries of the Christian Era.* 2 vols. New York: Schocken Books, 1971.

Moule, C. F. D. *Worship in the New Testament.* Richmond: John Knox Press, 1967.

Mowinckel, Sigmund. *The Psalms in Israel's Worship.* 2 vols. New York: Abingdon Press, 1962.

Nettl, Paul. *Luther and Music.* Translated by Frida Best and Ralph Wood. Philadelphia: Muhlenberg Press, 1948.

Neunheuser, Burkhard. *Baptism and Confirmation.* Translated by John J. Hughes. New York: Herder, 1964.

Oesterley, W. O. E. *The Jewish Background of the Christian Liturgy.* Gloucester, Mass.: Peter Smith, 1965.

Old, Hughes Oliphant. "The Service of Daily Prayer in the Primitive Christian Church—A Study of Acts 4:23–31." *Communal and Personal Prayer: A Resource Document.* New York: Advisory Council on Discipleship and Worship of the United Presbyterian Church, 1980.

Pedersen, Johannes. *Israel: Its Life and Culture.* 4 vols. London: Oxford University Press, 1959.

Petuchowski, Jakob J., ed. *Contributions to the Scientific Study of Jewish Liturgy.* New York: KTAV Publishing House, Inc., 1970.

Pierik, Marie. *The Psalter in the Temple and the Church.* Washington, D.C.: The Catholic University of America Press, 1957.

Quell, Gottfried and Johannes Behm. "$\delta\iota\alpha\theta\eta\kappa\eta$." *Theologische Wörterbuch zum neuen Testament* 2, pp. 105–37. Edited by Gerhard Kittle. 8 vols. Stuttgart: W. Kohlhammer, 1933–73.

Rabinowitz, Louis. "Does Midrash Tillim Reflect the Triennial Cycle of Psalms?" *The Jewish Quarterly Review* XXVI (1935–36): 349–68.

Regan, F. A. "Diés dominica and diés solis. The Beginnings of the Lord's Day in Christian Antiquity." Ph.D. dissertation, Washington, 1961.

Reichke, Bo Ivar. *Diakonie, Festfreude und Zelos.* Uppsala: A.–B. Lundequistska Bokhandeln, 1951.

Richardson, Cyril C. "The Date and Setting of the Apostolic Tradition of Hippolytus." *Anglican Theological Review* XXX (1948): 38–44.

Roetzer, W. *Des heilige Augustinus Schriften als liturgiegeschichtliche Quelle*. Munich: M. Hueber, 1930.

Rordorf, Willy, et al. *The Eucharist of the Early Christians*. Translated by Matthew J. O'Connell. New York: Pueblo Publishing Company, 1978.

Rordorf, Willy. *Sunday*. Translated by A. A. K. Graham. Philadelphia: Westminster Press, 1968.

Schlier, Heinrich. *Die Verkündigung in Gottesdienst der Kirche*. Cologne: J. P. Bachem, 1953.

Schnackenburg, Rudolf. *Baptism in the Thought of St. Paul*. Translated by George R. Beasley-Murray. Oxford: Basil Blackwell, 1964.

Schweizer, Eduard. *The Lord's Supper According to the New Testament*. Translated by James M. Davis. Philadelphia: Fortress Press, 1967.

Shepherd, Massey H., Jr. *The Paschal Liturgy and the Apocalypse*. Richmond: John Knox Press, 1960.

Srawley, J. H. *The Early History of the Liturgy*. Cambridge: The University Press, 1947.

Taft, Robert F. *The Great Entrance: A History of the Transfer of Gifts and Other Preanaphoral Rites of the Liturgy of St. John Chrysostom*. Orientalia Christiana Analecta 200 Rome: Pontificium Institutum Studiorum Orientalium, 1975.

Turck, André. *Evangélisation et catéchese aux deux premiers siècles*. Paris: Editions du Cerf, 1962.

Vermès, Géza. "Pre-Mishnaic Jewish Worship and the Phylacteries from the Dead Sea." *Vetus Testamentum*, vol. 9, pp. 65–72. Leiden: E. J. Brill, 1959.

von der Goltz, Eduard Freiherr. *Das Gebet der ältesten Christenheit*. Leipzig: J. C. Hinrichs'sche Buchhandlung, 1901.

Wainwright, Geoffrey. *Doxology: The Praise of God in Worship, Doctrine and Life*. New York: Oxford University Press, 1980.

Wainwright, Geoffrey. *Eucharist and Eschatology*. New York: Oxford University Press, 1981.

Watteville, Jean de. *Le sacrifice dans les textes eucharistiques des premiers siècles*. Paris: Delachaux & Niestlé, 1966.

Wellesz, Egon. *A History of Byzantine Music and Hymnography*. 2nd edition. Oxford: Clarendon Press, 1962.

Werner, Eric. "The Doxology in Synagogue and Church." *Hebrew Union College Annual* 19 (1945/46): 275–351.

Werner, Eric. *The Sacred Bridge*. New York: Schocken Books, 1970.

Westermann, Claus. "The Role of Lament in the Theology of the Old Testament." *Interpretation* XXVIII (1974): 20–38.

White, James F. *Introduction to Christian Worship.* Nashville: Abingdon, 1980.

White, James F. *Sacraments as God's Self Giving.* Nashville: Abingdon, 1983.

Willis, Geoffrey G. *St. Augustine's Lectionary.* London: Published for the Alcuin Club by S.P.C.K., 1962.

Winkler, Gabriele. "The Original Meaning and Implications of the Prebaptismal Anointing." *Worship* 52 (1978): 24–45.

Zahn, Theodor von. *Geschichte des Sonntags, vornehmlich in der alten Kirche.* Hannover: C. Meyer, 1878.

Zunz, Leopold. *Die gottesdienstlichen Vorträge der Jüden, historisch entwickelt.* Berlin: A. Asher, 1832.

THE REFORMATION AND PURITAN PERIODS

Alexander, J. Neil. "Luther's Reform of the Daily Office." *Worship* 57: 348–60.

Althaus, Paul, *The Theology of Martin Luther.* English translation by Robert C. Schultz. Philadelphia: Fortress Press, 1966.

Anderson, Marvin Walter. *Peter Martyr: A Reformer in Exile (1542–1562).* Nieuwkoop: B. de Graaf, 1975.

Balke, Willem. *Calvin and the Anabaptist Radicals.* Translated by William Heynen. Grand Rapids: William B. Eerdmans, 1981.

Barth, Karl. *La prière d'après les catéchismes de la reformation.* Neuchâtel: Delachaux et Niestlé, 1953.

Battles, Ford Lewis and Stanley Tagg. *The Piety of John Calvin.* Grand Rapids: Baker Book House, 1978.

Baxter, Richard. *A Christian Directory.* THE PRACTICAL WORKS OF THE REV. RICHARD BAXTER, vols. III, IV, and V. Edited by William Orme. 23 vols. London: James Duncan, 1830.

Baxter, Richard. *Christian Ecclesiastics.* THE PRACTICAL WORKS OF THE REV. RICHARD BAXTER, vol. V. Edited by William Orme. 23 vols. London: James Duncan, 1830.

Baxter, Richard. *Paraphrase on the Psalms of David in Metre, with Other Hymns.* London: Printed for Richard Baldwin, 1692.

Baxter, Richard. *The Reformed Liturgy.* THE PRACTICAL WORKS OF THE REV. RICHARD BAXTER, vol. XV. Edited by William Orme. 23 vols. London: James Duncan, 1830.

Beyer, Ulrich. *Abendmahl und Messe Sinn und Recht der 80, Frage des heidelberger Katechismus*. Neukirchen: Erziehungsverein, 1965.

Bosshard, S. N. *Zwingli, Erasmus, Cajetan: Die Eucharistie als zeichen der Einheit*. Wiesbaden: Steiner, 1978.

Bovet, Felix. *Histoire du psautier des églises réformées*. Paris: Grossart Libraire, 1872.

Bruce, Robert. *The Mystery of the Lord's Supper*. Translated and edited by Thomas F. Torrance. Richmond: John Knox Press, 1958.

Bucer, Martin. *Bericht auss der heyligen geschrift von der recht gottseligen anstellung und hausshaltung Christlicher gemeyn.* . . . Strasbourg: Matthias Apiarius, 1534. Reprint of the German text in *Martin Bucer's Deutsche Schriften*, vol. 5. Gütersloh: Gerd Mohn, 1978.

Bucer, Martin. *Deutsche Schriften*. Edited by Robert Stupperich. 6 vols. to date. Gütersloh: Gerd Mohn, 1960–.
   (Of special interest are Bucer's proposals to the city council regarding liturgical reforms, vol. 2, pp. 423–558; Bucer's treatment of liturgical subjects in the Confessio Tetrapolitana, vol. 3; Bucer's proposals for liturgical reform in the city of Ulm, vol. 4 and the Hessian church order in vol. 7.)

Bucer, Martin. *Grund und Ursach auss gotlicher schrifft der neuwerungen.* . . . Strasbourg: Wolfgang Kopfel, 1524. Reprint in *Martin Bucer's Deutsche Schriften*, vol. 1. Gütersloh: Gerd Mohn, 1960.

Bucer, Martin. *Psalmorum libri quinque ad Hebraicam veritatem traducti et summa fide.* . . . Geneva: Robertus Stephanus, 1554.
   (This work is particularly important for understanding the Reformed theology of praise and prayer.)

Bucer, Martin. "Psalter with Complete Church Practice: Strasbourg, 1539." English translation in Bard Thompson, *Liturgies of the Western Church*. Cleveland, Ohio: The World Publishing Company, 1961.
   (For the original text of various editions of the Strasbourg Psalter from 1524–37, see Friedrich Hubert, editor, *Die Strassburger liturgische Ordnungen*.)

Bucer, Martin. *Quid de baptismate*. Strasbourg: Matthew Apiarius, 1533.

Bucer, Martin. *A Treatise: How Almose Ought to Be Distributed*. Photo-reprint of the 1557 edition. Norwood, N. J.: W. J. Johnson, 1976.

Bullinger, Henry. *The Decades*. 5 vols. Translated by H. I. Edited for the Parker Society by Thomas Harding. Cambridge: The University Press, 1849. Photoreproduction. New York: The Johnson Reprint Company, 1968.
   (Of particular interest are the sermons on prayer, on the ministry of the Word, and on the sacraments.)

Bullinger, Henry. *De origine erroris in negocio eucharistiae, ac missae, per Heinrychum Bullingerum.* Basel: Thomas Wolff. 1528.
(This work has been called the first attempt at Dogmengeschicte. It gives important insights into the earliest Reformed understanding of the Lord's Supper.)

Bullinger, Henry. *Von dem vnuerschamptem fräfel.* . . . Zürich: Christoffel Froschouer, 1531.
(One of the most important documents on the Reformed understanding of baptism.)

Calvin, John. *Commentary on the Book of Psalms.* Translated by James Anderson. Grand Rapids: W. B. Eerdmans, 1963.
(For some time the preface to this commentary has been recognized as an important statement concerning Calvin's personal life. The text of the commentary, however, gives us equally important insights into Calvin's theology of worship.)

Calvin, John. *Institutes of the Christian Religion.* Edited by John T. McNeill. Translated by Ford Lewis Battles. THE LIBRARY OF CHRISTIAN CLASSICS, vols. XX & XXI. Philadelphia: Westminster Press, 1960.
(See particularly his explanation of the first four commandments, the chapter on prayer, and the chapters on the sacraments.)

Calvin, John. *Opera selecta,* vol. II. Edited by Petrus Barth and Dora Scheuner. Munich: Ch. Kaiser, 1952.

Calvin, John. *Sermons on the Ten Commandments.* Edited and translated by Benjamin W. Farley. Grand Rapids: Baker Book House, 1980.
(This collection of sermons is a good example of Calvin as preacher.)

Calvin, John. *Theological Treatises.* 3 vols. Translated by J. K. S. Reid. Philadelphia: Westminster Press, 1954.
(See particularly the Form of Prayers and the Short Treatise on the Lord's Supper.)

Capito, Wolfgang. "Brief an den Prediger . . . Leonhard von Liechtenstein. Uber das Buch vom Sabbath von Oswald Glait." *Elsass,* vol. 1. Edited by Manfred Krebs and Hans Georg Rott. Quellen zur Geschichte der Täufer, vol. VII. Gütersloh: Gerd Mohn, 1959.

Capito, Wolfgang. "De pueris instituendis ecclesiae Argentinensis." Strasbourg: Isagoge, 1527. *Monumenta Germaniae Paedagogica* 23, pp. 76–141.

Capito, Wolfgang. *Was mann halten soll von der spaltung zwischen Martin Luther und Andreas Carolstadtt.* Strasbourg: Wolff Kopphel, 1524.

Charnock, Stephen. *The Works of the Late Rev. Stephen Charnock.* 9 vols. London: Printed for Baynes, Paternoster Row, 1815.

Corda, Salvatore. *Veritas Sacramenti: A Study in Vermigli's Doctrine of the Lord's Supper.* Zürich: Theologische Verlag, 1975.

Cotton, John. *Singing Psalmes a Gospel Ordinance.* London: Printed by M. S. for Hannah Allen, 1647.

Cotton, John. *The True Constitution of a Particular Visible Church.* London: Printed for Samuel Satterthwaite, 1642.

Cotton, John. *The Way of the Churches of Christ in New England.* London: Printed by M. Simmons, 1645.

Davies, Horton. *Worship and Theology in England.* 5 vols. Princeton: Princeton University Press, 1965–75.

Davies, Horton. *The Worship of the English Puritans.* Glasgow: Dacre Press, 1948.

Dugmore, C. W. *Eucharistic Doctrine from Hooker to Waterland.* London, S.P.C.K., 1942.

Farel, William. *De la sainte cene de nostre seigneur Iesus et de son Testament confirme par sa mort et passion. . . .* Geneva: Jehan Crespin, 1553.

Farel, William. *Du vray usage de la croix de Iesus Christ.* Reprint edition. Geneva: J. G. Fick, 1865.

Farel, William. *La Manière et Fasson.* Neuchâtel: Pierre de Vingle, 1533. Reprint edition edited by Jean-Guillaume Baum. Strasbourg: Treuttel et Wurtz, 1859.

Farner, Oskar. *Huldrych Zwingli.* 4 vols. Zürich: Zwingli-Verlag, 1943–60. (Of particular interest is the chapter on Zwingli's preaching.)

Gagnebin, Bernard. "L'Histoire des Manuscrits des Sermons de Calvin." Supplementa Calviniana. Sermons inédits. Vol. 2, pp. xiv–xxviii.

Gérold, Théodore. *Les plus anciennes melodies de l'église protestante de Strasbourg et leurs auteurs.* Paris: F. Alcan, 1928.

Grötzinger, Eberhard. *Luther und Zwingli: die Kritik an der mittelalterlichen Lehre von der Messe-als wurzel des Abendmahlsstreites.* Zürich, Cologne and Gütersloh: Benzinger Verlag and Verlaghaus Gerd Mohn, 1980.

Henry, Matthew. *A Church in the House.* THE COMPLETE WORKS OF THE REV. MATTHEW HENRY. Edinburgh: A. Fullarton and Company, 1855. Reprint. Grand Rapids: Baker Book House, 1979.

Henry, Matthew. *The Communicant's Companion.* THE COMPLETE WORKS OF THE 'REV. MATTHEW HENRY, vol. 1, pp. 284–412. Edinburgh: A. Fullarton and Company, 1855. Reprint. Grand Rapids: Baker Book House, 1979.

Henry, Matthew. THE COMPLETE WORKS OF THE REV. MATTHEW HENRY. Edinburgh: A. Fullarton and Company, 1855. Reprint. Grand Rapids: Baker Book House, 1979.

Henry, Matthew. *Directions for Daily Communion with God.* THE COMPLETE WORKS OF THE REV. MATTHEW HENRY, vol. 1, pp. 198–247. Edinburgh:

A. Fullarton and Company, 1855. Reprint. Grand Rapids: Baker Book House, 1979.

Henry, Matthew. *Family Hymns: Gathered Mostly Out of the Translations of David's Psalms.* THE COMPLETE WORKS OF THE REV. MATTHEW HENRY, vol. 1, pp. 413–43. Edinburgh: A. Fullarton and Company, 1855. Reprint. Grand Rapids: Baker Book House, 1979.

Henry, Matthew. *A Method for Prayer.* THE COMPLETE WORKS OF THE REV. MATTHEW HENRY, vol. 2, pp. 1–95. Edinburgh: A. Fullarton and Company, 1855. Reprint. Grand Rapids: Baker Book House, 1979.

Hubert, Friedrich, ed. *Die Strassburger liturgischen Ordnungen im Zeitalter der Reformation.* Göttingen: Vandenhoeck und Ruprecht, 1900.

Jacobs, Elfriede. *Die Sakramentslehre Wilhelm Farels.* Zürich: Theologischer Verlag, 1978.

Jenny, Markus. *Die Einheit des Abendmahlsgottesdienstes bei den elsassischen und schweizerischen Reformatoren.* Zürich: Zwingli Verlag, 1968.

Jenny, Markus. *Geschichte des deutschschweizerischen evangelischen Gesangbuches im 16 jahrhundert.* Basel: Bärenreiter, 1962.

Jensen, Robert W. *Visible Words: The Interpretation and Practice of Christian Sacraments.* Philadelphia: Fortress Press, 1978.

Kingdon, Robert M. "Calvinism and Social Welfare." *Calvin Theological Journal* 17 (1982): 212–30.

Kittelson, James M. "Martin Bucer and the Sacramentarian Controversy: The Origins of His Policy of Concord." *Archiv für Reformationsgeschicte* 64 (1973): 166–83.

Knappen, M. M. *Tudor Puritanism.* Chicago: The University of Chicago Press, 1970.

(See particularly the discussions on the troubles at Frankfort, the doctrine of ceremonies, and the Vestiarian Controversy.)

Knox, John. *The Works of John Knox.* Edited by David Laing. 6 vols. Edinburgh: James Thin, 1895. Reprinted. New York: AMS Press, Inc., 1966.

Knox, John. *The Book of Common Order: Or the Form of Prayers, and Ministrations of the Sacraments, etc. Approved and Received by the Church of Scotland, 1564.* THE WORKS OF JOHN KNOX, vol. 6, pp. 275–334. New York: AMS Press, Inc., 1966.

Knox, John. *The Form of Prayers and Ministrations of the Sacraments, etc. Used in the English Congregation at Geneva, 1556.* THE WORKS OF JOHN KNOX, vol. 4, pp. 141–213. New York: AMS Press, Inc., 1966.

Knox, John. *A Narrative of the Proceedings and Troubles of the English Congregation at Frankfurt on the Maine, 1554–1555.* THE WORKS OF JOHN KNOX, vol. 4, pp. 1–68. New York: AMS Press, 1966.

Knox, John. *Prayers (Edinburgh 1564)*. THE WORKS OF JOHN KNOX, vol. 6, pp. 343–80. New York: AMS Press, Inc., 1966.

Lamb, John Alexander. *The Psalms in Christian Worship*. London: The Faith Press, 1962.

Leith, John H. *Assembly at Westminster: Reformed Theology in the Making*. Richmond: John Knox Press, 1973.

Leith, John H. *Introduction to the Reformed Tradition: A Way of Being the Christian Community*. Revised edition. Atlanta: John Knox Press, 1981.

Locher, Gottfried Wilhelm. *Die zwinglische Reformation im Rahmen der europäischen Kirchengischichte*. Göttingen: Vandenhoeck and Ruprecht, 1979.

Locher, Gottfried Wilhelm. *Im Geist und in der Warheit: die reformatorische Wendung im Gottesdienst in Zürich*. Neukirchen: Buchhandlung der Erziehungsverein, Vandenhoeck und Ruprecht, 1957.

Luther, Martin. *The Babylonian Captivity of the Church*. Translated by A. T. W. Steinhaeuser and revised by Frederick C. Ahrens and Abdel Rose Wentz. LUTHER'S WORKS, vol. 36. Edited by Helmut T. Lehman. Philadelphia: Fortress Press, 1959.

Luther, Martin. *The German Mass and Order of Service, 1526*. Translated by Augustinus Steimle. Revised by Ulrich S. Leupold. LUTHER'S WORKS, vol. 53, pp. 51–90. Edited by Helmut T. Lehman. Philadelphia: Fortress Press, 1965.

Luther, Martin. *An Order of Mass and Communion for the Church at Wittenberg, 1523*. Translated by Paul Z. Strodach. Revised by Ulrich S. Leupold. LUTHER'S WORKS, vol. 53, pp. 15–40. Edited by Helmut T. Lehman. Philadelphia: Fortress Press, 1965.

Luther, Martin. *The Order of Baptism, 1523*. Translated by Paul Z. Strodach. Revised by Ulrich S. Leupold. LUTHER'S WORKS, vol. 53, pp. 95–103. Edited by Helmut T. Lehman. Philadelphia: Fortress Press, 1965.

Luther, Martin. *The Order of Baptism Newly Revised, 1526*. Translated by Paul Z. Strodach. Revised by Ulrich S. Leupold. LUTHER'S WORKS, vol. 53, pp. 106–09. Edited by Helmut T. Lehman. Philadelphia: Fortress Press, 1965.

Marot, Clément. *Les psaumes de Clément Marot*. Edited by S. J. Lenselink. Assen: Van Gorcum, 1969.

McDonnell, Kilian. *John Calvin: The Church and the Eucharist*. Princeton: Princeton University Press, 1967.

McLelland, J. C. *The Visible Words of God: An Exposition of the Sacramental Theology of Peter Martyr Vermigli*. Grand Rapids: William B. Eerdmans, 1958.

McMillan, William. *The Worship of the Scottish Reformed Church: 1550–1638*. London: James Clarke and Company, 1931.

M'Crie, Thomas. *The Life of John Knox.* Glasgow: Free Presbyterian Publications, 1976.

Mulhaupt, Erwin. *Die Predigt Calvins, ihre Geschichte, ihre Form und ihre religiösen Grundgedanken.* Berlin: W. de Gruyter, 1931.

Müller, Johannes. *Martin Bucers Hermeneutik.* Quellen und Forschungen zur Reformationsgeschichte, vol. 32. Gütersloh: Gerd Mohn, 1965.

Neuser, W. H. *Die reformatorische Wende bei Zwingli.* Neukirchen: Buchhandlung der Erziehungsverein, 1957.

Oecolampadius, John. *Antwort auff Balthasar Huobmeiers buchlëin wider der Predicanten gespräch zuo Basel, von dem Kindertauff.* Basel: Andreas Cratander, 1527.

Oecolampadius, John. *Apologetica Ioann. Oecolampadii de dignitate eucharistiae . . . Antisyngramma.* Zürich: Christoffel Froschauer, 1526.

Oecolampadius, John. *De genuina verborum Domini: Hoc est corpus meum iuxta vetustissimos authores expositione liber.* Strasbourg: s.n., 1525.

Oecolampadius, John. *De risu pascalis Oecolampadi ad V. Capitonem theologum epistola apologetica.* Basel: J. Froben, 1518.

Oecolampadius, John. *Ein gesprech etlicher predicanten zuo Basel, gehalten mit etlichen bekennern des widertauffs.* Basel: Valentine Curione, 1525.

Oecolampadius, John. *Form und gstalt wie das Herren Nachtmal, der kinder Tauff, der Kranken haymsuochung, zuo Basel gebraucht und gehalten werden.* Basel: Thomas Wolff, 1526.

Oecolampadius, John. *Vnderrichtung von dem Widertauff, von der Oberkeit und von dem Eyd. . . .* Basel: Andreas Cratander, 1527.

Old, Hughes Oliphant. "Bullinger and the Scholastic Works on Baptism: A Study in the History of Christian Worship." *Heinrich Bullinger, 1504–1575, Gesammelte Aufsätze zum 400. Todestag.* Edited by Ulrich Gabler and Erland Herkenrath. 2 vols. Zürich: Theologischer Verlag, 1975.

Old, Hughes Oliphant. "Daily Prayer in the Reformed Church of Strasbourg, 1523–1530." *Worship,* L11 (1978): pp. 121–38.

Old, Hughes Oliphant. "The Homiletics of John Oecolampadius and the Sermons of the Greek Fathers." *Communio Sanctorum. Melánges offèrt á Jean–Jacques von Allmen.* Edited by A. de Pury. Geneva: Labor et Fides, 1982.

Old, Hughes Oliphant. *The Patristic Roots of Reformed Worship.* Zürcher Beiträge zur Reformationsgeschichte. Zürich: Theologischer Verlag, 1975.

Old, Hughes Oliphant. "The Reformed Daily Office: A Puritan Perspective." *Reformed Liturgy and Music* XII, 4 (1978): 9–18.

Owen, John. *The Works of John Owen.* 16 vols. Edited by William H. Goold. Reprint of the Johnstone & Hunter edition, 1850–53. Edinburgh: Banner of Truth Trust, 1976.
> (Owen represents the left wing of the Puritan Movement. His thought did much to shapte the liturgical practice of later Anglo-Saxon Protestants.)

Owen, John. "A Brief Instruction in the Worship of God." *The Works of John Owen.* Vol. 15. Edited by William H. Goold. Edinburgh: T. & T. Clark, 1862.

Owen, John. "A Discourse Concerning Liturgies and Their Imposition." *The Works of John Owen.* Vol. 15. Edited by William H. Goold. Reprint of Johnstone & Hunter edition, 1850–53. Edinburgh: Banner of Truth Trust, 1976.

Owen, John. *A Discourse of the Work of the Holy Spirit in Prayer.* (*1662*). OPERA. Edited by Russell. London: 1826. Also reprinted in The Works of John Owen, vol. 4. Edited by William H. Goold. Edinburgh: Banner of Truth Trust, 1976.

Parker, T. H. L. *The Oracles of God: An Introduction to the Preaching of John Calvin.* London: Lutterworth Press, 1947.

Patrick, Millar. *Four Centuries of Scottish Psalmody.* London: Oxford University Press, 1949.

Perkins, William. *The Art of Prophesying or a Treatise Concerning the Sacred and Only True Manner and Method of Preaching.* London: F. Kyngston for E. Edgar, 1607.
> (Perkins was one of the most influential Calvinist theologians of his day. He was a creative thinker and his ideas on worship had great influence.)

Perkins, William. *A Discourse Concerning the Gift of Prayer.* London: Printed by T. M. for Samuell Gellibrand, 1655.

Perkins, William. *Exposition of the Lord's Prayer.* London: John Lagatt, 1626.

Perkins, William. *A Faithful and Plaine Exposition Upon the First Two Verses of the Second Chapter of Zephaniah.* London: T. Creele for W. Welby, 1605.
> (This is in effect a work on the theology of worship.)

Perkins, William. *The Work of William Perkins.* Edited by Ian Breward. Appleford: The Sutton Courtenay Press, 1970.

Peter, Rodolphe. "L'Homiletique de Calvin." *Supplementa Calviniana. Sermon inédits.* Vol. 2, pp. xlix–lxi.

Peter, Rodolphe. "Rhetorique et Predication selon Calvin." *Revue d'histoire et de philosophie religieuses,* v. 55 (1975), pp. 249–72.

Preston, John. *Grace to the Humble as Preparation to Receive the Sacrament.* London: Thomas Cotes, 1639.

Preston, John. *The New Covenant, or the Saint's Portion.* London: J. Dawson for Nicholas Bourne, 1630.

Preston, John. *A Preparation to the Lord's Supper: Preached in Three Sermons.* London: John Dawson, 1638.

Preston, John. *The Saints Daily Exercise.* London: W. I. & Nicholas Bourne, 1629. Reprinted by Norwood, N. J.: Walter J. Johnson, 1976.
(An important work on the discipline of daily prayer.)

Proctor, Francis. *A New History of the Book of Common Prayer.* Revised and rewritten by Walter Howard Frere. London: Macmillan, 1949.

Reed, Luther D. *The Lutheran Liturgy.* Philadelphia: Fortress Press, 1947.

Richardson, Cyril C. *Zwingli and Cranmer on the Eucharist.* Evanston: Seabury-Western Theological Seminary, 1949.

Rous, Francis. *The Psalms of David Set in Meter, Approved by the Westminster Assembly.* London: Printed by J. Young for P. Nevill, 1643.

Scholl, Hans. *Der Dienst des Gebetes nach Johannes Calvin.* Zürich: Zwingli Verlag, 1968.

Sehling, Emil, ed. *Die evangelische Kirchenordnungen des 16. Jahrhundert.* Leipzig, 1905–13 and Tübingen: J. C. B. Mohr (Paul Siebeck), 1955–63.
(Of particular interest are the liturgical documents of Augsburg, Kempton, Lindau, and Memmingen found in volume 12 and the volume dedicated to the documents of Hesse.)

Shepard, Thomas. *The Works of Thomas Shepard.* 3 vols. Boston: Doctrinal Tract and Book Society, 1853. Reprinted. New York: AMS Press, Inc., 1967.
(Of particular interest are his works on the Sabbath, on the church membership of children and his passages on prayer and on preaching in his work, *The Parable of the Ten Virgins, Opened and Applied.*)

Smyth, Charles Henry. *Cranmer and the Reformation Under Edward VI.* Cambridge: The University Press, 1926.

Staehelin, Ernst. *Das theologische Lebenswerk Johannes Oekolampads.* Quellen und Forschungen zur Reformationsgeschichte, vol. 21. Leipzig: M. Heinsius Nachfolger, 1939.

Sternhold, T. and I. Hopkins. *The Whole Booke of Psalms Collected into English Metre by T. Sternhold, I. Hopkins and others.* London: John Daye, 1562.

Stephens, W. P. *The Holy Spirit in the Theology of Martin Bucer.* Cambridge: The University Press, 1970.

Sturm, Klaus. *Die Theologie Peter Martyr Vermiglis während seines ersten Aufenthalts in Strassburg, 1542–1547.* Neukirchen-Vluyn: Erziehungsvereign, 1971.

Tate, Nahum and Nicholas Brady. *A New Version of the Psalms of David Fitted to Tunes Used in Churches.* London: T. Hodgkin, 1698.

Thompson, Bard. *Liturgies of the Western Church.* Cleveland: The World Publishing Company, 1961.

Torrance, Thomas F. *The School of Faith and the Catechisms of the Reformed Church.* London: James Clarke & Co., Ltd., 1959.

Trinterud, Leonard John. *The Forming of an American Tradition: A Re-examination of Colonial Presbyterianism.* Philadelphia: Westminster Press, 1949.

Tylenda, Joseph M. "Calvin and Christ's Presence in the Supper—True or Real?" *Scottish Journal of Theology* 27 (1974): 65–75.

Vajta, Vilmos. *Luther on Worship.* Translated by U. S. Leupold. Philadelphia: Fortress Press, 1958.

van de Poll, Gerrit Jan. *Martin Bucer's Liturgical Ideas.* Assen: Van Gorcum, 1954.

Vermigli, Peter Martyr. *Defensio doctrinae veteris et apostolicae de sacrosancto Eucharistiae sacramento.* Zürich: Christoffel Froschauer (?), 1559.

Vermigli, Peter Martyr. *A discourse or traictise of Peter Martyr Vermill . . . wherein he openly declared his . . . judgment concernynge the Sacrament of the Lordes supper.* Translated by N. Udall. London: R. Stoughton, 1550 (?).

Vermigli, Peter Martyr. *Most Godly Prayers Compiled Out of David's Psalms by D. Peter Martyr.* Translated by C. Glemhan. London: W. Seres, 1569.

Vermigli, Peter Martyr. *Tractatio de sacramento Eucharistiae, habita in celebrima Universitate Oxoniensi . . . Ad hec Disputatio de eodem Eucharistiae sacramento in eadem Universitate habita. . . .* London: R. Wolfe, 1549.

Wakefield, Gordon S. *Puritan Devotion.* London: The Epworth Press, 1957.

Watts, Isaac. *A Guide to Prayer.* OPERA, vol. III, Edited by George Burder. 6 vols. London: J. Barfield, 1810.

Watts, Isaac. *Hymns and Spiritual Songs.* 3 vols. London: J. Humphreys, 1707.

Watts, Isaac. *The Psalms of David Imitated in the Language of the New Testament.* OPERA. Edited by George Burder. 6 vols. London: J. Barfield, 1810.

Yoder, John H. *Täufertum und Reformation im Gespräch.* Basler Studien zür Historischen und Systematischen Theologie, vol. 13. Zürich: EVZ-Verlag, 1968.

Yoder, John H. *Täufertum und Reformation in der Schweiz I*. Schriftenreihe des Mennonitischen Geschichtsvereins, vol. 6. Karlsruhe: H. Schneider, 1962.

Zurich Letters. Edited by Hastings Robinson for the Parker Society. 2 vols. Cambridge: The University Press, 1842–45.

Zwick, Johannes, "Bekantnuss der zwoelff Artickel des Glaubens von Jesu Christo, zu dem allmaechtigen Gott im Hymel." *Monumenta Germaniae Paedagogica*, vol. 23, pp. 76–141.

Zwick, Johannes. "Das Vatter unser in frag und betswyss für die jungenn kind ussgelegt ouch den alten nit undienstlich." *Monumenta Germaniae Paedagogica*, vol. 23, pp. 67–74.

Zwick, Johannes. *Nuw gsangbuchle von vil schonen Psalmen und geistlichen liedern.* . . . Zürich: Christoffel Froschouer, 1540.
(This hymnbook, drawn together for the Reformed church of Constance, is one of the most important documents for the history of Reformed liturgics. Zwick's preface is particularly interesting.)

Zwingli, Ulrich. *Action or Use of the Lord's Supper*. Zürich: Ch. Froschauer, 1525. Translated by Bard Thompson. Liturgies of the Western Church. Cleveland: The World Publishing Company, 1961.

Zwingli, Ulrich. *Of Baptism*. THE LIBRARY OF CHRISTIAN CLASSICS, vol. XXIV. Philadelphia: Westminster Press, 1953.

Zwingli, Ulrich. *Of the Clarity and Certainty of the Word of God*. THE LIBRARY OF CHRISTIAN CLASSICS, vol. XXIV. Philadelphia: Westminster Press, 1953.

Zwingli, Ulrich. *On the Lord's Supper*. THE LIBRARY OF CHRISTIAN CLASSICS, vol. XXIV. Philadelphia: Westminster Press, 1953.

Zwingli, Ulrich. *Refutation of the Tricks of the Catabaptists*. Selected Works. Edited by Samuel Macauley Jackson. Philadelphia: University of Pennsylvania Press, 1972.

Zwingli, Ulrich. *Selected Works*. Edited by Samuel Macauley Jackson. Philadelphia: University of Pennsylvania Press, 1972.

Index